AF470802

Great Motor-cycle Riders

By the same author

Encyclopaedia of Motor-cycle Sport

Great Motor-cycle Riders

Peter Carrick

Robert Hale · London

Robert Hale Limited
Clerkenwell House
Clerkenwell Green
London EC1R 0HT

Carrick, Peter
    Great Motor-cycle Riders
    1.   Motorcycle Racing — Records
    I.   Title
796.7'5'09   GV1060

ISBN 0-7090-2374-X

Photoset by Peter Carrick Associates
Printed in Great Britain by St. Edmundsbury Press,
Bury St. Edmunds, Suffolk
Bound by Hunter & Foulis Ltd

Contents

Acknowledgements

I am grateful to the individuals and publishers concerned for permission to use short references from existing material in this book: TT Special (G.S. Davison), The Story of MV Motor Cycles (Patrick Stephens), Motor Cycling Today, and Racing All My Life (Arthur Barker), Motorcourse, and Motor Cycle News.

I am also indebted to Sheena Atkinson, Pauline Rew, Ann Roome and Paul Smith for their help.

Illustrations

25   French Canadian Yvon Duhamel
26   Barry Sheene after his Daytona crash
27   Sheene at the 1978 Spanish Grand Prix
28   Marco Lucchinelli in 1983
29   'King Kenny' Roberts at Brands Hatch in 1980
30   Randy Mamola's return to grand prix racing in 1984
31   Freddie Spencer at the Yugoslavian Grand Prix of 1984
32   Eddie Lawson rides the fastest lap in the 1984 Spanish
     Grand Prix

Picture credits

Foreword

I am delighted to write this foreword to Peter Carrick's latest book. *Great Motor-cycle Riders* is a worthy addition to this popular writer's work and presents a dramatic and absorbing tribute to some of the greatest racing motor-cyclists of all time.

The subject matter is well chosen, for what motor-cycle enthusiast can resist a book which brings together so many of the sport's most magical names — Stanley Woods, Jimmie Guthrie, Les Graham, Geoffrey Duke, Bob McIntyre, John Surtees, Derek Minter, Bill Ivy, Phil Read, Mike Hailwood, Yarno Saarinen, Barry Sheene, Kenny Roberts, Freddie Spencer and many other giants of the racing circuits.

The author's painstaking research and compelling narrative bring the races, personalities, incidents and controversies to life in a vivid style. This is not merely a collection of individual biographies. It is a panoramic vision of the racing life through the feats, daring and skills of motor-cycling's greatest names over more than 80 years.

As such it will find a permanent place on my bookshelves and, I hope, yours too.

Murray Walker
BBC Motor Sport Correspondent

Preface

Great Motor-cycle Riders spans more than eighty years. In that time grand prix motor-cycle racing has changed dramatically. For a long time riders enjoyed little public status and received scant financial gain. Today, rewards can be considerable and have brought racers like Barry Sheene millionaire status.

In the years between the wars the sport was much less commercial. Most riders were left to ferret for any scrap of sponsorship they could get, negotiate their own deals with organizers, and attend meetings which gave them the best chance of bonus money. They bought and worked on their own machines, picked up spares where they could, made their own travel arrangements, and felt privileged if they had a part-time engine tuner they could call on occasionally.

Famous British factories like Norton, AJS, Rudge, Sunbeam and Velocette were in a powerful position to recruit the best riders to the comparatively few full-scale works contracts available. Riders were expected to race more for the honour of competing than for financial gain.

It was the Italian factories of Gilera and MV Agusta in the post-war years who poached Britain's best riders, tempting even the most patriotic with powerful multi-cylinder machines and lucrative racing contracts.

Then Honda, in the 1960s, invested prodigiously in their quest for worldwide racing domination. Riders like Hailwood and Redman were paid enormous sums to ride their brilliant, exotic machinery. Motor-cycle racing lost much of its once grimy image and the top riders enjoyed superstar status, as sales of commercial models soared.

As Honda was joined by Yamaha and Suzuki in the battle for

racing supremacy, there were extremely rich pickings for the top riders. Works contracts were negotiated direct with racing chiefs back in Japan. The obsession for grand prix success, as a springboard to extra sales in the showroom, finally got out of hand and even Honda were forced to cut back.

By then subsidiary companies which had been established in the United States and Europe were left to find much of the finance for their own racing programmes from their own budgets. But if the bike factories themselves cut their own investment in racing, they were able to attract an increasing level of sponsorship from outside organizations. Suzuki GB, for instance, received support from Texaco and Forward Trust while they had Sheene under contract. And there developed more opportunities for riders to boost their income with private deals with equipment and clothing firms and other organizations.

While many of the top riders were now encouraged to let agents and PR professionals handle their 'spin-off' deals, those fighting for success and recognition still found the path ahead difficult and uncertain. The battle for financial support was every bit as hard as it had been for the foraging tyros of the 1940s and 1950s. The division in status and financial rewards between a works contracted rider competing in a full programme of grand prix events and a struggling privateer, forced by financial constraints into galloping around less prestigious home circuits, is enormous.

Now, with American racers dominating the grand prix scene, there is still plenty of money in the sport for riders who win races and find a special place in the hearts of the crowd.

In *Great Motor-cycle Riders* it has been impossible to include every racer who might deserve attention. But in honouring the comparative few, the overall tribute is to them all.

1. When 50 mph was Fast

Even in the early days of the twentieth century the men who raced motor-cycles were national and international heroes. They dashed over dirt roads and rugged countryside, and adventure, not money, was their motive. Their machines were crude, notoriously uncomfortable and absurdly limited compared with the finely tuned power bikes of today. Yet, with no protection for head or hands and wearing only lightweight everyday clothing, their courage and skill were unquestionable.

The motor-cycle dates back to the late 1800s, though its birth was so protracted and complex that no individual can rightfully claim sole credit. Numerous pioneers from many countries looked expectantly towards automotive travel. As early as 1876 Dr Nicolaus Otto and Eugen Langen in Germany patented a working application of the famous four-stroke principle of piston and valve action in a cylinder. In 1885 Gottlieb Daimler and Wilhelm Maybach built a wooden framed two-wheeler incorporating belt drive. In 1887 Felix Millet produced the first multi-cylinder motorcycle and a year later John Boyd Dunlop developed his pneumatic tyre. Not until 1894, however, a year when Hans Renolds introduced his roller chain, did Heinrich Hildebrand and Alois Wolfmuller's design become the first commercial two-wheel vehicle to be called a motor-cycle. It was said to be capable of travelling at 28 mph. Four years later Colonel Henry Holden in Britain was planning the limited production of the world's first four-cylinder motor-cycle and at the turn of the century, in the United States, the Indian motor-cycle company brought out its earliest model.

At first it was exciting enough simply to ride one of the new contraptions. As design advanced and machines were made more practical, there came the natural urge to see how far and how fast they could go. Motor-cycle racing had arrived. In 1897 the *Horseless Vehicle Journal* recorded that a race had taken place between a motor-cycle and an ordinary pedal-cycle, and although the pedal-cycle won by some 300 yards, the publication commented astutely that it would be a bold man indeed who would say that the cycle would always be the victor. Pedalling gear, it is interesting to recall, was necessary on motor-cycles for many years to assist in scaling hills when motor power alone was not enough.

While doubtless numerous private challenges were contested in all manner of places during the formative years, organized racing developed faster on the Continent than in Britain. The Friedenauer cycle track in Germany and the Exelberg circuit in Austria were centres of activity. Races, speed trials and motor-cycle competitions in France were staged in many places, including Nice, Lille and the Parc des Princes in Paris and on the popular Circuit des Ardennes.

Canning Town, Crystal Palace and Herne Hill were among the popular early venues in Britain. Harry Martin was a contemporary hero at Canning Town, recording a standing start mile in 1 minute 24 seconds on a 2¾ hp Excelsior in 1903. He later became the first motor-cycle rider to break the 60 mph barrier, in speed trials at Dublin's Phoenix Park. The redoubtable Martin, known both as 'the English Cannonball' and as 'the wizard', the latter because of his rare ability as an engine-tuner, rode in jersey and breeches, with no gloves and with his soft peak cap turned back-to-front in the style of the day. He wore goggles, but many early photographs show him racing with them strapped round his forehead. His chain-driven Excelsior machine was made in Coventry and bore many similarities to pedal-cycles of the day, as well it might, for Excelsior were not alone as a business with origins in pedal-cycles which then saw the potential in 'motor'-cycles. Primitive by later standards, the bike had thin tyres, spoke wheels, drop-down handlebars and a puny frame. The fuel tank hung from a conventional crossbar, and the engine, which Excelsior could have bought in from one of a number of sources, was mounted in front of the forward frame member. Excelsior built their first motor-cycle in 1896, and the popular belief is that the first motor-cycle ever sold in Britain was an Excelsior.

Matchless is another British motor-cycle from the pioneering days. Founded in 1899, the company fitted a variety of engines to their frames, including de Dion and JAP. Racing success came through founder H.H. Collier's sons, Charlie and Harry. They made history in 1907 by capturing the honours with JAP-powered Matchless machines in the first Tourist Trophy race on the Isle of Man. In the single-cylinder category Charlie completed the 158 miles in 4 hours 8 minutes 8 seconds (an average speed of 38.22 mph), while Harry clocked the fastest lap at 41.81 mph. Harry won in 1909, Charlie again in 1910, with Harry second. In just three years Charlie Collier increased his average for the race from 38.22 mph to 50.63 mph. That same year he reached 91.37 mph over the flying mile on a special JAP-engined 998cc V-twin Matchless racer.

The Collier brothers were active and successful motor-cycle racers on all the British short cycle tracks of the day. Charlie was third in the first official full-scale motor-cycle race to be held at the legendary Brooklands circuit near Weybridge in Surrey. This magnificent track, the world's first purpose-built motor-racing circuit, was opened in June 1907, but not until February 1908 did the first motor-cycle race take place there. This was a private encounter won by W.C. McMinnies on a Triumph against O.L. Bickford on a Vindec, and it proved to be such an exciting spectacle that the British Automobile Racing Club adopted the idea as a means of broadening the appeal of their forthcoming Easter Monday programme.

Thus, on 20 April 1908, the first full-scale motor-cycle race to be held at the famous circuit took place, twenty-one of the top riders appearing on the starting line on a variety of machines which ranged in engine size from 331 to almost 1,000cc. Collier, on an 861cc British JAP-powered Matchless, could do no better than finish third, but the day's undoubted hero was Will E. Cook. On a fine day and racing over two laps of the Brooklands circuit (5½ miles) he scored a handsome win by more than half a mile, never being challenged. His not inconsiderable prize for those days was twenty sovereigns. Cook's average speed of 63 mph was below his best practice times because of a strong wind and the relatively high gearing of his 984cc NLG-Peugeot machine, the largest and most powerful bike in the race.

NLG (North London Garages) made motor-cycles from 1905 to 1912, with normal production versions being powered by 499cc single and 770cc V-twin JAP engines. Peugeot had been in business earlier, this famous pioneer of the motor-cycle and car industries having been established as early as 1899. But for Cook (affectionately known as 'Wee-Wee') the telling combination of a Peugeot engine mounted in an NLG frame brought lasting eminence, for just a year later, on 16 June 1909, and racing the same machine once more at Brooklands, he was overall fastest in Record Time Trials with a speed over the flying kilometre of 75.93 mph. Earlier that year Cook, a compulsive racer and an outstanding enthusiast, faced near disaster as he raced up the Members' Banking and, after the bend just beyond the Finishing Straight, looked certain to disappear over the top of the circuit until he recovered control. That same year, at the first race meeting organized by the newly established British Motor Cycle Racing Club, Cook finished second in a two-lap scratch race and was second again at the Whitsun weekend meeting in the Metropolitan Motor Cycle Handicap, in which motor-cycles competed alongside cars. Cook's overall position was eighth.

In 1909 and 1910 Will Cook made a number of attempts to better the long-standing flying-start kilometre and flying-start mile world records of Frenchman Henri Cissac, putting confidence in his NLG machine packed this time with a massive 2,713cc JAP engine, one of three 'specials' built by the JAP concern for attempts on the records. Around Whitsun he reached 84.247 mph for the flying kilometre to secure the unlimited track record for Brooklands, but the speed fell short of both the British and world records. The other two special JAP engines had gone to Charlie Collier and Harry Bashall. Fitted to one of Charlie's Matchless machines, it might have given greater hope of a world record, but the awesome power was too much for the bike to be sufficiently controllable at speed, even in the hands of the skilful and experienced Collier. At the last meeting that year at Brooklands, on 11 November, Will Cook once again attacked the records and over the flying-start kilometre distance sensationally averaged more than 90 mph, but the speed was unofficial and only hand-timed because the electrical equipment had failed to work at the vital moment. A further valiant attempt that day ended in failure.

Undaunted, Will Cook took his machine back to Brooklands in October 1910 and at the end of the 100-mile Reliability Trial once more set out to outstrip Cissac's records. Frustrating delays and mechanical problems, however, bedevilled Cook's efforts, and although he made two starts, the first ended when a driving-belt fastener broke, and the second was thwarted because of poor visibility. These latest failures were demoralizing even for the redoubtable Cook, who afterwards sold the machine, as indeed did Harry Bashall his version. The experience proved that engine power (for the monster JAP power unit was indeed a fearsome thing) is not necessarily enough alone to win races and break records. In some respects it was to be a hard lesson to learn, for more than fifty years later the mighty Honda, it seemed, had not fully realized the significance, if racing success is to be achieved, of the fine counter-balance necessary between motive power, frame design and handling characteristics. When they hired Mike Hailwood in the 1960s with the sole object of securing the 500cc World Championship, then held by MV Agusta and Giacomo Agostini, their response to failure was to add power, and they, too, finally had to abandon the attempt.

The cavalier days at Brooklands were noted for the daring and dash of many colourful riders whose inspired deeds, though often crude and unscientific by modern standards, nonetheless pointed the sport towards a more organized and sophisticated future. Along with the brilliant Collier brothers, who repeatedly won races and triumphed in other motor-cycle events, and Will Cook, there were enduring characters such as Harry Bashall and Frank McNab, winners of the first 1,000cc and 500cc hour-long races to take place at Brooklands; Guy Lee Evans, who gave a Brooklands crowd its first sight of the American Indian machine; Frank Applebee, an Isle of Man Senior TT winner in 1912; and a great many others, including of course Harry 'Wizard' Martin, whose staggering per-formances on a 340cc machine in August 1910 were enough to shatter the 500cc class flying-start kilometre and mile records. For a 350 machine in those days his record-breaking speeds of 68.28 mph and 65.97 mph were sensational.

As early as 1909 Matchless Motors ran an official racing team comprising Harry and Charlie Collier and Bert Colver, and in October that year they finished first, second and third in the 8½ miles Handicap event for machines of between 450 and 1,000cc. One of the most interesting Brooklands results a year later, however, was the convincing display of a strong Indian contingent in the One-Hour TT Race. Ridden by Charlie Bennett, Walter Bennett and Guy Lee Evans before a vast crowd, the 638cc Indian machines had moved well ahead of the rest of the field at the end of the first lap and never fell back.

From the early 1900s British enthusiasts wanting to race motor-cycles were at a grave disadvantage. While their counterparts on the Continent of Europe were free to race on public roads without restriction, British riders were handicapped by a rigidly enforced speed limit, first of twelve miles an hour and later twenty miles an hour. This gave limited opportunity for the testing and development of machines, and British riders were soon falling behind their Continental rivals. In France, particularly, development surged ahead, with concentration on race 'specials' built for outright speed. Speed was all-important, and racing without rules was normal. This attitude led to grossly overpowered machines which offended British taste. Branded a monstrosity on this side of the Channel was Maurice Fournier's massive 22hp machine of 1903. It weighed 360 lb (163.3 kg), had a 2,340cc twin-cylinder Buchet special engine, and was said to be capable of a top speed of 80 mph. Its performance was certainly impressive, for when Fournier brought it to Britain to race against the British rider Barden at the Canning Town track in 1903, the Frenchman quickly and decisively won the first three of the five scheduled races, making further competition unnecessary. He also claimed the stake of £1,000!

From the very earliest days France had found its racing excitement in rugged competition. The epic inter-city marathons were torrid affairs, the first of which was held as early as 1895. The French ace Bucquet riding a French-built Werner machine soon became a national hero, winning the Paris-Vienna race and similar events, and was again in the lead when the fated Paris-Madrid marathon was dramatically abandoned at Bordeaux.

The race had started at Versailles with motor-cyclists being flagged off in pairs at minute intervals. Bucquet, after a battle with Demester, was the first to complete the 119 kilometres to Châteaudun, but already the race was getting out of hand. On public roads, with motor-cars competing alongside bikes and with little if any crowd control, the hazards were obvious for all to see. Public enthusiasm was enormous, and spectators put themselves at grave risk as they stretched out onto the road to catch a glimpse of oncoming or disappearing cars and motor-cycles as they thundered through great dust clouds which built up from the primitive un-made roads. Three million people are said to have lined the roads, and there had been so many accidents and casualties, some fatal, by the time the competitors reached Bordeaux that the French authorities called off the race.

These inter-city marathons were unique spectacles and fired the public imagination, but they were grotesque affairs, and after 1903 France replaced them with the annual International Cup Race, competed for in 1904 by five nations — Austria, Denmark, France, Germany and Great Britain.

Though under the auspices of the French Auto-Cycle Club, this first International Cup Race was shabbily organized and shamefully administered with little adherence to the rules. Regulations were brazenly flouted and gamesmanship was rampant. The British team of three riders, led by long-distance specialist Tom Silver, faced an effective Continental vendetta and had so many punctures after nails had been thrown onto the track that they had to retire. In the end it was all too much even for the French authorities, who had no alternative but to annul the results. The French made a better attempt at organizing the second International Cup Race in 1905 but could not completely resist the temptation to bend the rules, running their eliminating trials on the Dourdon course, where the race was to take place.

This second International Cup competition became recognized officially as one of the earliest authenticated motor-cycle road races. To be fair, the French had tightened up the supervision of machines eligible for entry and stiffened the administration but in so doing had unhappily bolstered international rivalry to the extent that the atmosphere was tense — and the race was to end in high drama. The French ace Demester, on a twin-cylinder Griffon, was an easy favourite, and he led convincingly at the start, with Germany's Mueller next, followed by Campbell of Britain and Toman of Austria. Last to be flagged away was C.V. Wondrick, the Austrian rider, on his rugged Laurin-Klement machine. Meantime, Demester had made a good start and was riding well as he came round to begin his second lap. Then his luck ran out and he was delayed by a broken belt and punctures, enabling Wondrick, who was riding superbly, with excellent cornering technique, to move into first place, three seconds ahead of Demester. Toman, Austria's favourite rider, crashed on his first lap and was forced to retire.

On lap 3 the race became a battle between Demester and Wondrick, and the French ace was showing great form. He had made up for his earlier misfortune and looked a good prospect to win, being placed just 1 minute and 45 seconds behind race leader Wondrick. On lap 4 he gained a further nineteen seconds on his Austrian rival, but a further puncture set him back. Undeterred, he changed the wheel and set off once more in pursuit, but the cause was lost and he finished second to Wondrick, some seven minutes behind. Wondrick, whose rugged machine absorbed the severest stresses of the tough course superbly, shattered all previous records for the Dourdon course, covering the 270 kilometres in 3 hours 5¼ minutes to give a race average speed of almost 54.5 mph. France's Joseph Giuppone, on a Peugeot, was the third man home. Indeed, he was the only other rider to finish. The British challenge, after some promising moments, evaporated. J.S. Campbell's JAP-powered Ariel suffered all manner of problems, and he finally had to retire. C.B. Franklin's JAP broke an inlet valve, and the final member of the three-man British team, Harry Collier on his JAP-powered Matchless, was forced to pull out on the fifth lap after tyre problems.

With national feeling running high throughout the race, controversy now surrounded the results, as protests against the French accused Demester of breaking the rules by changing the whole wheel, and not the tyre, when he punctured. Ironically, the French themselves before the race had insisted on the rule which now disqualified their ace. So Austria won the cup through Wondrick, with Giuppone elevated to second place.

But, anyway, the Continental approach to racing was not liked by the British riders, who felt machines should be closer in design and styling to touring and not, as was the French way, artificially created 'specials' built for speed alone, with overpowered engines, skeleton-like frames, puny tyres and inadequate brakes. The savage quest to save weight and therefore increase speed was madness in British eyes, and a movement for a British road race limited to touring bikes gained momentum.

With racing outlawed on mainland roads because of the authority's unyielding attitude on speed limits and their persistent refusal to close roads temporarily for racing to take place, the eliminating trials for the British team destined for the International Cup Race of 1905 had been held on the Isle of Man. Desperate to secure a venue for British riders to run their own kind of race, the Auto-Cycle Club, formed in 1903 and the forerunner to the present-day Auto-Cycle Union (the British governing body of the sport), turned again to the Isle of Man. They found the Manx Government once more understanding, enthusiastic and responsive, and plans were quickly made. It was an historic move and the start of what was to become perhaps the greatest series of motor-cycle road races in the world, the legendary TT (Tourist Trophy) Races.

The regulations specified machines 'similar to those sold to the public', there was no weight or capacity limit, and efficient silencers were obligatory, as were ordinary-type saddles and mudguards, and two-inch tyres. Pedalling gear was allowed, but there was a restriction on fuel, qualified as 90 mpg for single-cylinder machines and 75 mpg for the 'twins'. Ten times round a short course to give a race distance of 158 miles was a good test for both rider and machine, despite a compulsory ten-minute 'rest' stop after five laps.

So on 28 May 1907 the first TT Race began, before a bemused smattering of onlookers, competitors being despatched in pairs at one-minute intervals. On the dirt-surfaced roads, punctures were frequent, and there was a dramatic moment when the eventual winner of the twin-cylinder class, H. Rembrandt Fowler on a Norton-Peugeot machine, ploughed through another rider's blazing machine as he chugged up towards Kirkmichael. There were twenty-five starters (eighteen single-cylinder and seven twin-cylinder machines), and nearly half of them valiantly completed the course, despite (or was it because of?) having to carry cumbersome and heavy tool-kits. Frank Hulbert and Jack Marshall on Triumphs made history as they set off first, to be followed by the Collier brothers, Harry and Charlie. Charlie, on his pedal-assisted Matchless, took the lead on the first lap, with Marshall second, brother Harry third and Hulbert fourth. Marshall's machine punctured on lap 3 and was delayed ten minutes, but he later made good ground on Charlie Collier, who nonetheless rode out the eventual winner at an average speed of 38.23 mph, with a fuel-consumption average of 94.5 mpg, safely above the permitted 90. In the twin-cylinder class, Rem Fowler's winning average of 36.22 mph was completed in 4 hours 21 minutes 53 seconds, and he registered the fastest lap at 42.91 mph.

The establishment of road racing on the Isle of Man and the increasing status and influence of Brooklands were to provide the British motor-cycle industry with the impetus and opportunity it had lacked at the turn of the century. Machines could now be tested against endurance standards and momentary excesses of strain and stress, not only in the laboratory and on the test bench but also in realistic race conditions on road and track. British riders were able to ride more frequently and develop their race techniques to enable them to compete on fairer terms with European and American rivals. This led in the 1920s and 1930s to Britain's world superiority in motor-cycle manufacture and to the dominance of British motor-cycle riders.

But on the other side of the Atlantic the motor-cycle industry had been developing impressively. The two major factories, Indian and Harley-Davidson, had been founded in 1901 and 1903 respectively, and both were soon involved in racing. Within a decade reports began to reach Britain of some remarkable speed records set up in the United States and when it was claimed that Indian rider Jake de Rosier had raced for an hour on his 994cc bike and had covered more than 84 miles, Britain's Brooklands speed riders put it down to America's basic preoccupation with, and acceptance of, the extravagant and the exaggerated. But in 1911 the American rider travelled to Britain and in a three-race match with Charlie Collier secured an historic American victory at Brooklands.

When the American arrived at Brooklands, he was already an international hero, having just a week before shattered three world records, while Charlie Collier was a world champion in his own right on his JAP-powered 985cc Matchless. The champions would race against each other three times, over distances of two, five and ten laps of the 2.75-mile banked circuit, for prize money of £130. It was Saturday, 15 July 1911, and large crowds gathered in ideal racing weather to witness the battle between Britain and America, Charlie Collier against Jake de Rosier.

Tension was high at 3 pm as the rivals appeared for the first race. Harry Collier wheeled his brother's machine to the start and Jake's British host, Sydney Garrett, wheeled out de Rosier's machine. The contrast in the two bikes was interesting. The American's Indian, with 28-inch diameter wheels and thin tyres, looked lean and gaunt against the rugged, more workmanlike appearance of the British rider's Matchless. For Brooklands' bumpy track Jake fitted wider handlebars and a pair of knee grips to assist handling. The Matchless had two-foot-long exhaust pipes. De Rosier's racing fashion was close-fitting brown leathers, while Collier wore a white pullover and riding-breeches. Both had soft aviator-style helmets.

The two riders chatted amiably as they walked down from the

paddock. A rolling start had been decided for all three races, and the excitement mounted as the two riders followed the start car. Then, as they came abreast and the two machines were dead in line, the red start flag, held high by an official in the car, was brought down and the first race was on. Charlie moved to the front first as they climbed the Members' Banking, but Jake had pulled level again at the Railway Straight. The battle continued, with Collier again in front by several lengths at a crucial stage on the second lap. The Matchless tore down the finishing straight fractionally ahead of the Indian, but a magnificent piece of riding soon took Jake ahead. Charlie tucked his head lower and closed the gap, but as they flashed across the line the American was ahead by just one length, to win the opening encounter at a speed of 80.59 mph. Had Collier not allowed de Rosier to throttle up first at the last bend, it might have been a different story.

As if to demonstrate his learning from the first encounter, Charlie Collier roared his Matchless into the lead from the start of the second, five-lap race and relentlessly surged forward in a superb exhibition of riding. Jake, head down, travelled in Charlie's slipstream at speeds in the high seventies, and then the crowd caught its breath as Jake was seen to wobble badly before recovering control. In an impressive demonstration of the new art of slipstreaming, an innovation for Brooklands, Jake was content to be 'pulled' along by Charlie, but on the dramatic fourth lap there was no sign of the American as Charlie swept on to complete the five laps without once surrendering the lead. The American had been forced out with a burst front tyre while travelling at more than 80 mph, but fortunately he was not injured.

All now depended on the third and final race. There was a dramatic delay as, with both riders set to go, it was discovered that Jake's machine had one or two loose nuts. A spanner was sent for. Tension was at fever pitch as a false start was declared, and then a carbon brush in Jake's magneto was discovered to be broken. But then the two riders were away — ten laps (27.18 miles) before them. With two races gone, it was now generally accepted that the American had slightly the faster machine, but Charlie's Matchless was tough and had perhaps greater endurance than the thoroughbred Indian. It was a well-balanced contest, with the odds perhaps slightly in favour of the British rider.

Charlie led from the start, but at the end of lap 1 the American pulled out of his slipstream to put himself a wheel ahead. There was little between them at the end of the second lap. At the end of lap 3 Jake was two lengths in front, but Collier rode manfully and with great skill and, with throttle wide, he roared down the Railway Straight some ten lengths ahead. The crowd was now shouting for a British victory, but desperate luck was to thwart the British challenge. Machine vibration dislodged the ignition switch from the 'on' position, and Charlie had to locate the problem and set it right. His speed dropped, and as he struggled to correct the fault, the American seized his chance and raced well ahead. Seeing that Charlie was in trouble, Jake sat up in the saddle and eased back, thinking he had the race won. Charlie did not concede defeat and rode like a demon so that Jake had to get his head down again to make certain of victory, flashing over the line some twenty seconds ahead of the Briton. America had won the race, the series and the prize money.

British racing had learned a lesson from the American: that speed alone is not necessarily enough. Tactics and the wisdom to keep close to your rival, nursing your machine along in his slipstream, and making your supreme effort when it matters most, dashing for the flag, can also be important and are sometimes enough to win races.

2. The Golden Years for British Bikers

In the years between the wars, motor-cycling came of age. It was the golden days of the industry, with British riders on British machines dominating the sport. Bikes had become more dependable and advanced by then, but their performance was still rugged. Motor-cycling for many held the promise of adventure — and, for the legendary few, fame. Barnstorming characters such as Jimmy Simpson, Jimmy Guthrie, Graham Walker, Percy Hunt, Alec Bennett, Freddie Frith, Harold Daniell, Wal Handley, Freddy Dixon and Stanley Woods charged from one race success to another on the Isle of Man, at Brooklands and on the Continent. Riding Norton, AJS, Sunbeam, Rudge, Velocette, Matchless and Douglas machines, they were virtually unbeatable.

It was in the early 1920s that these great names began to make an impact on the Isle of Man. Alec Bennett's first TT victory was in 1922, when he was first home in the Senior TT on a Sunbeam. His average speed for the 226½ miles race was 58.31 mph, and he also recorded the fastest lap at 59.99 mph. Stanley Woods registered his first TT win in 1923, in the Junior event on a Cotton at a race average of 55.73 mph. That year a sidecar TT was held for the first time and was won by the ebullient Freddie Dixon on a Douglas-powered combination, with Walter Denny riding passenger. Dixon's victory crowned a remarkable week of success for the Douglas factory, for Tom Sheard won the Senior event on a Douglas bike, and Alfie Alexander managed third place in the Junior race. Mind you, Dixon's success was not without anxiety. Until Harry Langman ran his Scott combination into the wall at Braddan Bridge on the final lap, Freddy was in second place and did not look like improving.

In 1924 Alec Bennett brought the famous Norton factory their first TT victory in the all-important Senior event. Until then Norton's approach to racing had been tepid and casual. The factory were concentrating on making first-class motor-cycles for the general public, and they tried to win races on machines which were far too close to their standard road bikes to gain much success on the track. Norton's executive Bill Mansell decided to go more positively for racing success in 1924 and engaged Alec Bennett to ride for the factory. It turned out to be a wise choice, for Bennett, whose Senior TT victory two years earlier on the Sunbeam had broken the lap record by almost 4 mph, won again, this time for Norton and in sensational fashion. His 1924 Senior win was by 87 seconds (from Harry Langman on a Scott and Freddy Dixon on a Douglas), and it was the first time in the TT Races that a race average speed had exceeded 60 mph. Bennett's time was 61.64 mph, though Dixon's fastest race lap was 63.75 mph.

Alec Bennett's career was remarkable. He did not race all that often, yet when he retired, at thirty-two, he had won more TT Races than any other rider at that time. Born in Ireland, Bennett spent time in Canada after seeing war service as a fighter pilot, but he had a driving ambition to ride in the TT, then the centre of the sporting calendar. His first outing was in 1921, when he finished fourth on a Sunbeam in the Senior event. After his win for Sunbeam in the Senior race the following year, and his record-breaking victory on the Norton in 1924, he won the Junior on a Velocette in 1926, also registering the fastest lap at 68.75 mph, and the Senior on a Norton in 1927; in the Junior event in 1928, again on the Velocette, he won at an average of 68.65 mph with the fastest lap at 70.28 mph, a new record and the first-ever 70 mph lap to be recorded in the Junior class. He also scored exciting success on the Continent, winning the French Grand Prix four times and the Belgium Grand Prix twice.

Velocette machines were made by the Veloce Company of Birmingham, a highly respected company which had been established in 1904. The factory had been interested in Isle of Man racing since 1913, when Cyril Pullin finished 22nd in the Junior TT on a 'works' machine. It was Alec Bennett, however, who first brought them racing prominence, with his Junior TT win in 1926. Bennett was proprietor of a Southampton firm of motor-cycle dealers, handling Velocette among other makes. He was so impressed with the factory's latest 350cc overhead-camshaft 'K' model that he convinced Percy Goodman, elder son of the founder, that, with race modifications, he could ride it to victory in the Junior TT. Bennett was still under contract to Norton, but as they were not producing a 350cc racer at that time, he was free to pick up a Velocette ride. Despite an unscheduled pit stop at the end of the first lap, incipient pre-ignition and a tumble at the deceptive Nook while in sight of home, Bennett was as good as his word, winning in convincing style and bringing Velocette the prestige bonus of a victory by the outstanding margin of ten minutes, from Jimmy Simpson on an AJS. The achievement was all the more impressive because 1926 was the first year that alcohol fuel was prohibited, and for that year the race distance had been increased by one lap (to a total of 264 miles) of the severe and demanding Mountain Course. Bennett's machine was so much better than the opposition that he deliberately 'toured' round on the first lap, allowing his engine to warm up thoroughly before opening the throttle wide.

Bennett's victory two years later provided all the impetus Velocette needed to market an over-the-counter racer, the first factory to do so. It was a major development in the sport because until then only those riders who could get hold of a factory-type racer had any real chance of track success. Over the years Velocette, never one of the giants of the industry in terms of money and resources, nonetheless were remarkably inventive. They used coil ignition at a time when it was unusual, an alloy cylinder head and throttle-controlled lubrication, and as far back as 1928 had pioneered foot gear change. Bennett's 1928 TT victory machine incorporated the first positive-stop foot gear change, widely recognized throughout the industry as an important advance and soon to be adopted by other factories. That same year they were also seriously experimenting with pivoted-fork rear springing, though rigid frames were continued in use until 1936; and they also contributed to the development of the modern racing seat.

Velocette's history is distinguished. In 1928 alone, the famous Velocette '350' smashed no fewer than fifty world records. The first 350cc machine to exceed 100 mph was a Velocette, and at the famous Montlhéry track in France, on 18/19 March 1961, a Velocette which was astonishingly close to standard specification became the first machine in the world to exceed a 100 mph average over twenty-four hours. The banked circuit was not in good condition and riders were forced up to the top of the banking to avoid wide gaps which had over the years developed between the concrete slabs, inevitably subjecting the machine to the additional hazards of an accelerating rate of tyre wear. But the eight-man Anglo-French team of riders, which included Britons Bertie Goodman and Bruce Main-Smith, nonetheless exceeded the magical 100 mph average for the 24 hours, the official figure being 100.05 mph. On the way to this particular new record, the Velocette '350' collected five other world records, reaching new figures for 12 hours and 24 hours in the 750 cc and unlimited classes for solo motor-cycles.

As Continental factories began to show their superiority in the days just before the outbreak of the Second World War, Velocette countered with an exciting supercharged vertical twin 500cc machine with geared cranks and shaft drive. Known as 'the Roarer', it showed outstanding promise in the hands of Stanley Woods, but the war intervened. After hostilities Velocette did not support an official works team, and the fate of 'the Roarer' was sealed when the official international body for the sport, the Fédération Internationale Motocycliste (FIM), banned the use of superchargers in 1946. Bravely, Velocette fought on into the early post-war years with their unblown singles and showed they were still capable of the odd sensation when, in 1947, Velocette machines secured the first four places in the Junior TT. This first post-war TT was a direct confrontation between Velocette, with twenty entries, and Norton, who had twenty-eight entries. The only two remaining riders were mounted on AJS and Excelsior machines. On the first lap just one minute separated the first six riders, with Bob Foster on the Velocette leading Norton-mounted Harold Daniell. Maurice Cann (Norton) set the fastest lap to then on his second time round, but Foster soon bettered his time. Norton's challenge disappeared with the retirement on the fourth lap of their best hopes, Daniell and Maurice Cann. Foster raced on to win in 3 hours 17 minutes 20 seconds at an average speed of 80.31 mph, with David Whitworth recording the fastest lap of the race at 81.61 mph.

Sadly, along with all the greatest names in British motor-cycle racing, there was to be little glory left for Velocette when racing resumed after the Second World War. Freddie Frith brought them the Junior TT title again in 1948 and yet again in 1949, setting the fastest lap on both occasions, at 82.45 mph and 84.23 mph. When the world championship series was inaugurated in 1949, Frith brought Velocette the 350cc world title, and Bob Foster came back into the reckoning a year later to repeat the honour for the famous factory. But that was the end. Velocette were to be no match in the future for Norton, who were themselves soon to be eclipsed by the powerful multi-cylinder machines from Italy. Fortunes thereafter faded for Velocette, and at the end of 1952 the racing department was closed down. The company went into voluntary liquidation early in 1971.

The tough Mountain Course on the Isle of Man and the consistent use of Brooklands for testing and speed trials combined to provide the British motor industry with the 'battle courses' it required for the positive and swift development of its products. Riders gained their courage and acquired their skills in one of the toughest apprenticeships it was possible to find. The Isle of Man was the greatest and most arduous motor-cycling natural road-race circuit in the world, in motor-cycling's swashbuckling days of the 1920s. The TT course quickly became the standard by which other courses were judged, and the racing men and racing machines from Britain dominated motor-cycling for nearly twenty years. There was enormous public enthusiasm, and huge crowds witnessed the most important events.

The most outstanding racer of them all, during these golden years, many would argue, was a small Irishman called Stanley Woods. He raced incredibly fast yet was such a master of technique that he seldom seemed to be in danger of falling off. He was always dashing but never impetuous, and his remarkable achievements were secured with such a refreshing degree of modesty that he was everybody's favourite. In the 1920s and 1930s he was publicly acclaimed in the style of international entertainers and top television personalities of today, and his riding skills were so well defined that he seemed capable of winning on all but the slowest and most unreliable of machines. His versatility was legendary and in those pre-war days when specialization had not become a fetish, or essential to ultimate success, he was considered the greatest all-rounder. He rode with success in motocross (then called scrambles), trials, sand racing in both solo and sidecar events, speedway even, sprinting, hill climbs, grass-track racing and record attempts, though his ultimate reputation derived from his prowess in road racing, both on the natural road courses, such as the Isle of Man and Dundrod in the Ulster Grand Prix, and on the shorter circuits built specially for racing. His reputation extended to the Continent, and he was no mean performer on the dirt roads of far-off Australia.

Stanley Woods was born in Dublin in 1905 and rode in the TT Races for the first time in 1922 as a works rider for the Cotton company in the Junior race. Never one of the giants of motor-cycle racing, Cotton had been founded only two years before and were eagerly looking round to make their mark. Even so, when the seventeen-year-old Stanley Woods wrote to them stating how good a rider he was and asking for a bike to ride, they were so taken aback that they gave him one! His début on the Isle of Man was spectacular. While taking on fuel at the pits, his engine caught fire, but despite this sensation he managed to finish fifth. Cotton were delighted, and Woods rode for them again in 1923 and 1924.

Interestingly, two other riders who were to become all-time greats on the Isle of Man made their début in the TT in 1922 — Wal Handley, riding an OK bike in the Lightweight race, and Jimmy Simpson, riding a Scott in the Senior. Both retired.

Because of the steadily increasing speed capability and improved reliability of the lower-capacity machines, the Junior and Lightweight TTs were in 1923 increased from five laps of the Mountain circuit to six, giving a total race distance of 226½ miles, the same as for the Senior race. Woods was handily placed in the early stages of the Junior race, positioned fourth behind Jimmy Simpson on an AJS, Charlie Hough, also riding AJS, and Bert Le Vack on a New Imperial. Hough dropped out, Simpson broke down and after Le Vack had also retired, the race for victory was between Stanley Woods and George Dance on a Sunbeam. Woods' slow fifth lap enabled Dance to put 2½ minutes between them and all looked set for a Sunbeam win, but then Dance broke down on the Mountain with victory almost in sight, leaving Stanley Woods to record his first TT win (and the first for Cotton) at a race average of 55.73 mph, which, incidentally, was the fastest race speed recorded on the Island that year. Woods was also entered for all solo TTs in 1923, but he retired in the Lightweight event (again riding a Cotton), and retired once more in the Senior, riding a Scott.

For two more years Stanley Woods failed on the Island in terms of results. In 1924, again riding for Cotton, he retired in both the Junior and Senior races, and in 1925, riding a New Imperial in the Lightweight event and a Royal Enfield in the Junior, he suffered two more retirements. It was not surprising, therefore, that, when someone suggested him to Norton for a works ride, the famous factory was not keen. The recommendation came from a Dublin motor-cycle dealer who was a friend of Norton's race chief, Bill Mansell. Grudgingly Norton invited Woods to try his luck in 1926, and he repaid them handsomely. He won the Senior TT convincingly, being four minutes ahead of second-placed Walter Handley, and registered a new race average record speed at 67.54 mph. He later became fully employed at Norton and with the famous 'cammy' model scored good victories the following year in major grand prix events in Holland (the Dutch TT in 1927 being granted international status), Belgium and Switzerland.

Riding in the Senior TT on the Isle of Man in 1927, however, Stanley Woods' fortunes faded. He rocketed away from the start in determined mood and, from a standing start, raised the lap record to 70.70 mph. His second lap was even better, and he pushed up the lap record to 70.90, going round in just six seconds under 32 minutes. It was the first time that particular milestone had been reached. At the end of the fourth lap Woods came in to refuel holding a commanding lead of some four minutes over Alec Bennett, racing in second place. In those days, however, sadly for Stanley Woods, rider instructions and information were scant and not always precise, and he was simply told that he was in the lead and he should keep going. The Irish rider, given no clear idea how close or far behind Bennett was, raced on at a hectic pace. His clutch could not cope and he was forced to retire on the fifth lap. When Woods later knew the extent of the lead he had held over Bennett, and that he could have maintained first position without putting the Norton under such unrelenting strain, he was determined not to fall victim to a similar misfortune again. He devised his own signalling system and five years later, when used for the first time, it brought him a spectacular victory.

Altogether Stanley Woods won ten TT races between 1923 and 1939. On four further occasions he was forced to retire while in the lead and was beaten only fractionally into second place in four other TT races. He set a record by competing in the TTs for eighteen successive years. His tally of TT wins has even today been exceeded by only one other rider — Mike Hailwood — and equalled only by the fifteen times World Champion, the former Italian ace Giacomo Agostini. In just nine years from 1930 Woods won thirty-nine international events at home and abroad. His achievement is all the more remarkable when you consider that in the 1920s and 1930s, when Stanley Woods was at his peak, the number of top races a rider could compete in was considerably fewer than today. The racing calendar internationally was far less crowded, the home racing programme more limited, and the present form of the World Championships, with its extended series of races all over Europe, had not begun.

Woods stayed with the Norton factory for eight years, from 1926 to 1933, bringing them victory on the Isle of Man in 1926, 1932 and 1933. The latter two years were supreme. He won both the Senior and Junior races both years. In 1932 the Norton contingent of Woods, Guthrie, Percy Hunt and Simpson faced strong opposition from Rudge who, two years earlier, had finished first and second in the Senior race and first, second and third in the Junior event. In 1931 Norton had hit back, filling the first three places in the Senior and the first two places in the Junior, with Norton-mounted Simpson and Hunt putting up the fastest laps respectively in both classes. Only Nott, in third place in the Junior event, had kept the Rudge flag flying, so the factory were keen to strike back at Norton in 1932. It was a lost cause. In the Senior race Woods won from Guthrie by more than one minute in a Norton-1,2,3. In the Junior his victory over Wal Handley on a Rudge by almost two minutes was a good ride indeed, for his average speed for the race of 77.16 mph was some 3½ minutes faster than Percy Hunt's victory ride in the corresponding race the previous year, and he even exceeded Hunt's fastest lap of that same year by almost two miles an hour.

As the 1933 season opened, it was hard to see how Stanley Woods could better his performance of 1932, but on the Island he once again rode brilliantly and was totally unassailable. In the Junior event it was soon obvious that Norton would make the running, with Woods, Simpson, Guthrie and Hunt surging ahead of the competition. Stanley led from the start, and after Hunt had broken the lap record at 78.85 mph, Woods replied the very next lap with a speed of 79.22 mph. Simpson made a manful effort to reach the magic 80 mph lap, a landmark he had secured for the TTs for the first time in the Senior event two years previously, but his engine gave up the struggle, and Woods finished first at a race average of 78.08 mph. Norton again dominated the Senior race, with Stanley Woods in supreme form. Not only did he win but he set up new race and lap records, and in both he smashed through the 80 mph barrier. His race average was 81.04 mph against his 79.38 mph the previous year, and his fastest lap was 82.74 mph, against Jimmy Simpson's 81.50 mph the year before and 80.82 mph in 1931.

Stanley Woods raced in a bygone age, before the days of super-bikes, colourful riding-leathers, multi-million-pound sponsorships and space-age helmets, but his jaunty personality and gifted riding made him everybody's hero. In action he was a joy to watch — so deceptively controlled and disarming. He was the supreme exponent of his time; a superb tactician; precise in knowing about the machine he was riding, meticulous in race preparation, yet relentless in his scent for success. He once did a final lap of the historic North-West 200 on a flat tyre! He won the Ulster Grand Prix seven times when it was the fastest road race in the world. Nobody knew the Isle of Man course better, and his many victories there were against formidable riders backed by ambitious factories. His uncanny use of the road seemed almost instinctive, and nobody could outbrake him on the bends and stay in the saddle.

After eight years Stanley Woods left Norton, unable to fall in with their policy of riding to team orders. Norton by then so dominated racing that their riders were competing against one another as much as against rival factories, and they began to dictate which rider would take the flag. After bringing Norton victory in both the Senior and Junior TTs at record race and lap speeds in 1933, Woods travelled to Northern Ireland for the Ulster Grand Prix with his mind made up to leave the famous factory. Norton had made it clear that they did not want him to win the 500cc event there, and he might well have defied them had it come to it. But events took a hand, other Norton works entries retired and Woods was left with a clear field to race on to win without breaking any team rules.

The Italian Moto Guzzi factory, founded in 1921, began at this time to look towards racing honours to get their name known and had already contested the TTs with distinction back in 1926, their Italian rider Pietro Ghersi finishing second in the 250cc race, though his placing was later withdrawn because he used a spark plug which was different from the one he had used in practice. They now acquired the services of Stanley Woods, who, after racing their machine to fourth place in the Lightweight race in 1934, brought them brilliant success in 1935. He beat the Rudge machines of Tyrell-Smith and Nott to win the Lightweight TT at a race average of 71.56 mph and, despite poor visibility, broke the lap record at 74.19 mph. It was a significant win on two counts, because the single-cylinder Guzzi was the first spring-framed motor-cycle to win a TT and the first foreign bike to finish first in any TT since Godfrey's win on an Indian in the Senior race back in 1911. The next day Woods rode a two-cylinder Guzzi to victory in the Senior race, again recording the fastest lap at 86.53 mph, a new record. His phenomenal record now included three TT doubles in four years and five out of a possible six fastest laps.

Towards the end of his career Woods moved to Velocette and in the Senior race on the Isle of Man in 1936 finished second, setting up a new lap record at 86.98 mph (the fastest lap ever recorded in the TTs to that time). In the Lightweight race he again set the fastest lap, this time on a DKW machine, at 76.2 mph. He was second again in the Senior on a Velocette the following year and in 1938 made it three second places in a row in the Senior event, narrowly missing victory after an unsuccessful battle with Norton works rider Harold Daniell. He won the Junior comprehensively for Velocette by almost four minutes from team rider Ted Mellors, Woods' average for the race being 84.08 mph. He also set the fastest lap at 85.30 mph and was clocked at a phenomenal 109 mph on the run down to Brandish.

That autumn Prime Minister Neville Chamberlain returned from his Munich meeting with Adolf Hitler waving a piece of paper and declaring it was 'peace in our time', but Britain continued to prepare vigorously for war. Despite the international tension, however, Germany and Italy 'fielded' strong teams on the Isle of Man in 1939. There were three supercharged BMWs in the Senior event, NSU teams in both Senior and Junior races, and all three classes were contested by DKW. From Italy there were 250cc and 500cc entries from Guzzi, and a pair of Benellis. British works team entries came from AJS, Velocette and CTS. It was to be Woods' last appearance in the TTs. Back on the Italian Guzzi for the Lightweight race, he recorded the fastest lap before retiring with mechanical problems. He finished fourth in the Senior on the Velocette, and in the Junior event justice was done as he raced his Velocette to victory by eight seconds from Harold Daniell on the Norton. It was Stanley Woods' tenth TT victory, and in all the TTs in which he had finished he had never missed being on the leaderboard. There was plenty of racing left in Stanley Woods, but within a few months the world was locked in war and the great Irish rider was forced into premature retirement. By the time peace returned, it was too late for him to race again. But the legend lived on, and eighteen years later, to mark the Jubilee celebrations of the TT Races in 1957, Stanley Woods returned to the Island to take a second-string Guzzi round the famous course at 86 mph; and he was there to greet Mike Hailwood when the young rider surpassed his record of ten TT victories.

The last Island races for the great Stanley Woods were also marked by a moving and sad ceremony on the day following the Lightweight race when a memorial to Jimmy Guthrie was unveiled. Guthrie had ridden with Woods in the Norton team and made an indelible mark on the sport over some seven years in the 1930s. When he was signed by Norton in 1931 to ride their new machines with redesigned overhead camshafts, he had already won the 350cc German Grand Prix and brought AJS victory in the Lightweight TT of 1930. When Stanley Woods was supreme in 1933, Guthrie, a redoubtable Scot from Hawick, was finishing third in the Junior TT and fourth in the Senior, but in 1934 he showed outstanding dash and skill to become only the third man to complete a Senior and Junior TT double, beating Jimmy Simpson in both races and riding the fastest lap at 80.11 mph in the Junior event.

Only the ingenuity, gamesmanship and guile of the astute Stanley Woods prevented Guthrie's repeating the double the following year in one of the most dramatic and epic races ever to take place on the famous Island. Guthrie on the Norton had already made sure of the Junior when the first sensation occurred. The Senior race could not take place on the day scheduled because of bad weather, and as the riders stayed back on the Island, thousands of fans had to leave disappointedly for home, the Senior race still un-run. Never before in the twenty-eight years' history of the famous races had a race been postponed.

But more drama was to come. Mist on the mountain delayed the start the following day, but at 11.30 am the first rider finally got away, and soon Jimmy Guthrie, taking the first lap at more than 84 mph, was half a minute up on his team-mate Walter Rusk, in second place, with Stanley Woods holding third place on the powerful Guzzi twin. Woods quickly gained time on Rusk, but on Guthrie he could make little impression. The Scotsman was really flying as he hoisted the lap record to 85.5 mph. Woods gained time as Guthrie pulled into the Norton pit to refuel, in the process beating Guthrie's new lap record with a brilliant circuit at 85.66 mph. In a desperate attempt to make up ground on the Scot, Woods decided against a mid-race refuel, but he was still 32 seconds adrift with just two laps to go. Guthrie seemed certain of victory when this sensation-packed race had the crowds gasping in disbelief. The remarkable events which were crucial to the outcome began at the end of Woods' penultimate lap. Reckoning that Woods would be forced to pull in to refuel, thus adding further to the 26 seconds he was now in arrears, the Norton pit crew passed the message to their station at Ramsey, and Guthrie was signalled that the race was virtually won and he could ease up. The result was that his seventh and last lap was some nine seconds slower than his sixth. So what? He was roared home to winner's champagne and a grandstand crowd who were convinced that Jimmy Guthrie had won a magnificent race to collect the Senior Trophy for 1935. Guthrie was already being hailed the victor.

Meantime Stanley Woods had made two momentous decisions. Even his pit crew, ready with the hoses, were taken by surprise when he flashed past them in front of the grandstand crowd without even a glance in their direction and disappeared over the brow of Bray Hill on the last lap. After pit signals had let him down and cost him victory in the Senior TT of 1927, he had recruited his own timekeepers and their signals now told him that he was still mathematically in with a chance if he could keep the Guzzi going without refuelling and could force the machine over its accepted limits without it blowing up. He explained later that he had decided to ignore all the engine's safety margins. He squeezed every fraction of performance out of the Italian machine. It absorbed the abuse as the revs mounted — up and over the safety margin of 7,700 and on to more than 8,200 rpm in certain stretches — in excess of 121 mph. He raced the last lap at a record 86.53 mph, and as he approached the end he had made up the time on Guthrie. The grandstand crowd, jubilant at Guthrie's stirring performance, now hushed as Woods powered his Guzzi towards the finishing line. Then, unbelievably, the official announcement came over the loudspeakers: Stanley Woods is the winner — by four seconds!

It was a desperate disappointment for Guthrie, but he had other successes to enjoy that year, winning the Swiss Grand Prix as well as the German and establishing a new world one-hour record of

114.092 mph at the high-speed Montlhéry circuit in France. The Swiss and German Grands Prix fell to the likeable Scot once more in 1936, and that same year he turned the tables on Stanley Woods by beating him in the Senior TT by 58 seconds. He made a remarkable impact on the Continent by winning the Swiss Grand Prix for the third year running in 1937 but had mixed fortunes on the Isle of Man that year, winning the Junior race but retiring in the Senior. A few weeks later Jimmy Guthrie crashed on the last lap at the Sachsenring circuit, while leading in the German Grand Prix, and was killed.

Thus, two years on, in the last TT Races before the outbreak of the Second World War, on the day following the Lightweight race, the Jimmy Guthrie Memorial was unveiled by the Island's Lieutenant Governor, at the Cutting where the brilliant Scots rider had retired on his last TT race, the 1937 Senior event.

To be a great motor-cycle rider, however, it is not essential to win a lot of races. Jimmy Simpson, a contemporary of both Woods and Guthrie, only once won a TT race, but in ten Isle of Man rides he finished outside the first three only twice. His fame, though, stems from the lap speed milestones he achieved on the Isle of Man. He was the first rider to complete a TT lap at 60 mph, 70 mph and 80 mph, and altogether he made eight fastest laps in his twelve years of Island racing. He first rode in the TTs in 1922 on a Scott machine, but from then until he retired in 1934 he rode AJS in twelve races and Norton in twelve races. He always raced with plenty of vigour and not too much respect for his machines, and in his 26 TT rides he retired fifteen times. He worked at Norton for a spell, but afterwards took on a Rudge ride for the Lightweight race of 1934. Rudge had been suffering severe financial problems, and a year before an official receiver had been called in to run the company's affairs. The racing department was shut down, but private-entry Rudges were still to be seen racing under the banner of former works rider Graham Walker. Simpson's ill fortune in having to retire in so many TT outings changed in 1934, and for the very first time in his thirteen years of TT riding he rode in three races and finished in all of them.

Simpson was a likeable, well-respected rider who always gave good value for money and the crowd loved him. His win in the Lightweight race of 1934 — the first time incidentally he had entered the Lightweight event — was one of the most popular to take place on the Island. Ironically, Rudge's financial and commercial collapse had no effect on their racing results in the Lightweight event that year, for they occupied the first three places, Simpson leading Nott and Walker over the finishing line. Simpson's time for the race was 3 hours 43 minutes 50 seconds (race average 70.81 mph), and he also raced the fastest lap at 73.64 mph. In the Senior and Junior events he rode Norton machines, and the crowds were delighted when he finished second in both races, behind Guthrie in each case. At the end of the Senior event he simply got off his machine and retired from racing. As the former editor of the *TT Special,* G.S. Davison, once wrote, 'The TT was never the same without him.' Simpson had also ridden successfully in European events and in 1930 became the fastest road racer in the world with a record lap of 84.63 mph in the Ulster Grand Prix. Fittingly, he scored a number of wins on the 'European' circuit in his retirement season, taking Grand Prix honours in Holland, Belgium, Germany, Switzerland and Northern Ireland, in the 350cc event, and in Switzerland in the 500cc class. Fourteen years after his last race, the Jimmy Simpson Trophy was established as a special award for riders who are fastest round the TT course.

Jimmy Simpson's special 'speed' laps were in 1924, 1926 and 1931. It was in the Junior race of 1924 on an AJS that he broke the 60 mph lap barrier, recording 64.24 mph. Two years later, this time on a 500cc AJS in the Senior event, he reached 70.43 mph, and in 1931 he was riding for Norton in the Senior event when he reached 80.82 mph to record the fastest lap ever raced on the Isle of Man. The very next year, again on a Norton, he pushed the record still higher, going round at 81.5 mph, before retiring. Simpson was a hard, uncompromising rider, and to this extent he was the victim of his own philosophy, for he generally demanded too much of his machines. But in 1934, as he prepared for the Lightweight TT, he had already decided to retire at the end of racing that week, and for once he was willing to relax his naturally aggressive style of riding. Even so, it is said that on the first lap the Rudge engine partially seized and it was only the pit manager's insistence that he continue riding that brought him his long-awaited and fully justified first and only Tourist Trophy.

The Second World War foreshortened many riders' careers and ruined others, and there was an unfamiliarity about many of the riders when racing resumed in 1947. The immaculate Stanley Woods was no longer present. Jimmy Guthrie's death was still mourned. Jimmy Simpson's particular brand of cavalier riding had yet to be equalled, though his last race was now more than a decade in the past. Other pre-war stars, such as Mellors, Tyrell-Smith, Rusk, Nott, Walker and 'Crasher' White, were strangely absent from those early post-war results on the Isle of Man.

Some names, however, did survive to rekindle past glories. It was in 1936 that Freddie Frith, a quiet lad from Grimsby and earlier an apprentice stonemason, first joined the Norton works team. His interest in motor-cycling had begun in the early 1920s when he competed in local grass-track meetings near his home, and he travelled to the Isle of Man for the first time in 1930 when, in the Manx series, he finished third on a KTT Velocette. Five years later, in the same competition, he won the Junior race at race and record speeds, and in the 500cc class he led for five of the six laps. So he was an able candidate when Norton went in search of a replacement for an injured Walter Rusk in 1936. Frith's TT début was remarkable, for in an astonishing Junior race he not only won by a 5½ minute margin but cracked the lap record three times to finish with a new lap record of 81.94 mph. The battle between the established Guthrie and new-boy Frith was sensational. In good weather Guthrie set a cracking pace from the start and led for the first four laps, smashing his own lap record, but Frith held on grimly in second place. With 130 miles gone, only one second separated the two Norton riders, but when Guthrie's chain came off on the fifth lap, Frith raced into the lead. It was a remarkable victory because Guthrie's existing lap record of 80.11 mph, which had stood since 1934, was shattered five times — twice by Guthrie himself.

This was the race in which Guthrie was first disqualified for allegedly receiving help from a marshal in restarting after losing his chain; then received an admission from the stewards that they had made a mistake; and finally had to accept their judgement that they could not alter the finishing order to reinstate him in second position, though they did suggest that he receive the value of the prize for the second-placed rider.

In the Senior event that year, Frith by no means disgraced himself, finishing third behind Guthrie and Woods. The following year he did even better. Riding one of the new twin-cam Nortons, he beat Stanley Woods on a Velocette in a nail-biting contest to take the Senior TT, at the same time setting the fastest lap, and in the

Junior race he finished second to team-leader Jimmy Guthrie and shared the fastest lap with him.

Frith's battle with Woods in the Senior was a classic. Norton's formidable team considered Woods the major opposition, though the Italian champion, Omobono Tenni on the reliable Guzzi, and Jock West on a BMW could not be ignored. In the early stages Guthrie and Frith led Woods to put Norton in a strong position, but Woods soon passed Frith, and at record-breaking speed Guthrie and Woods raced out a three-lap duel which was talked about for years. When Guthrie's engine packed in, Norton's hopes were pinned on Frith. It was a lot to ask, but he opened the throttle wide and with just one lap to go had pulled up on Woods, both then sharing first place at a record average speed of 87.88 mph. With a new record lap of 90.27 mph, the first lap in excess of 90 mph in the history of the TT, Frith raced on furiously, and as Stanley Woods finished ahead of Frith, all he could do was wait to see if the young man from South Humberside would beat his time. With a new race average of 88.21 mph, Freddie Frith managed a remarkable win, finishing just fifteen seconds ahead of Woods.

In just two seasons Frith's riding on the Isle of Man had established him among motor-cycling's hierarchy, and although his performances were less good in 1938 and 1939, he was still considered one of the all-time greats and a familiar name to latch onto when racing resumed in 1947. An accident on a practice 500cc Guzzi kept him out of Isle of Man racing that year, but in 1948 he returned to triumph in the Junior event. He had switched from Norton to Velocette, and on one of the two new Mark VIII KTT machines which had been assigned to him and Kenneth Bills, Frith led the race from beginning to end. He also set the fastest lap at 82.45 mph.

For 1949 Velocette produced seven special engines, two to 500cc specification and five 350s. One was fitted into the Mark VIII KTT frame for use by Freddie Frith, and after a close battle with Bill Doran on a works AJS he once again secured the Junior TT for the factory, registering the fastest lap at 84.23 mph. The win contributed to an outstanding season for Freddie Frith. That year the pre-war European Championship was replaced by the new series of World Championship races which Velocette contested vigorously in the 500cc and 350cc classes. Frith's performance was exceptional. He won all five rounds, in Switzerland, Holland, Belgium and Northern Ireland, as well as on the Isle of Man, to become one of Britain's three first World Champions in that inaugural year of the new series. Les Graham topped the 500cc class, and Eric Oliver won the sidecar series. Frith so commanded the 350cc series that he ended the season fifteen points ahead of the class runner-up, Reg Armstrong, on an AJS.

Sadly, Freddie Frith decided to retire at the end of 1949 to set up a motor-cycle establishment in Grimsby, but for his outstanding contribution to the sport he became the first motor-cyclist to be awarded the Order of the British Empire. Frith was a neatly composed, stylish rider of extraordinary talent, and his retirement, so soon after re-starting his career after the war, was mourned by thousands of fans.

Another rider for whom the war stunted a sparkling career was Harold Daniell, a Londoner born in 1910 who continued to ride competitively until 1951. He started riding seriously in the late 1920s, and after a number of good outings on AJS machinery he switched to Norton in the mid-1930s, riding works bikes in Continental races and a highly tuned Steve Lancefield special in home races. In 1937 he won an impressive number of events on British circuits, but his outstanding successes came immediately prior to, and after, the Second World War. In 1938 he beat Stanley Woods by fifteen seconds to take the Senior TT, also establishing the fastest lap at 91 mph, and he was a winner once again in the Senior in the first Island races to be held after the war, beating Artie Bell by twenty-two seconds. He made it a hat-trick of Senior TT wins in 1949. Bespectacled, chunky for a motor-cycle racer, Harold Daniel nevertheless had much talent and plenty of courage. His win against Woods in 1938 was against all the odds. The legendary Irishman had already notched a record nine victories on the Isle of Man, yet it was Daniel's first TT win there. Moreover, his 91 mph record lap was the first time the Mountain Course had been circuited under 25 minutes, and this enormous achievement stood until 1950, when Geoffrey Duke eclipsed it by 2.33 mph.

After the war motor-cycle racing was never quite the same again. The gutsy, breezy characters were gradually replaced by a new breed of racer, more sophisticated, more aware of their own value. The days when British riders on British machines dominated the world were drawing rapidly to an end. In little more than a decade there would emerge the phenomenon of the Japanese, with Honda making prodigious investment in the sport.

But before dropping the curtain on this first golden age for British racing motor-cyclists and the British motor-cycle industry, there were other great riders who need to be mentioned. There was Howard Davies, who in 1921 became the only man to win the Senior TT on a 350cc machine. There was Walter Handley, who won TT trophies in all four solo classes — Senior, Junior, Lightweight and Ultra-Lightweight. There was Freddie Dixon, the only rider to win both a solo and sidecar TT, Percy Hunt, Geoff Nott, Graham Walker, Walter Rusk, Jock West and many others.

3. Top Racers on the Championship Circuit

Motor-cycle road racing in the 1950s was dominated by two rare talents. Geoffrey Duke won his first world titles in 1951 and was virtually unbeatable until 1955, after which John Surtees became supreme right up to 1960. Between them these two extraordinary British riders secured thirteen world titles and won sixty-seven grand prix races in just ten years. For style, skill and sheer impact they were in a class of their own, and their careers were boosted by a significant upsurge of public interest in road racing at an international level at that time, brought about mainly by a new points-scoring series of races held under the new World Championship banner. Their fan following set new levels, and they were sporting heroes admired and respected far beyond the frontiers of motor-cycle sport.

Duke was generally accepted as the first of a new style of motor-cycle racer, alert to developing opportunities, conscious of his own worth to a factory with racing ambitions, and happy to benefit from his own public image. With his smart new one-piece racing-leathers he brought a touch of fashion and class to the track. Before that it had never occurred to riders to wear anything but the standard, baggy two-piece outfits. In 1951, with five wins in the 350cc class and four wins in the 500cc class, he became the first-ever double World Champion. In the next four years he was 350cc World Champion in 1952 and 500cc World Champion three years running, in 1953, 1954 and 1955. Such was his command in the 500cc class in 1955, his last great season as a world champion, that he finished up eight points ahead of Armstrong, having won four of the eight grand prix rounds.

Geoffrey Duke was only thirteen when he first took to motor-cycle riding. Two years later he owned an ancient 175cc Dot. He was just beginning to become seriously interested in the sport when, at eighteen, he became an army despatch rider during the Second World War. Afterwards he bought a 350cc BSA and worked for the factory as a tuner of their trials machines. As a member of the BSA trials team, his talent was noticed by Irish rider Artie Bell, and it was not long before Duke had offers of work from both AJS and Norton. On advice, he moved to Norton and attracted their attention with his all-round riding ability. He had always been versatile, competing in trials and scrambles, and was still riding successfully in off-road competition when Norton supplied him with a road-racing Manx Norton in 1949, on which he won the Junior Manx GP on the Isle of Man. Within a year he was in the Norton works team and the envy of all aspiring racers, for at that time Norton had the best and most successful racing team in the world.

Duke appeared in his first TT races in 1950. Once in the public eye, he was an immediate sensation — trim-fitting leathers and an immaculate riding style, even for those days when racers stuck firmly to the saddle anyway. His mastery of the famous Norton 'featherbed' machine was exceptional as he swept into corners at high speed, cranking the machine over to exciting and extreme angles. On the Island he won the major Senior race with a new race record, and his new lap record, at a searing 93.33 mph, was more than 2½ mph faster than the previous best, set by his Norton team-mate Harold Daniell. He won further World Championship rounds in Italy and Ulster and could have clinched the world title in his first season had not the tread come off his rear tyre at the Belgian Grand Prix with the famous Italian Gilera team well beaten. In the 350cc class he ran second on the Isle of Man and in Holland and third in Belgium and Switzerland, and showed a glimpse of his future success with a win over AJS rider Les Graham at the Italian Grand Prix. That year he ended the season in second place in both the 500cc and 350cc classes of the World Championship.

In 1961 Duke left no one in doubt that he was the finest motor-cycle racer in the world. Contesting the World Championships once more for Norton, he won the 350cc round on the Isle of Man and in Belgium, France, Northern Ireland and Italy. In this class his final tally of 40 points was a record for the World Championships which was to stand for ten years. He had a tougher fight in the 500cc class, but Duke (with 35 points) clinched the title, and his double World

Championship, by finishing the season just four points ahead of the Italian Gilera star, Alfredo Milani, with Umberto Masetti, also on a Gilera, in third place with 21 points. For his contribution to motor-cycle racing, Duke became the second rider, after Freddie Frith, to receive the OBE. His outstanding talent also earned him the Segrave Trophy and the Sportsman of the Year title.

Not only on the track was Geoffrey Duke a credit to his sport. He was composed, confident and articulate, and although he did not shirk the responsibility to fight when he considered a principle needed defending, he was assured, reasoned and quiet: a fine ambassador. He was also a staunch patriot, increasingly troubled by the seeming inability of the British factories to galvanize themselves for what was to turn out to be a death-battle with Continental competition. Internationally, Germany was banned from competing in those early post-war years as a retribution for the atrocities perpetrated by the Nazis, but Italy escaped the ban and, once the World Championships were established in their new form, in 1949, was quick to take up the challenge again. From the start of the new championships Italian riders on Italian machines dominated the lower-capacity classes, securing the 125cc and 250cc titles in 1949, 1950 and 1951. Through Velocette, AJS and then Norton, piloted by Duke, Britain managed during these years to maintain its premier position, though a dangerous precedent was set in 1950 when Umberto Masetti rode a Gilera to become the 500cc World Champion, pipping a fast-emerging Geoffrey Duke by a single point.

The Italians' great ambition was to consolidate their position in the heavier, more prestigious classes, most particularly in 500cc racing. With this in mind Gilera worked hard to improve the handling characteristics of their powerful and very fast multi-cylinder racers. They also realized that to win World Championships they needed to have the best riders — and they were British. They set out to tempt them away from AJS, Velocette and Norton. Sadly, this became less of a problem as time went on and as the British factories played into the Italian hands. In short, British bikes had been best for far too long. Why should a war change things? British factories relied too much and for too long on the single-cylinder and twin-cylinder machines that had dominated racing in pre-war days, but against the multi-cylinder bikes from Italy they were fast becoming less competitive. Their dependability was no longer enough.

Against the Italians' aggressive racing policy, British effort seemed puny, suffering, it appeared, from meagre investment, only tepid ambition, lack of foresight, little will to accept challenge, and appalling complacency. Britain's top racers were faced with increasing problems in finding a competitive ride on British machinery. Even after Cecil Sandford and Les Graham, however reluctantly, had finally accepted the inevitable and moved to the Italian MV Agusta factory, Norton seemed unwilling or incapable of acting positively to retain the services of Geoffrey Duke.

In 1952 Duke on the Norton was left to fight a desperate rearguard action. While he deplored the trend towards British riders racing foreign machines, he was left to wage an unequal battle against the big Italian factories, who now had Fergus Anderson (Guzzi) and Cecil Sandford (MV) in the lighter classes and Les Graham (MV) contesting the 250cc and 500cc rounds. Norton continued triumphant in the 350cc class, and Duke once again took the World Championship with ease, winning in Switzerland, on the Isle of Man and in Holland and Belgium. In the 500cc class it was a different story, but despite the British/Italian challenge in the form of Les Graham on the MV, it was the Italian, Umberto Masetti, on the Gilera who ironically took the premier title from Duke. In the Senior TT Duke was forced to retire with clutch trouble, after setting the fastest lap at 94.88 mph, but he managed second place in both Holland and Belgium. In a desperately disappointing season he then crashed in a minor German event at Schotten and was out of action for the remainder of the season. Fortunately he had already done enough in the 350cc class to secure that particular world title.

After receiving widespread acclaim, which even included a 'well done' piece by no less an authority than *The Times,* for deciding to 'stay with Britain' for the 1953 season, Duke had an eleventh-hour change of heart, finding it impossible in the end to decline an offer made by Commendatore Giuseppe Gilera to join his works team. Thus began the second and even more successful part of Duke's sparkling motor-cycle racing career. In a sense Norton accepted the inevitable courageously and, after seeing their other star rider, Reg Armstrong, depart to Gilera along with Duke, quickly reorganized their squad, depending in 1953 on Jack Brett, the wild Rhodesian racer Ray Amm and Australian Ken Kavanagh. They made a spirited challenge to the might of Italy and in the opening round, on the Isle of Man, did magnificently, Amm and Kavanagh finishing first and second in the Junior event and Amm and Brett racing through in similar positions in the Senior race, ahead of Armstrong on the Gilera. In the Senior, Duke began in sizzling style with a record lap of 96.38 mph, but tragedy struck on the next lap when the likeable Les Graham lost control of his MV while racing down Bray Hill at 130 mph and was killed. Duke later raised the lap record to 97.2 mph, only to see Amm better it with a round at 97.41 mph. When Duke tweaked the Gilera a shade too much at Quarter Bridge and came off, his petrol tank being too damaged for him to continue, Amm was left with a clear field, and it was first blood to Norton. But with wins in Holland, France, Switzerland and Italy, and a second place in Northern Ireland, Geoffrey Duke went on to make certain of the 500cc world title.

Duke stayed with Gilera to the end of his classic racing career. He won the 500cc World Championship again in 1954, by an important 12 points margin, and in 1955 he secured his sixth world title, once more claiming the prestigious 500cc crown. So convincing was his performance in the Senior TT that year that his average of 97.93 mph over the seven laps was higher than the previous lap record.

By now the always stylish Duke was approaching thirty-three, while a promising rider some eleven years his junior had already begun to excite crowds at home circuits, stimulating track-side talk of a new world champion in the making. Duke's young rival was a Londoner called John Surtees, son of famous racer Jack Surtees. As a nineteen-year-old, Surtees had already created something of a sensation with repeated wins at home circuits such as Brands Hatch, Cadwell Park and Castle Combe, and at Silverstone in the Hutchinson 100 race, riding his tuned Manx Norton, he had shown his contempt for Duke's fame and experience by outriding him so positively that he might well have beaten the Gilera-mounted rider had he not been forced out with engine problems.

But the future was by no means certain for Surtees. Norton, who had supported a number of riders unofficially in 1955, Surtees among them, had decided to withdraw from racing in 1956 and, with the retirement of their expert development manager Joe Craig, there was little future there for a talented rider with ambitions to be world champion. In the Ulster Grand Prix of 1955 Surtees had scored a convincing victory in the 250cc class on a German NSU, but the German factory, which had strongly supported racing since Germany had been permitted in 1951 to compete once more in international races, was finding it hard, as indeed were all the British factories, to sustain any kind of racing policy. Italy provided the best opportunities and MV in particular, for the ill-fated Ray Amm, on whom the Italian factory pinned such hopes, had been killed on his first outing for MV, on Easter Monday 1955, at Imola. MV boss Count Agusta was looking earnestly for a replacement, and John Surtees came highly recommended by Bill Webster, their unofficial talent-scout in the UK. Gilera also showed interest, but after testing the MVs thoroughly at the Monza circuit, going round only fractionally slower than the existing lap record, Surtees decided to accept Count Agusta's offer and he signed for MV.

It should be made clear that not every rider would automatically have jumped at the chance to ride MV at that time. Both Les Graham and Ray Amm had been killed riding the Italian machine, and their native rider, Carlo Bandirola, had 'fallen' repeatedly, leading many observers to raise considerable doubts about the handling characteristics of the bikes when ridden at speed. Nonetheless, Surtees backed his own judgement and after sampling the bikes at Monza had no hesitation in joining what was a formidable MV works team.

The palpitating prospect now was a season-long clash between Geoffrey Duke on the Gilera and John Surtees on the MV, in anticipation an epic duel. Disappointingly, it did not materialize. At the Dutch Grand Prix of 1955 the discontent felt by a number of 'private' riders at the start money being offered led to an unprecedented riders' revolt, and their action was supported by a number of works riders, Duke among them. For this Duke, along with Armstrong and several others, was suspended by the FIM for six months and so could not take part in the World Championships until July 1956. Meantime, John Surtees started his grand prix career in magnificent style, thundering round the Mountain Course on the Isle of Man in the Senior event at an average 96.57 mph for the 264¼ mile race and setting the fastest lap at 97.79 mph. He looked certain to make it a Senior/Junior TT double, but with only a quarter lap to go he ran out of petrol, stranding him up on the mountain. In the following Dutch TT in June, Surtees scored a comfortable 500cc victory from Walter Zeller riding a BMW, in the

The pioneering days of motor-cycle racing. Harry Collier (or is it brother Charlie?) competing in the 1909 TT Races on the Isle of Man.

Jake de Rosier shattered three world records in America before coming to Britain to race against Charlie Collier at the famous Brooklands Circuit in July 1911. The American on his Indian machine won two of the scheduled three races.

The golden years for British motor-cycling, with Norton supreme. Jimmy Simpson (36) and Jimmy Guthrie (29) photographed with V. N. Brittain at the Senior TT in June 1934. That year Guthrie won the Senior and Junior TT double, with Simpson runner-up in both events. Simpson on a Rudge won the Lightweight race.

The incomparable Stanley Woods. He established a racing legend in the 1920s and 1930s, and his record of ten TT victories established in 1939 has to this day been bettered by only one rider (Mike Hailwood) and equalled by only one (Giacomo Agostini). He rode on the Isle of Man every year from 1922 until 1939, winning the Junior race on a Velocette on his last appearance there.

Geoffrey Duke was one of the most stylish riders and one of the most successful. He won the prestigious 500cc World Championship three years running from 1953 on the Italian Gilera machine. He scored a 500cc and 350cc double World Championship on a Norton in 1951. Duke is seen here (seated) with Norton team-mates Ken Kavanagh, Reg Armstrong and Len Parry.

John Surtees took over from Duke as World Champion, riding for the Italian MV factory, in 1956. Before his retirement in favour of car-racing in 1960, his phenomenal run of success brought him 500cc and 350cc World Championships in 1958, 1959 and 1960. He is the only man to become World Champion racing motor-bikes and cars.

Note the ancient-looking streamlining. Leading the 125cc race at the German Grand Prix of 1955 is the Italian lightweight ace, Carlo Ubbiali. Unmatched on lighter machinery, Ubbiali would undoubtedly have become better known had he moved up to the more prestigious 500cc class.

Trials riding is the most skilful of motor-cycle sports, and the king for many years was Britain's Sammy Miller. Belfast-born, he was also a wonderful ambassador for his sport. His natural style and outstanding ability won him eleven British titles in as many years.

Motocross is a spectacular sport and there has never been a more colourful character than the Belgian Joel Robert. Competing in the 1969 Polish 250cc Motocross Grand Prix, Robert becomes airborne, swinging his CZ machine into impossible-looking angles.

Honda's most famous team captain, Jim Redman rode for the Japanese factory during its most successful racing days in the 1960s. On the Honda, in top-flight 250cc and 350cc racing, Redman was virtually unbeatable for a number of years.

Dominating speedway in the late 1950s and early 1960s, the New Zealander Barry Briggs is seen in practice at Wembley for the 1961 British Speedway Championships. He was World Champion four times and took the British Riders Championship five times in a row from 1965.

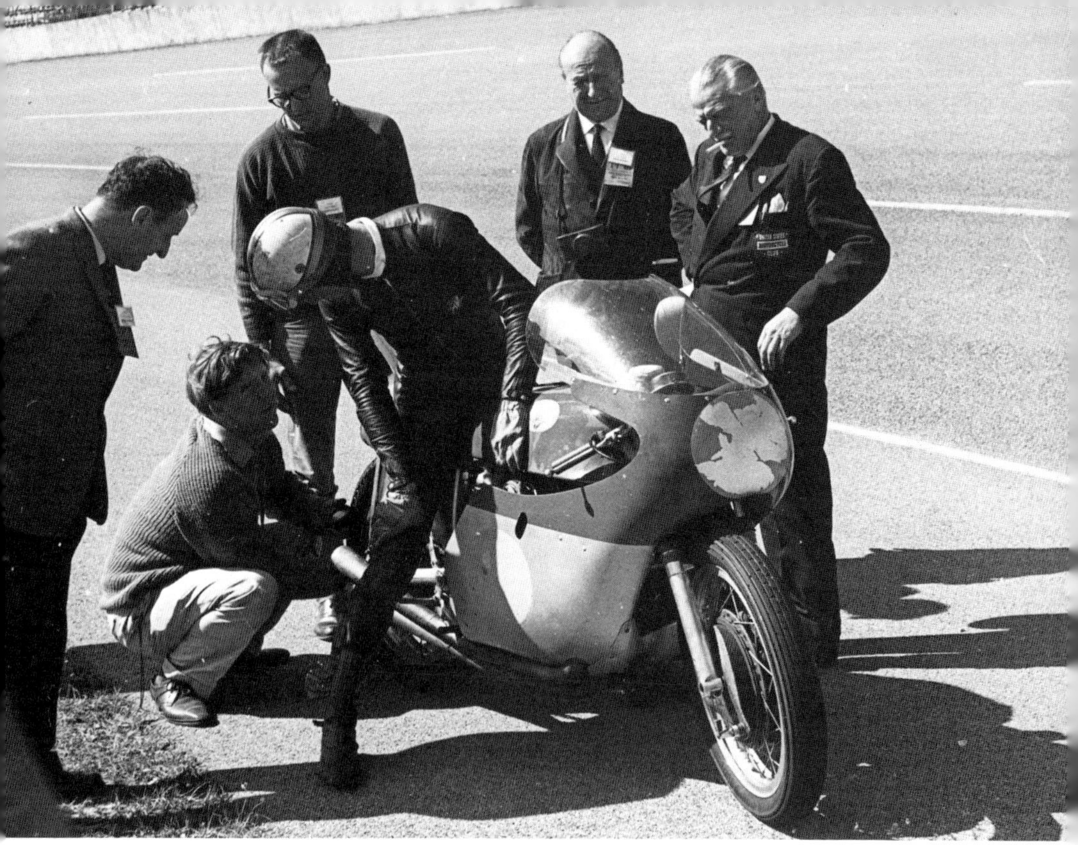

The late and great Mike Hailwood pictured at Daytona during his successful attempt at the One Hour Record in 1964. Extreme right is Stan Hailwood and tending the MV machine is famous sprint expert and motor-cycle journalist Charlie Rous.

Two of the most famous motor-cyclists of all time meet on the Isle of Man at the 1975 TT Races. Geoffrey Duke looks on as Mike Hailwood signs yet another autograph.

No rider has been World Champion more often than the fifteen-times crowned Giacomo Agostini. His five 350cc and 500cc double World Championships is also a record. The handsome Italian (inset) is seen winning for the last time on the famous MV 500 at the German Grand Prix of 1977.

No rider has a superior record in racing lighter machines than the incredible Angel Nieto. The famous Spaniard (2) is seen in a close battle with Holland's Jan de Vries at the Swedish Grand Prix of 1972.

process breaking Geoffrey Duke's existing race and lap records established only a year before. Excitement was intense as riders prepared for the Belgian Grand Prix in July, for John Surtees, eager to capitalize on his successes on the Isle of Man and in Holland, would be facing Geoffrey Duke, now out of suspension, on the Gilera, for the first time.

In *The Story of MV Agusta Motor Cycles* (published by Patrick Stephens), I describe the event as follows:

> According to Surtees' recollection of the race, practice times had shown how difficult it was going to be for the MVs to hold the Gilera, the latter with modified ratios to incorporate a special fourth gear which was to be used for the long uphill stretch from Stavelot. From the start, Surtees took the MV to the front and held the lead for five laps. Then the Gilera roared past and Surtees was faced with having to decide whether to run the risk of taking off in pursuit and possibly over-revving the MV, or to settle for second place and six valuable championship points. He had virtually decided on the latter tactic — perhaps most sensibly — when the unlucky Duke had to retire with valve trouble on the thirteenth lap.

Surtees also won the 350cc event to score a magnificent double victory.

With three rounds to go, Surtees looked a hot favourite for the 500cc world title. His position seemed impregnable, with 24 points against his nearest rival, Walter Zeller, on a BMW, who had fourteen. Indeed, just one more victory would remove all doubt, and although in a less strong position in the 350cc table, there was a good chance that he might make it a double championship success.

The next round was at the Solitude track in Germany. In the 350cc race Surtees was handily placed, but Bill Lomas, riding an Italian Guzzi, was making him work hard to keep in touch. Lomas entered the bend first, Surtees rushed after him, but the front wheel of the MV slipped on loose sand and the bike spun out of control. Surtees was flung across the track, hit the banking and lost consciousness. He was rushed to hospital at Stuttgart and was lucky to escape with only a badly broken and bruised arm, which later had to be permanently pinned. The crash put him out for the remainder of the season. Could Geoffrey Duke capitalize on his rival's misfortune? It did not seem possible as he had to retire in the German Grand Prix with electrical problems, and in the Ulster Grand Prix he came off while trying to keep ahead of a persistent John Hartle on a 'works' Norton. Duke came back to win the final round of the championship at Monza, but Surtees had done enough in the early rounds to clinch the 500cc world title.

Ill-luck persisted for the unfortunate Duke into the next season. In a pre-championship meeting at Imola, he crashed heavily in the warm-up race and so badly injured his shoulder that he missed four of the six classic rounds. He returned for the Belfast meeting, finishing third behind the Italian Libero Liberati and Bob McIntyre, both Gilera-mounted, and in the final race at Monza he was second to Liberati. Worst of all was the shock announcement at the end of 1957 of the retirement from racing of Gilera, along with those of Guzzi and Mondial. Duke, however, maintained his interest in racing and had outings on BMW and Norton in 1958 and was on a Norton again in 1959. He even won the Swedish Grand Prix of 1958, but it was a token victory. Some years earlier Duke had tried car-racing, and in 1960 he had another go, but a crash in Sweden the following year ended his racing career altogether.

Geoffrey Duke remained an inspiration to thousands of ambitious racers for years. They tried to copy his amazingly deceptive style — unhurried, precise, disciplined — and only then discovered the extent of his genius. It looked so easy, to see him in action. It proved so hard when you tried it yourself. His thoughtful, intelligent approach to racing gave him a keen and lively perception of all aspects of the sport. He said that the British industry would collapse unless policies and attitudes were changed, and he shouted in the wilderness about the oncoming threat from Japan. As he packed away his leathers for the last time, it had been almost forty years since, as a very small boy, he had watched races on the sands at Southport and Wallasey and climbed up to ride pillion behind his older brother. The lad from Lancashire was said to have picked up his early knowledge of engines by haunting local garages and he was only thirteen when he pooled his cash with a friend to buy his first motor bike for just ten shillings. Years later his suggestions and advice on machine development to both Norton and Gilera contributed significantly to their continued success.

Although out of racing, Duke kept close to it. Now thirty-seven, he had raced successfully for twelve seasons and in 1960 sponsored the famous Sammy Miller. He went to live on his beloved Isle of Man.

His inspired and courageous move in 1963, though doomed to

failure, showed how devoted and committed he was to the ideals of the sport. Count Agusta, the autocratic boss of MV Agusta, had decided to continue to back racing after most of the rival Italian and German factories pulled out in the late 1950s. His machines, ridden by John Surtees, Gary Hocking and Mike Hailwood, had raced virtually unchallenged from one world championship to another, and the sheer predictability of the results had taken much of the edge out of racing. Duke somehow managed to persuade Gilera to bring their old racing machines out of mothballs, formed Scuderia Duke and signed Derek Minter and John Hartle to spearhead his challenge. It was a brave and expensive move. The old Gileras were still magnificent machines and very fast and could have posed a serious threat to MV.

Unfortunately, Duke's challenge was beset with misfortune. After showing the Gileras' paces in tests at the famous Monza circuit, both Hartle and Minter lapping consistently at around 116 mph, and at early season non-championship races at Silverstone and Brands Hatch, the season looked poised for a tremendous battle between MV and Duke's private venture with the Gileras. Sadly, disagreements between Hartle and Minter, and then Minter and Duke, did nothing to encourage success, and then Minter crashed heavily and suffered a broken back. Phil Read was drafted into Minter's place, but Minter made a good recovery and returned to the team in Ireland. Further niggling disagreements with Duke, however, plus some misfortunes in one or two races, and the challenge was gone. The turning point was certainly the hideous crash of Derek Minter at Brands Hatch, which kept him out of the team. More than one noted authority in the sport believes to this day that had Minter not crashed, he would have been World Champion in 1963, and Geoffrey Duke's inspired move would have ended in sensational triumph.

With Geoffrey Duke retired from racing, John Surtees became the new hero. Never to quite the same extent the crowd favourite that Duke had been, Surtees nonetheless became a popular champion, admired and respected for his skill and courage. His style was more vigorous, somewhat less compact, and he never developed the same kind of relationship with the fans, but he is still the only man ever to have become World Champion riding motorbikes and racing cars. It is a pity that Surtees' career coincided with the withdrawal from top-flight racing of most of the Italian grand prix teams. As a team rider for MV Agusta he was for some years required to overcome only non-factory opposition, and for this reason there is a tendency in less generous assessments to downgrade his performances. This is unfair. John Surtees was an outstanding and worthy champion, taking the world title seven times between 1956 and 1960.

Surtees, like Duke, had started motor-cycle racing while still in his teens, inspired by his father, Jack, a noted sidecar rider. Young John soon became his father's sidecar passenger, but he wanted to race solo and, although under age, he entered his first meeting, a grass-track event at Luton, while only fifteen. He came off while in third place. After leaving school he went to Stevenage to work for the famous Vincent factory and at seventeen won his first major road race, at Brands Hatch, on a 500cc Vincent Grey Flash which he had picked up from scrap and worked on himself. From his prize money he eventually bought a Manx Norton and showed such promise that in 1955 he was recruited to the famous Norton works team. He was ambitious and keen to do well in world championship events, but Norton were coming to the end of their racing road. When he could see there was no prospect of his becoming World Champion while riding for Norton, because by then the factory were not contesting a full programme of world championship races, he accepted the offer from MV and raced to his first world title that same year.

In 1958, 1959 and 1960, in a phenomenal run of success, John Surtees became World Champion in both the 350cc and 500cc classes. With little to challenge the mighty MV, Surtees applied his talent to beating previous records, and he raced magnificently. In 1958 he swept to victories in every grand prix event, in both the 350cc and 500cc classes, his name being absent only in the results from Sweden where, with maximum points secured from other rounds, Count Agusta decided it was not worth attending the meeting. Even so, Surtees won the championship by eight points (in the 350cc class) and twelve points in the 500cc class. If MV as a factory had little to oppose them, Surtees had John Hartle for a team-mate, and he was a tough, adventurous rider who could run Surtees close for speed on a good day. Such was Surtees' consistency, however, that when he was timed during the Grand Prix at Monza, only two-tenths of a second difference was recorded between his first and twentieth laps. What precision!

In 1959 John Surtees won every race in the 350cc World

Championship and every race in the 500cc World Championship, a feat never before achieved by any rider. In France, on the Isle of Man, in Germany, Sweden, Northern Ireland and Italy, he stormed ahead of the field, well on his way to his career-record of thirty-eight victories in World Championship events. In the 500cc Championship in 1959 he won all seven rounds at new record speeds. Despite such a performance critics talked of hollow victories because of the lack of works opposition, but Surtees' personal talent was never in question. The attacks were made from the standpoint of racing itself, and who could deny that grand prix competition in the heavier classes had become far too boring and predictable for its own good? But in 1960 there was still no opposition to MV, and Surtees, for the third year running, took both titles.

John Surtees was an outstanding engineer, and his wide technical knowledge was applied with benefit by MV in sorting out their frame and mechanical problems. It would also be hard to find a more dedicated rider. His career in motor-cycle racing was foreshortened by the racing policy of Count Agusta. The MV boss was only interested in collecting world titles and increasingly denied Surtees rides in other events. Consequently, while he had ridden in perhaps some 70 events during his first season with MV, his programme had been cut down to no more than twenty in 1959. He had already been tempted to have a few car rides and had showed much promise, so at the end of 1960, with that quiet deliberation which characterized his personality, John Surtees said farewell to MV and motor-cycle racing and moved into motor-racing, becoming Formula 1 World Champion in a Ferrari in 1964.

Like most riders of his time and before, John Surtees took naturally to the Mountain Course on the Isle of Man, accepting its dangers as a natural challenge to his courage, skill and intelligence. To win there gave added satisfaction, and he enjoyed many successes. He won the Senior and Junior TTs in 1958 and again in 1959 and so in 1960 was on the verge of two exciting records. No rider had yet secured that coveted Senior trophy three times in a row, nor had any rider done the Senior/Junior TT 'double' in three successive seasons. Barring mechanical failure, an in-form John Surtees was very likely to scale both these heights. In the Junior TT Surtees made a brilliant start. On the opening lap he set a new class record at 98.26 mph, and he did even better the second time round, lapping at 99.2 mph, but from then on the potential 'double' was lost. His MV developed problems and he lost bottom gear, then fourth gear, and as the race progressed it was obvious that the engine was losing compression. Meantime, team-mate John Hartle took the lead, and in the end Surtees did well to finish in second place, just 1 minute 55.4 seconds behind Hartle. Even so, Surtees' 99.2 mph lap was the fastest raced in the event.

In the Senior race it was a different story. Surtees was in devastating form, roaring round the Mountain Course on his opening lap at an astonishing 103.03 mph — almost two miles an hour faster than the previous lap record. His second lap was even faster, at 104.08 mph, the MV kept going and he was totally in command, winning the race at an average 102.44 mph, with John Hartle second and a youthful Mike Hailwood finishing third on a Norton. It was a fitting reward to a rider who had given such dedication to the sport of motor-cycle racing. He thus became the first rider to win the Senior TT three times in three successive years, and his win also enabled him to equal Stanley Woods' record of four Senior TT wins.

There is no question that, first, Geoffrey Duke and then John Surtees dominated international motor-cycle road racing in the 1950s. In a way, ambitious contemporaries could count themselves unfortunate to have been born into the same era, because the presence of Duke and Surtees blocked opportunities which might otherwise have gone to other riders. But there were other great riders during this period, for greatness cannot always be measured by results and success. Some riders were more exciting, others more prepared to dredge up their last fraction of courage in the name of their sport. If you could make reliable comparisons, which indeed you cannot, it is possible that certain riders, who fought laboured battles riding less exotic machinery and struggled on without the benefits and obvious advantages of a 'works' ride, did better than Duke and Surtees. Who can tell?

Any account of motor-cycle racing in the 1950s would certainly be incomplete without mention of, for instance, Les Graham. Here was a rider of immense ability, yet for whom fate played its most cruel hand. When Count Domenico Agusta's motor-cycle racing ambitions extended beyond Italy and settled on the new World Championships instituted in 1949, he looked with envy towards Britain. Italy was not short of good riders, but few were world class.

Those who were had contracts with other major factories, but Les Graham caught the Count's eye when finishing second to Geoffrey Duke in the Italian Grand Prix at Monza in 1950. Graham was no novice even then. Indeed, with wins in Switzerland, Northern Ireland and a second place in Holland, he had in 1949 become the first-ever World Champion in the 500cc class while under contract to Britain's AJS factory. The MV boss could see in Graham a rider of world class, but the additional bonus Les could offer was his outstanding ability as a mechanic, skills which could be applied to the fast but then patently unreliable four-cylinder MVs. British factories had already seen their best days, and Graham was becoming increasingly concerned and frustrated by AJS's attitude towards the future, and to racing in particular. In contrast, Italy seemed buoyant in terms of motor-cycle activity, and he was impressed at the development and the different attitude there.

Les had a lively temperament which suited him for the short-circuit racing in Britain, and at Cadwell Park in the last years before the Second World War he had caught the attention of fans and observers alike with his infectious enthusiasm and obvious skill. After serving as a bomber pilot in the war, for which he won the DFC, he joined the AJS team when racing recommenced, and in spite of the famous 'Porcupine' twin being temperamental, he managed to bring that first 350cc World Championship to Britain. It was on the AJS that Les Graham suffered what many judge to be his greatest disappointment. His ambition was to win the Senior TT, and in the 1949 event he was in a commanding lead when, at Bray Hill on the final lap and with less than two miles to the end of the race, his magneto failed and he was left to coast to a standstill and, thereafter, to push into finish. As famous motor-cycling commentator Murray Walker once said: 'It was so typical of him that as he crossed the line he had a broad grin on his face.'

So it was logical that, given the opportunity, he should join MV for 1951. He put every effort into making the bikes more reliable, and after working hard and bringing in experts such as forks specialist Ernie Earles, he made progress, finishing runner-up in the 500cc World Championship in 1952. The Isle of Man was the background to a titanic struggle with Reg Armstrong on the Norton, which Graham just failed to win. When that year he won the Italian Grand Prix at Monza, he enjoyed a standing ovation from the crowd. Another winter of intense work on the bigger MVs put him in a good position to take the championship for the Italian factory in 1953.

So secure did Graham see his future with MV that at the start of the 1953 season he decided to leave Britain and set up home with his wife and two sons in Italy. But sadly, it was not to work out. On his favoured Isle of Man, Graham started well, racing his MV in record-breaking time to win the Lightweight TT, taken as a good pointer to possible success in the more important Senior race the following day. But on the second lap, as recorded elsewhere, Les Graham lost control while travelling at speed into the dip at Bray Hill and was killed instantly. So devastated was Count Agusta by Graham's death that he withdrew the MV team from the 500cc Championship, and his machines did not reappear in that class until the final Italian round at Monza where, fittingly, Umberto Masetti brought the MV Agusta home first from the Gileras of Armstrong, Duke, Colnago and Milani.

Les Graham was significant to MV Agusta in another way. Indirectly he was responsible for the events which led to the factory achieving their first World Championship with a British rider in the saddle; and, incidentally, it was the first time ever that a British rider had won a World Championship on a foreign machine.

This particular World Champion was Cecil Sandford. He had started grass-track racing and scrambling in 1947 and two years later switched to road racing. He made his début on the Isle of Man in 1950, riding a Velocette. He retired in the Senior race and finished 33rd in the Junior — hardly impressive perhaps for a potential World Champion; nor did he perform much better in 1951. Yet, dramatically, everything was to change. Sandford was not new to the grand prix circuit, and after finishing in fifth and sixth place, he scored more heavily in 1951 with a second place in the 350cc race of the Swiss Grand Prix and a fourth place in the Belgian Grand Prix. In 1952 British factories were on the verge of racing capitulation, but in a final fling Velocette provided Sandford with a works 348cc KTT, and he also had a BSA entered in the Senior. Les Graham, though under contract to ride MV in the Senior, enthusiast that he was, decided to ride Velocette in the Lightweight and Junior races. It was always something of a challenge for British riders, even those with works contracts, to perform well on the Isle of Man, and few could resist in those days taking on as many rides as they could get. Even so, Graham somewhat overdid the enthusiasm when he found himself faced with the prospect of riding in all four solo classes. He went to see Sandford, arriving unexpectedly at his home in Warwickshire. He offered Sandford one of his rides and, because Sandford was slimmer than Graham, it seemed sensible that he should ride the lighter, more manageable 125cc MV, leaving Graham to concentrate on the heavier bikes. So they now had three TT rides each. It was all so casual that there was no contract, not even a signed slip of paper. Sandford told me many years later: 'Les came and asked me if I was interested in the MV ride. I said I was and that was it.'

To the uninitiated spectator the race itself was very ordinary. Sandford made excellent time from the start and, in his own words, 'It was simply a matter of keeping it going at the right speed.' At a race average of 75.54 mph he beat Italian ace Carlo Ubbiali by 1 minute 40.2 seconds to take the trophy, and Sandford also set the fastest lap at 76.07 mph. It was all deceptively simple. What the crowds did not know was that Graham and Sandford had discussed tactics before the race and had gone round the course together. Sandford said later that a lot of thought had gone into the race and he could recall that Les and he had decided, for instance, which side of the road he should ride on during various sections of the course to gain the most benefit from the wind, deciding to take shelter from a hedge or wall if the wind was blowing from that direction.

Having shown his skill on the small MV on the Isle of Man, plans were hurriedly made for Sandford to continue contesting the World Championships. Graham took him back to Italy to square things with Count Agusta and it was then time for the Dutch TT at Assen. Again Sandford outstripped Ubbiali to win this popular event, which generally in later years attracted a crowd well in excess of 100,000. A third place in Germany, at the Solitude circuit, and another win in Northern Ireland had Cecil Sandford poised to take the 125cc World Championship, and he made the issue certain with two more third places, in Italy and Spain. After making such an impact, MV were keen to sign Cecil to a firm contract. It was for two seasons, 1953 and 1954, and the contract was good for those times, reported Sandford years later. 'I was paid a basic sum and everything I won I kept; and I had all my expenses paid. It was a good deal.' Though new to MV, Sandford was also at other times in his career a works rider for AJS, Guzzi and DKW, as well as Velocette, and in 1957, at the end of which he retired, he also claimed another distinction by becoming the first British rider to win the 250cc World Championship.

Another great motor-cycle rider of the 1950s was Fergus Anderson. He was one of a small group of British racers who in the early days realized the value of competing on the Continent, being a member of what was probably the first 'Continental Circus'. He rode Rudge and Velocette machinery and in the Senior and Junior TTs in 1939 was aboard German DKW machines, but he had disappointing results. His greatest success was achieved after moving to the Italian Moto Guzzi factory in 1950. He finished second in the 250cc World Championship in 1952 and was third in the same class a year later, but it was after he persuaded the factory to make a 350cc version of their highly successful four-valve 250 that he brought them the championship. With wins in Belgium, France and Switzerland, and a second place in Italy, he finished the season just four points ahead of his Guzzi team-mate Lorenzetti to take the world title. At the peak of his success Anderson retired to run the competitions department at the Moto Guzzi headquarters at Mandello del Lario, but in 1955 he left on a point of principle, being denied a free hand in the running of the race team. He was then forty-seven, but wanted to ride again. An approach to the German NSU factory was unsuccessful but he was later offered a works BMW 500cc machine. Racing this machine at an international meeting at Floreffe in Belgium, he crashed and was thrown while chasing John Surtees and was killed. Fergus Anderson was an intelligent rider and well respected and liked as a person. While with Moto Guzzi he lived for a number of years with his wife and family on the shores of Lake Como, close to the factory, and enjoyed life on the Continent. In the 1930s he was a working journalist in Hamburg and later was well known to British enthusiasts for his 'Continental Chatter' weekly column in *Motor Cycle*.

Over the years motor-cycle racing has been rich in characters. One of the most outstanding and exciting was the Southern Rhodesian Ray Amm. His epic duels with the legendary Geoff Duke in the early 1950s still quicken the heartbeat for those who saw and remember them. Slim, religious and a gentleman, Amm on a racing motor-cycle was totally committed, and his abandoned style and sheer bravery, with total disregard for his own safety, made him one of the most colourful characters in the sport in the 1950s. He came to Britain in 1951, joining the Continental Circus and racing all over Europe. Joe Craig, Norton's brilliant team-leader, spotted his potential in 1952, and Amm joined the Norton team. When Geoffrey Duke left Norton for Gilera, Amm took over as team-leader. He turned down tempting offers from foreign factories, preferring to ride British machines for as long as possible, but his passion for racing competitively eventually took over, and he signed, somewhat reluctantly, for MV. Soon the sport was left to mourn the passing of this outstanding racing personality. Tragically, in his very first race for the Italian factory, he crashed on a slippery second-gear corner in the 350cc event at Imola on Easter Monday 1955 and was killed.

In a brief but memorable career, Ray Amm is remembered for his spectacular One Hour Record, at 133.71 mph, on the extraordinary Norton 'Kneeler' in 1953. At Montlhéry, in two days of record-breaking with team rider Eric Oliver, in which more than sixty new times were set, Amm improved the previous 1939 record of Italian Piero Taruffi on a supercharged Gilera, by more than six miles per hour. Also that year he established for Norton a new 350cc lap record at the North-West 200 race in Northern Ireland.

One of Ray Amm's greatest moments, however, must surely have been on the Isle of Man when, in that same year, he captured the Senior and Junior TT double. It was an outstanding performance which brought him the distinction of becoming only the fifth rider in the forty-six-year history of the Tourist Trophy races to gain that elusive 'double'. Dismissing all thought of personal safety, Amm thrust his Norton in the wake of Geoffrey Duke in the Senior event, and although theoretically his machine was miles slower than Duke's powerful multi-cylinder Gilera, he somehow managed to catch and pass him on the Mountain. Breaking course and lap records, his fastest lap, of 97.41 mph, was almost three miles per hour faster than Duke's previous record set the year before. He also raced the fastest lap once again in the Junior event and crowned a remarkable spell of racing by leading all the way and finishing in record time.

Everyone has a favourite rider and some of those who followed motor-cycle racing in the 1950s will welcome being reminded of the names of Bill Lomas, Dickie Dale, Reg Armstrong, Artie Bell, Keith Campbell, Bob Foster, Werner Haas and Tarquinio Provini.

Lomas, a dogged, single-minded individual, has in some respects been undervalued by history. The name does not punch out clearly from the past, yet he won two World Championships in the 350cc class, in 1955 and 1956, and was third in the 250cc in 1955. This was also his best year on the Isle of Man, where he won the Junior TT and Lightweight TT, was fourth in the Lightweight 125cc TT and was seventh in the Senior race. Bill Lomas was a good friend of Les Graham, and after the latter's death Count Agusta tempted Lomas from the German NSU factory with a well-paid three-year contract to ride MV machines. Earlier Lomas had been with Bob Foster in the Velocette team, where he began to get noticed, and then came a spell with AJS before his signing for NSU. His first rides for MV in 1952 had mixed results. He finished second in the 125cc event in the Ulster Grand Prix but was thwarted with mechanical problems in Italy and Monza.

There was talk in 1953 that Lomas would team with Graham in the MV line up, but nothing came of it. His talent was obvious, however, and he was a natural choice for Count Agusta after Les Graham's fatal accident. At that time MV was not the all-conquering force in racing they were to become, and in the short time that Lomas rode for the Italian factory he was put under a lot of pressure from faster NSU and Guzzi machinery. Lomas broke off his contract within a year, complaining that Count Agusta would not listen to his ideas to improve the machines and condemning the factory's trackside organization, but he insisted the break was amicable and, indeed, was invited to ride a new MV in the Lightweight 250cc TT the following year.

Although by this time Bill Lomas had moved on to Guzzi, he accepted MV's offer of the Lightweight ride and proved his worth by winning the race handsomely. After this important win Lomas claimed that Count Agusta was keen to get him back in the MV team and that he could have named his own price, but he had been impressed by the 350cc Guzzi and thought his best chances of a world title to be in this class. He did, however, continue to ride the MV in the 250cc Championship and in Holland crossed the line first but was relegated to second place by the international jury for taking on fuel without stopping his engine. It was to be a costly blunder. Germany's Herman Peter Müller took the championship which could have been Lomas's but for the points he forfeited in Holland.

Dickie Dale's record is far less impressive, though he was constantly in demand by the Italian factories in the 1950s to ride their exciting machines. In 1949, as a member of Guzzi's four-man squad on the Isle of Man, he might well have won the Lightweight 250cc but on the last lap, while in the lead, his engine failed. After four years with Guzzi he moved to Gilera in 1953, riding their exotic four-cylinder machines alongside Geoff Duke and Reg Armstrong. Then he moved after a year to MV, winning the final round of the 500cc class in Spain to finish fifth in the Championship. In 1956, once more with Guzzi, he tied for second place in the 350cc World Championship. Towards the end of his career he rode BMW with Duke again, and then Benelli machines, but it all came to an end in 1961 when he crashed at Nurburgring and was killed.

Reg Armstrong was another famous rider from this era whose reputation has perhaps been more enduring though in terms of results his career was less productive than Dale's. During the eight years he raced motor-cycles, the Dublin-born Armstrong had contracts with AJS, Norton, Gilera and NSU. Always neat and coolly calculating, there was nothing spectacular about Armstrong's style. His climb to top-class racing was steady and logical, and he always gave the impression of being happiest when riding as number two to a more obvious front man. On the Isle of Man his best performances came in 1952 on the Norton. He won the Senior event and came second in the Junior race. That year he also won the German Grand Prix at Solitude and was second in Northern Ireland, and in the 500cc class he also won in Germany, to complete a convincing 'double'. He started racing at seventeen and retired when only twenty-eight.

Another brief racing career, but this time enforced, was that of Artie Bell. He became interested in racing as a teenager and progressed to such an extent that in 1938 he ran second to the famous Bob Foster in the gruelling North West 200 race. The Second World War came at just the wrong time for Bell, but he returned to racing in the 1940s, and in 1947 he was invited to join the official Norton squad under the legendary Joe Craig. That year, on his first visit to the Isle of Man, he caused a sensation by leading in the Senior event for three of the seven laps, finishing second to Harold Daniell and sharing the fastest lap, at 84.07 mph, with P.J. Goodman on a Velocette. He won the Senior in 1948, also finishing third in the Junior, was third and fourth respectively in the Junior and Senior events of 1949, and crowned three superb seasons with another win, this time in the Junior TT, with a second place in the Senior. His winning ride in the Junior also included the fastest lap at 86.49 mph. He seemed poised for even greater events in 1950 but sustained severe injury to his left arm in a crash at the Belgian Grand Prix, and his career as a works rider was ended.

Keith Campbell came into grand prix racing later, in the mid-1950s, after gaining some prominence and the 350cc Championship in his home country of Australia. It was a bad time to fight for a works ride because both Norton and AJS were on the point of withdrawing from racing. Then his part in the mass protest at the Dutch Grand Prix, because private riders felt they were not being paid enough, kept him out of grand prix action for six months, but in 1956 he signed to ride for Guzzi, then producing arguably the most specialized and effective 350cc and 250cc single-cylinder machines in the world. In the 500cc class Guzzi also had their fabulous V8, still generally considered to be one of the most exciting and exotic machines ever raced.

Campbell's best season was 1957. He was second on the Isle of Man in the Junior 350cc event and rode home first in Holland, Belgium and Northern Ireland to win the World Championship comfortably with a total of 30 points against Bob McIntyre's and Libero Liberati's 22 points each in second and third place. His memorable win in the Belgian Grand Prix that year, which included a new lap record, is still considered one of his best-ever rides.

In 1958, with Guzzi now officially retired from racing, Campbell continued as a private entrant contesting the classic round. In the 350cc series he was third in Belgium and third again in Holland, outstanding performances when you consider he was riding his own Norton, which had no real chance of winning against the powerful works MVs of Surtees and Hartle. At the Belgian Grand Prix he raced magnificently in the 500cc class finishing between Surtees and Hartle to snatch second place. At the Cadours circuit later that year he won the 350cc race but was killed in the 500cc event.

An earlier champion by a few years was Bob Foster, whose career, like that of Artie Bell mentioned earlier, was disappointingly interrupted by the Second World War at a significant stage. A dedicated enthusiast and an impressive all-rounder in his earlier days, Foster turned seriously to road racing in the early 1930s, competing in the Manx Grand Prix on a New Imperial. The factory sponsored him the following year, and as New Imperial began to run into serious financial problems, Foster beat Tyrell-Smith on an Excelsior and Geiss on a DKW to win the 250cc Lightweight TT. It was to be the last win in this class by a British rider on a British-made machine. After the race New Imperial announced their withdrawal from racing and Foster was left to soldier on as a privateer. He later rode an AJS and, after the war, a Triumph and then a 500cc Guzzi twin. Velocette signed him for their 350cc machine, and in 1947 he won the Junior TT at an average 80.31 mph. On the Velocette 'Fearless Foster', as he was then known, did well in the 350cc class of those first post-war World Championships to finish in third position, behind Freddie Frith and Reg Armstrong, but he achieved a major ambition the following year, taking the 350cc world title with wins in Belgium, Holland and Northern Ireland. He finished six points ahead of Geoffrey Duke. He then retired.

Two 'foreign' riders who gained a respected following in the UK at this time were Werner Haas and Tarquinio Provini. Curiously, Germany has not earned much of a reputation for producing motor-cycle racers who have rated highly internationally, but Werner Haas is a distinguished exception. This happy-go-lucky, pint-sized Bavarian produced some electrifying rides on the ultra-fast NSU machines in the mid-1950s and his memory is all the more vivid by the tragic circumstances of his death, only some four years into his grand prix career, in an airplane crash.

Haas burst onto the international scene in 1952 when on a German NSU machine he swept aside the might of the all-conquering Italian Mondials to win the 125cc German Grand Prix, and in the 250cc class of the Italian Grand Prix that same season he came within a fraction of upsetting the predictions, finishing just behind the year's World Champion, Enrico Lorenzetti, on the speedy Guzzi. Werner Haas' brilliant displays helped to convince the German NSU factory that they could make a name for themselves in the new World Championships, and they mounted a full-scale racing assault in 1953 and 1954, producing machines which, in the skilful hands of Haas, were virtually invincible. Against formidable opposition in the 125cc class which included such riders as Les Graham, Cecil Sandford, Carlo Ubbiali and Reg Armstrong, Werner Haas raced to an astonishing world title, winning in Holland, Northern Ireland and Italy and finishing second in the TT on the Isle of Man and in Germany. His performance in the 250cc class was no less impressive. He raced second to Fergus Anderson on the Isle of Man, was first home in

Holland and in Germany and finished second in Northern Ireland and Italy.

Virtually unknown to big-time racing before 1952, even in Germany, his dramatic double World Championship was only the second recorded in the short history of the new series, and he was the first German to gain the distinction. In 1954 Ruppert Hollaus' exceptional form, with four grand prix wins in four races, left little room for Haas to consolidate his reputation in the 125cc class, but in the 250cc series he was in a class of his own. He won the first five grands prix, out of the seven-race series, to take the class championship for the second year running. With three world titles and ten championship wins in just two years, Werner Haas set a record which even today has not been equalled by any other German rider.

Another rider who found fame in the lighter classes was the Italian, Tarquinio Provini. Prominent for some ten years from the mid-1950s, he was an intelligent and skilful rider, particularly at home in wet conditions. In 1956 a third place in the German Grand Prix and a second place in the final round in Italy, both results in the 125cc class, were the prelude to an outstanding season in 1957. The Italian Mondial concern had made a sensational racing comeback with superbly engineered, streamlined double overhead camshaft single-cylinder machines, and aboard one of these Provini swept to victory on the Isle of Man, at the Dutch TT, in the Belgian Grand Prix and in Northern Ireland to take the 125cc World Championship in sensational style. That same season he was runner-up to team-mate Cecil Sandford in the 250cc series. Left without a ride at the end of 1957 by the dramatic retirement from racing of the three Italian factories Gilera, Guzzi and Mondial, Provini switched to MV and in the 250cc class brought the famous Italian factory their second World Championship. Winning four of the six rounds, he dominated the series. He rode for MV again in 1959 before switching to a Morini 250cc machine. In 1964 he rode the four-cylinder Benelli, but by this time the Japanese were fast developing their stranglehold on the World Championships, and although the Italian champion won some grand prix events during two more years, he was not able to capture another world title. Riding the Benelli on the Isle of Man in 1965, he finished fourth in the Lightweight 250cc race but fell in the Junior, fracturing his pelvis. The injury forced his retirement from racing.

In the World Championships Italy has a proud heritage. From

the beginning in 1949 the country was strongly represented, in both riders and machinery. Nello Pagani, Bruno Ruffo, Dario Ambrosini and Umberto Masetti were legends in their own country, and riding those superbly engineered Mondial, Guzzi, Benelli and Gilera machines, they quickly made an impact on the early years of the post-war championships.

Probably Italy's greatest rider in the days before Agostini was the unassuming Carlo Ubbiali, who specialized in racing lightweight machinery. Few would dispute the claim, for this small, slim motor-cyclist won more world titles than either Geoffrey Duke or John Surtees. He was World Champion nine times in as many years.

Born in Bergamo in 1929, Ubbiali started his racing career when he was twenty, and within two years he was a World Champion. His natural ability was soon spotted by the Mondial factory, then dominating 125cc racing. He joined their works team in 1949 and remained with them for three years, capturing his first World Championship in 1951, when he was just twenty-two. In 1953 he raced for the first time for MV, Count Agusta importing his talent to team with that of British rider Cecil Sandford for a combined assault on the 125cc World Championship. Ubbiali did well to win in Germany and finish second in Holland, but that year the 125cc title went to Werner Haas on the German NSU machine. At this stage the NSUs were superior to the MVs, and despite Ubbiali's valiant battle the Italian's outstanding ability as a rider could not make up the difference in the two marques and the greater experience and efficiency of the NSU mechanics.

Ubbiali's experience on the MVs in these early years was not wasted, however, and when NSU withdrew from racing, MV with Ubbiali as their chief rider in the class were poised to take over. In the next five years Carlo Ubbiali won six out of a possible ten World Championships, at the same time clinching seven victories in the most rugged contest of all, the TT Races over the Mountain Course on the Isle of Man. In 1956 he became only the second rider to achieve a 125cc/250cc World Championship double in the same year, and his nine world titles stood as a record until 1967. Murray Walker, that shrewd observer of motor-cycle sport over many years, put Carlo Ubbiali's success down to three outstanding characteristics: '. . . he was a magnificent tactician and rode with craft and guile showing none of the temperament sometimes displayed by Italian riders; he was sympathetic to machinery and was able to get the maximum out of an engine without bursting it; his diminutive stature made him physically ideal to ride in the two smaller solo categories.'

The likeable and well-respected Ubbiali had a storming season in 1956. In the 125cc class he won five out of the six grands prix and finished second in the sixth. In the 250cc class he again won five out of the six championship races, being beaten only by Taveri, also on an MV, in the Ulster Grand Prix in Belfast. The Mondial factory some years before had been responsible for attracting a lot of much-needed attention to the lighter machine classes with superbly built double-overhead camshaft machines produced by Alfonso Drusiani. The 125cc Mondials were faster than most of the opposition in the 250cc machine class, and it was on such a machine that Ubbiali had achieved his first World Championship in 1951. Since those days the rapidly improving MVs, in the hands of Ubbiali particularly, had reduced the original Mondials to far less potent opposition, but for 1957 the new and beautifully streamlined 125cc and 250cc Mondials which had been introduced in 1956 had sufficient power to be a major threat to Ubbiali.

In the opening round at Hockenheim, Ubbiali scored an outstanding double, winning both 125cc and 250cc races, but on the Isle of Man in June the writing was on the wall. Provini on the Mondial won the 125cc race, and Sandford, again on a Mondial, triumphed in the 250cc class. Further 125cc wins by Provini in Holland and Belgium, with a second place in Northern Ireland, gave him the title. Despite a win in the final round in Italy, Ubbiali could do no better than finish third in the final world rankings. In the 250cc class Ubbiali was down to fifth position at the end of the season. When Mondial, along with Gilera and Guzzi, announced their withdrawal from racing at the end of the 1957 season, the way seemed clear for Ubbiali on the MV to regain his position almost unopposed, but Ducati stepped in with a new single-cylinder machine featuring their desmodromic valve gear. Carlo had to fight hard to regain his 125cc title, being just seven points ahead of Gandossi on the Ducati at the end of the season.

In 1959 and 1960 lightweight grand prix racing was dominated by Carlo Ubbiali. With little outside opposition, the battle for places was fought within the MV camp, with Ubbiali being seriously pressed by team-mate Provini in 1959. In the 125cc class he just squeezed ahead of Provini to finish the season two points ahead, and in the 250cc class he beat Provini by a margin of twelve points to give him his second World Championship within a single year. In 1960 the Rhodesian Gary Hocking, also riding an MV, gave Ubbiali his most serious opposition, but again the Italian was supreme, with a six-point margin in the 125cc class and a four-point margin in the 250cc class. He thus became the rider with the greatest number of titles in the entire history of World Championship racing. He also amassed fifteen national titles.

By then Honda, in the vanguard of the Japanese invasion of motor-cycle racing, were becoming interested in the World Championships, and the Italian factory were also under increasing pressure from the ultra-fast East German MZ two-strokes. As the acknowledged top rider in the world of lightweight machinery, Ubbiali could have anticipated lucrative works rides with the Japanese factories. Indeed, he turned down attractive and tempting offers from that quarter and, instead, at the end of 1960, decided to retire from racing after fourteen years of competition.

Ubbiali's most successful years with MV tended to be over-shadowed by the factory's outstanding achievements in all classes and in particular by the success of John Surtees in the heavier, more glamorous classes, the British rider capturing most of the glory. It is hardly surprising, therefore, that when Ubbiali's retirement co-incided with that of Surtees, MV decided to quit World Championship racing. Even into the 1980s Ubbiali's record had been bettered by only three other racers — Agostini, Nieto and Hailwood. No wonder he was a national hero in Italy, where he is regarded by many of his countrymen and -women as the best Italian motor-cycle racer of all time.

4. Off-road Heroes

Not everyone attracted to motor-cycles took to the road. From the earliest times off-road racing found its fanatics. As the sport developed overall, the various elements were more clearly defined and the organization improved. Scrambling (known also as motocross), trials riding, grass-track racing and speedway (known earlier as dirt-track racing) all developed a serious following and generated their own heroes.

Trials riding is generally acknowledged to be the most difficult motor-cycle sport of all, and often riders who went on to make their name in motocross and road racing learned their craft in trials. It is not one of the most glamorous aspects of motor-cycle sport, but to be a successful trials rider you need a precisely controlled riding technique, close unity with your machine and a sensitive feeling for balance. You also have to think carefully and clearly about what you are doing, for speed alone is not enough to win a trial. Trials courses are littered with boulders, rocks and streams, and the rider must keep going, negotiating these and other impediments, keeping his feet off the ground and himself on the bike. The trial is really as old as motor-cycling itself and developed from the need of riders to test their machines against those owned by other riders. At first it was enough for riders simply to complete the course, usually over roads and hills, and they were entitled to an award if they finished within a certain time. As riders improved their technique and as machines themselves became more capable of absorbing the rigours of the trial, a tougher test was necessary. That is when observed sections were introduced, where points were lost for stopping and other infringements. Machine control is allied to a special kind of physical strength in all the best trials riders, for often the demands of the trials course will mean the rider has to stand high on his bike, easing it round rocks or down crevices. And that is gruelling.

Acknowledged as one of the greatest trials riders of all time is Sammy Miller, the impish Belfast-born rider who was also one of the best ambassadors for the sport. Although Miller's first rides were across country, he moved into road racing to achieve a number of notable successes and then graduated to his phenomenal career in trials via grass-track events and scrambling. He moved seriously into trials riding about 1958 and caused a sensation with his natural style and incredible ability. He won eleven British titles in as many years, was five times winner of the Scottish Six Days Trial and won the famous Scott Trial seven times, including both the premier and veteran's awards in 1970. Much of Sammy Miller's success was on the famous 500cc Ariel, but he was also remarkably successful at the end of 1964 when he switched to Bultaco to ride their 250cc two-strokes. His outstanding career ended with his retirement in 1970, though he continued to work for the Spanish factory, designing and developing the famous Sherpa machines which put Spain so far ahead of the world at that time in the production of their trials bikes, and to run a team of riders in the top international events.

Sammy Miller apart, other great names in trials riding include Gordon Jackson, who was prominent on the British scene in the 1950s before the emergence of Sammy Miller and, after Miller's best years, Gordon Farley, Martin Lampkin and Mick Andrews. A new World Championship was started in 1975, and after Lampkin on a Bultaco had taken the first world title, the remarkable Finnish rider Vrjo Vesterinen was unbeatable, taking the championship for three years running, in 1976, 1977 and 1978. Vesterinen's bid to win four World Championships in a row was upset by Bernie Shreiber, who took the title in 1979, the first American-born rider to collect a World Championship in trials riding.

Scrambling, as it was originally called in Britain, now known universally as motocross, is a development of trials riding. It has its own style of racing exuberance as dedicated enthusiasts charge uninhibited through mud and dirt. The whole object is to keep going, and the rider who reaches the finishing line first is the winner. Early motocross races were far too long, putting unreasonable strain on riders and doing nothing to focus or sharpen the interest of spectators. Today's shorter courses, including climbs and descents and demanding S-bends, maintain spectator interest and excitement and test a rider's stamina and skill to the limit. For sheer daring and exhibitionism, the motocross 'leap' as a rider charges along an incline and becomes airborne as the ground below drops suddenly away, is the supreme thrill and spectacle of the sport. Although its origins go back to 1924, motocross developed into a specialized sport of immense popularity only after the end of the Second World War.

In Britain all-rounders such as Len Heat and Alfie West dominated, but with increasing specialization the Lancashire-born Jeff Smith became the undoubted 'king' of 500cc motocross. In 1970 he received the MBE, to become the first motor-cyclist outside road racing to be so honoured. Smith, starting his competitive career after the Second World War in trials, won a gold medal in the 1951 International Six Days Trial on a Norton. He took up scrambling when he was twenty and was soon dominating the British scene. He won the British title for eight successive years. Riding for BSA, he won his first World Championship in 1964 and repeated his success the very next year. Jeff's refreshing assessment of the qualities needed to win motocross events expressed during his heyday scuttles the concept of bull strength, a bonehead mentality — and little else: 'The only time it is important to lead the field is when crossing the line at the end of the last lap. I am content to stay in about seventh or eighth place until the leaders have sorted themselves out.' It is a philosophy which brought Jeff Smith the richest honours motocross could provide. He was always a most respected and admired rider.

In 250cc motocross Britain's biggest draw for many years was the remarkable Dave Bickers. Extremely popular with motocross crowds, Bickers was a familiar figure in his green sweater and white helmet. He knew while in his teens that he wanted to make scrambling his career and gained valuable experience alongside his inspiration, mentor and friend, Brian Stonebridge, riding on the Continent. It was in Switzerland, as a member of the famous Greeves team, that he recorded his first grand prix win. That was in 1960, and that same year he went on magnificently to take his first European Championship (equivalent then to the World Championship, which was not introduced until 1963). He collected the title again in 1962 and won six 250cc A-CU Stars, forerunner of the British Championships, before retiring in 1969. Bickers told me in 1967: 'It's all a matter of confidence. Once you make yourself believe you are capable of beating your rivals, you then go out to prove it in the cold objectivity of actual results.' It is a positive philosophy which kept Dave Bickers at the forefront of British 250 cc motocross for many years.

Internationally, motocross has produced some astonishing characters and riders of amazing consistency and dedication. Paul Friedrichs of East Germany, riding a CZ machine, was the first rider to win three 500cc World Championships, and he gained them all in three years running, 1966 to 1968. The tragedy of Friedrichs was that he might have done even better and figured more prominently in world motocross had he not been the victim of the 'cold war' and East-West political tensions. He would be allowed to emerge from the shadows of the Iron Curtain to perform in Western Europe only infrequently, and only then in certain grand prix races. A policeman from Erfurt, East Germany, Friedrichs was twenty-six when he won his first world title. At his best his control of his machine was exceptional, and his mental strength and concentration were impressive, enabling him to rise above the pressures and tensions of top-class competition. Such was his skill that he could dominate even top-class championship events, winning both legs in magnificent style. One particularly memorable occasion was the West German Grand Prix in 1967, an event which the East German authorities had not previously allowed him to enter. His career was bedevilled by political bogeys and visa regulations, and it was at the West German Grand Prix in 1969 that political drama erupted when the official programme listed Friedrichs' country as East Germany and not the official German Democratic Republic. He protested and threatened to walk out on the race, and officials had to apologize. Even then, although they announced his country correctly over the loudspeaker system, they refused to play the East German national anthem or fly the East German flag.

Other great riders of 500cc motocross bikes were Graham Noyce, the first British rider to win the 500cc World Championship (in 1979) since the brilliant Jeff Smith in 1965, the Belgian Roger de Coster and André Malherbe, who won his first world title in 1980, and the legendary Finnish rider Heikki Mikkola. De Coster's record is phenomenal. Riding for Suzuki, he won his first 500cc World Championship in 1971 and won the title again in 1972 and 1973. He was successful again in 1975 and once more in 1976, bringing him a total of five World Championships. Heikki Mikkola's first world title in 1974 was followed by further success in 1977 and 1978, and in 1976 he also won the 250cc World Championship.

De Coster's successes came through determination and persistence. In 1967, 1968 and 1969 he could not improve on fifth in the World Championship, but in 1970 CZ, the factory sponsoring de Coster, decided to switch him from the 500cc class to the 250cc competition in a bid to counter the inroads being made in that class by the Japanese Suzuki company. The Belgian did well in an obviously losing battle that year against the formidable Suzuki pair of works riders, Joel Robert and Sylvain Geboers, but he was more concerned at the lack of support he was receiving from the CZ factory. At the same time Suzuki had witnessed his skilful and determined riding, which more than once caused Robert and Geboers problems, and were quick to offer him a contract at the end of the season. It was with the Japanese factory that Roger de Coster won his World Championships.

One of de Coster's great rivals was the Finnish rider Heikki Mikkola, an undemonstrative figure in the flamboyant world of motocross but whose special brand of ferocious, totally dedicated riding brought him the distinction of a World Championship in both the 250cc and 500cc series. Mikkola started his racing career with the Husqvarna factory in 1964, and for thirteen years he rode for the famous Swedish factory, winning the 500cc World Championship in 1974 and the 250cc crown two years later. In his early days he was an excellent all-rounder, competing successfully in other sports such as ice speedway and even ski-jumping, at which he became an area champion in 1968, but motocross was the sport in which he excelled. After his sensational title-winning performances in 1974 and 1976, he made the shock decision to quit Husqvarna, as their race effort began to recede, and joined Yamaha, who then wanted to dislodge Suzuki from their top perch in the 500cc Championship, which Roger de Coster had captured for them in the two previous seasons. Mikkola's début on the Yamaha in Holland was disastrous. He was thrown over the front of his bike and dislocated his left shoulder. But the tough Finn's ruthless dedication did not let injury push his ambition off course, and that same year he beat de Coster to the title. It was Yamaha's first World Championship in the motocross series, and he won the title for them again the very next year.

Perhaps the greatest character of all in motocross, however, and certainly one of the greatest champions of all time, was the Belgian Joel Robert. He was controversial, unpredictable, given to throwing tantrums, obsessive, at times impossibly temperamental and belligerent — but his talent on a motocross bike was never in question. He specialized in 250cc motocross, taking his first World Championship on a CZ machine in 1964. With the CZ he won the title again in 1968 and 1969 and after switching to Suzuki totally dominated the world series, taking the title three more times in three years, 1970 to 1973, to become the most successful motocross rider in the history of the sport. Born in 1943, Joel Robert took to motocross at sixteen and made such an impact that he was World Champion when he was twenty, the youngest-ever rider to hold the title. He was a gifted, instinctive rider, but temperamentally so unreliable that fans hated or loved him. Among the well-documented outrageous antics perpetuated by Joel Robert was the time that he became so incensed, after three false starts, that he rode out from the start line for about fifty yards, stopped, threw his bike down and sat beside it, refusing to move. He would hit a spectator who provoked him and would respond instinctively if something upset him, like hammering the engine of his bike in rage after a breakdown and having to push his machine back to the start.

Robert was a tough, forceful character who delighted in ridiculing convention. He smoked a lot, drank lavishly at times, kept irregular and late hours and generally lived a hectic and self-indulgent life, but once on that motocross machine he took a great deal of beating. It is disappointing that his rip-roaring image has submerged to an extent the conventional side of his character — his obvious talent on a motor-bike and his prodigious control which made him a superb master of his craft. For you need more than brashness, a prima-donna mentality and an inflated ego to make your way to a World Championship, and Joel Robert's skill was abundant.

Grass-track racing does not command the public following of motocross, but its Cinderella image does not deter its dedicated enthusiasts, who like its clubby atmosphere and the way you can get close to the action. It is something like speedway, but held on grass, and power sliding (speedway's spectacular characteristic) is also important in grass-track racing. It has a long history, plenty of meetings being held in the 1920s. The A-CU introduced their Star Winners competition in 1962. This was followed by the British Grass-Track Championships in 1965 when, in that inaugural year, Dave Baybutt collected both 350cc and 500cc titles. Popular grass-track riders of the 1950s included such personalities as Austin Cresswell, Monty Banks and Arthur Stuffins, along with Reg Luckhurst, but Alf Hagon and Don Godden were dominant in the 1960s and 1970s. Godden won his first A-CU Star in that first year, 1962, in the 350cc class, and in 1963 and 1964 he dominated the British scene, winning Stars in both 350cc and 500cc categories. He won the 500cc class yet again in 1965. He was 500cc British Champion in 1967 and once more in 1972. Hagon was National Champion in both 350cc and 500cc classes in 1954, 1959 and 1962. He also took the 350cc National Championship in 1960, 1961 and 1964.

Speedway, in contrast to grass-track racing, is very much a public spectacle and grew to become the second largest spectator sport in Britain. It has blossomed over the years from its relatively shabby, fairground-type beginnings into a sophisticated professional sport with a mass following. It had its foundings in the United States when early motor-cyclists took to the horse-trotting tracks in the early 1900s. A closed-circuit race at the New South Wales Agricultural Show in Australia was the prelude to growing public interest there in dirt-track racing, and the sport came to Britain in 1927 when what was reported as the first dirt-track meeting to be held in Britain took place over a quarter-mile sandy circuit, incorporating two straight sections and two corners, at the Military Ground on Camberley Heath. The first licensed speedway in Britain was held at High Beech, Essex, on 7 April 1928, attracting a massive crowd of some 30,000, ten times the number expected. The Australian star Billy Galloway gave a spectacular demonstration of riding, and soon regular meetings were taking place all over the country. In 1928 the first evening meeting under floodlighting was held. The first speedway leagues were formed the following year.

In the early days it was the American and Australian stars who blazed the British trail, but as speedway became more international, Britain and the continent of Europe developed their own heroes. The first World Championship was held under the auspices of the FIM in 1936, with riders from America, Australia,

Sweden, New Zealand, Britain, Germany, Canada, France, Denmark, Spain and South Africa competing. Lionel van Praag won the run-off against Britain's Eric Langton to take that first world title. In 1937 Jack Milne from the United States became World Champion, and in 1938 the title went back to Australia through the superior riding of Bluey Wilkinson.

In the immediate post-war years, riders such as Tommy Price, Fred Williams and Australia's Jack Young, who was World Champion in 1951 and 1952, made an enormous impact, along with Fred Williams, Ronnie Moore, Peter Craven and Ove Fundin, all of them World Champions. One of speedway's greatest characters was Split Waterman. His cavalier approach and his personality on and off the track kept him in the news, but although he was an exceptionally dashing and skilful rider, he was never a World Champion. He came very close in 1951, but Jack Young beat him to the title.

Jack Young is one of three well-remembered names of speedway — Jack himself from the 1950s, Jack Parker, who was prominent in the 1930s and 1940s, and Peter Craven, prominent in both the 1950s and 1960s. Jack Young was the first rider to win the World Speedway Championship two years running, 1951 and 1952. He began speedway racing in Australia in the 1940s and moved on to the British scene in 1950, joining the second-division side Edinburgh. He won the Scottish Championship three seasons running, and on his specially tuned JAP-engined machine, with Ronnie Moore as partner, he was top scorer for Australia in the first Test Match against England at Harringay. In 1952 he moved to West Ham for the record fee of £3,750 (it remained a record for more than twenty years) and finished his riding days in Britain with Coventry.

The other Jack — Jack Parker — made his début in speedway, or dirt-track racing as it was then called, in 1928 after being active in motor-cycle trials, as a member of the official BSA team. The following year, at the start of league speedway, Parker became captain of Coventry, and he was later to captain a number of clubs including Southampton, Harringay and Belle Vue. After a memorable battle he won the World Championship from Vic Huxley in 1931. He finished in fourth place in the World Championship in 1937, and as war came and speedway was abandoned, his career was disappointingly interrupted. He rode again after the war, winning the British Riders' Championship in 1947. In 1949 he finished second to Tommy Price in the World Championship. After riding successfully in Australia he retired in 1953.

Born in Liverpool in 1951, Peter Craven was an outstanding ambassador for speedway and a brilliant rider. He appeared in the World Final first in 1954 and sprang to prominence by beating both Barry Briggs and the then current World Champion Ronnie Moore, to win his first World Championship in 1955. He became World Champion again in 1962, taking the title outright with a sensational fourteen-point victory at Wembley. Peter Craven's career was tragically ended on 20 September 1963 when, as skipper of Belle Vue, he crashed in a match against Edinburgh and died in hospital four days later.

In almost fifty years of speedway, two riders seem to stand out with British enthusiasts: Barry Briggs and Ivan Mauger (pronounced Major). Born in Christchurch, New Zealand, Briggs rode for British teams Wimbledon, New Cross, Southampton and Swindon. He was World Champion in 1957, 1958, 1964 and 1966, and he took the British Riders' Championship five times in a row from 1965, to become a legend in his own lifetime. His balance was remarkable. His boyhood hero, Ronnie Moore, was the inspiration of a young Barry Briggs who, determined to make a name for himself in his hero's sport, quit his office junior job in a Christchurch, New Zealand, advertising agency to journey to Britain. His riding was so undisciplined at the start that some of the established riders tried to get him banned, but unsuccessfully. His riding was remarkably consistent and he stayed at the top of his sport through most of the 1960s, one of speedway's greatest attractions. In business he was no less successful and built up a flourishing motor-cycle business in Southampton, operating an agency for the Czechoslovakian Jawa concern. His success on the track with Jawa machinery did much to promote the make in the United Kingdom. A crash at Wembley in 1972 meant the loss of a finger, and soon after he announced his retirement. For his contribution to his own specialized brand of motor-cycle sport Barry Briggs received the MBE in the Queen's Birthday Honours list of 1973, the first speedway rider to receive such recognition. Before retiring yet again at the end of the 1975 season he was persuaded back to lead his old club Wimbledon, and just when everyone must have felt that Briggs had now definitely come to the end of his racing days, he was hauled back from retirement yet again to assist Hull, before finally leaving the speedway track for good.

Following fellow-countrymen Ronnie Moore and Barry Briggs to speedway glory was Ivan Mauger who, like Briggs, was born in Christchurch, New Zealand. His début in British speedway was in 1957 with Wimbledon, but his first two seasons in the UK were so disappointing that he returned home, disillusioned. Not until 1963 did he try his luck in Britain again, this time joining Newcastle Diamonds. He was an immediate success, becoming Provincial Riders' Champion in 1963 and 1964, European Champion in 1966, third in the World Championship in 1967, and he gained his first coveted World Championship in 1968. He was individual World Champion again in 1969 and in 1970, yet again in 1972 and, astonishingly, in 1977 and once more in 1979. Six-times World Champion (he is the only rider with the distinction) is certainly a magnificent record.

Consistently outstanding, Ivan Mauger built a well-earned reputation for starting strongly and finishing that way. Rumour has it that he made more money out of speedway than any other rider. In 1976 he received the MBE, the first speedway rider to be honoured while still active in league racing and only the second speedway rider to receive the MBE. Mauger also won the world 1,000-metre long-track title in 1971, 1972 and 1976. He is considered to have been the most dedicated speedway rider of all time. His sixth record-breaking World Championship in 1979 was achieved before 130,000 spectators in the Slaski stadium at Chorzow, Poland, just one month before his fortieth birthday. With fourteen points he took the title outright, gaining victory over defending champion Ole Olsen in his last race. Only Michael Lee, Britain's latest superstar who was to take the world title himself in 1980, beat the New Zealander, in heat 10. Mauger's faultless riding brought him wins in his other four rides. He beat the Finnish rider Thomsen, and his devastating start in his race against Moran left the American behind. After being beaten by Lee, he overcame the challenge of the Australian Sanders and went on to crown a series of superb rides with victory over Olsen.

5. Riding for Honda

Towards the end of the 1950s motor-cycle racing took a dramatic new turn. It all began on the Isle of Man in the summer of 1959, when, to the astonishment and, let it be said, amusement of many onlookers, a team of riders from faraway Japan entered the TT Races for the first time. Honda at that time was an unfamiliar name, and nobody gave much for their chances. Japan was known more for cheap watches and cameras painstakingly copied from European examples. Only once in the entire fifty-two-year history of the island races had a Japanese rider taken part — Kenza Tada, who in 1930 finished an almost unnoticeable 15th on a Velocette in the Junior event. So there was little to suggest that motor-cycle racing was on the verge of a revolution.

The 1959 team of Japanese riders and mechanics, led by their thirty-year-old American rider-manager Bill Hunt, were pleasant, friendly, and well-behaved and, despite having travelled some 7,000 miles to compete, were there, according to Hunt, simply to finish and, if possible, to win the manufacturers' team prize. Their incursion into European racing, on their own admission, was tentative, exploratory. Having not raced their machines outside their own country before, their idea was simply to see how they would fare against the world's top competition in the world's toughest road race. Almost an academic exercise.

It all seemed innocent enough at the time, but looking back there were indelible signs that Honda's laid-back approach was perhaps not quite as unambitious as it seemed on the surface. Short-circuit racer Derek Minter said that nobody took much notice of them at first, but the machines went better and lasted longer than anybody thought they would. One of the Isle of Man's greatest riders of all time, Bob McIntyre, said the 125cc machine which the Honda camp allowed him to ride for the basis of a newspaper article had the performance of an average 350. There was no denying that their workshops were impressive, immaculately kept and superbly equipped, and racing authority John Griffith, looking beneath the surface, noted the clever design and superior detailed workmanship of their machines.

With the brilliant World Champion John Surtees in full flight, taking the Senior and Junior events, and Tarquinio Provini winning both the 250cc and 125cc Lightweight TTs, there was little room left for Honda to make an impact on the results. But despite the excitement elsewhere, Honda's activity 'down race' in the 125cc event was to prove the most significant event of all on the Island that year. Although unimpressive in practice and lacking pace in the race, the Hondas were nonetheless sufficiently reliable to finish in sixth, seventh, eighth and eleventh places, to gain the manufacturers' team prize. The Japanese had done what they set out to do.

Encouraged by their performance, they set to work. Amazingly, in the space of three short years, they were dominating motor-cycle racing. With exotic machinery, elaborate organization and enormous financial investment, Honda would create a new dynasty in motor-cycle racing, giving the sport a totally new dimension. Just two years later Honda machines were dominating the lightweight classes of the World Championships, being ridden to world titles in both the 125cc and 250cc series. A year later they added the 350cc world title, and in 1963 they were by far the largest motor-cycle company in the world, with annual production running at 1¼ million machines. Not only had they swept aside most of the competition from other parts of the world, but Honda, through their foresight, investment, dedication and clever sales strategy, had created a whole new market for motor-cycles. Racing success, too, had played its part in their phenomenal domination of world markets.

The rider largely responsible for their racing triumphs was a cool, calculating professional called Jim Redman. Honda's assault on the TT Races in 1959 had been with a team of Japanese riders under the astute leadership of American rider-manager Bill Hunt. They quickly learned the lesson that dependence on their own riders was hardly likely to bring them the grand prix successes they wanted. They signed Australians Tom Phillis and Bob Brown to bolster the team. Phillis became their first team captain. He rode his first race for Honda on the Isle of Man in 1960, being joined there for the TTs by fellow-Australian Bob Brown. Neither made much impact, and for Brown, 1960 brought early tragedy. Practising on the Honda-4, at a combined motor-cycle and car meeting later in the season, he crashed and was killed. The same fate, sadly, was in store for Tom Phillis, but not before he had brought Honda one of their two world titles in 1961. That year Phillis started the 125cc season well, with a good win from Ernst Degner on the faster MZ at Barcelona in the Spanish Grand Prix. It was to herald a season-long scrap between the Australian and the Eastern European rider. Degner won in the German Grand Prix, but Phillis won in France, Holland and Argentina and, with second places in Belgium and East Germany, he took the World Championship for Honda with 48 points against Degner's 42. He also did well in the 250cc class, finishing second behind Mike Hailwood, also racing a Honda which had been placed at the UK importer's disposal by the factory in Japan. Honda indeed were already applying enormous effort to gain inroads into top-class racing, giving rides to a large number of 'private' racers. This concentration enabled Honda-mounted riders to occupy four of the top five positions in the 125cc table at the end of the season, and in the 250cc class all five top positions.

Jim Redman had seized his chance with Honda when Tom Phillis had been injured in 1960, practising for the Dutch TT at Assen. Phillis recommended him to the Honda officials, and after a test ride he was given bikes for the Assen event, finishing fourth in the 125cc race and seventh in the 250cc event. He displayed enough potential to satisfy Honda, who signed him up to race alongside Tom Phillis. The very next year, however, on the Isle of Man, Phillis was killed when he hit the wall at Laurel Bank. Never a reckless rider, Tom Phillis nonetheless enjoyed a challenge. He had the vision to see the potential in Honda in the early days when most Europeans were looking at the Japanese factory's efforts with some amusement. And when in 1962 Honda decided to bid for the Junior TT crown with a race special bored out to 285cc, Phillis jumped at the chance to confront the all-conquering MV Agustas, ridden by Mike Hailwood and Gary Hocking. In fact it was Phillis who persuaded Redman, who was originally down to ride the bike, to let him have a go against the faster Italian machines. He was obviously moving very quickly and pushing up against the limits when the fatal accident occurred.

Despite the shock of Phillis' death, and also those, that same year, of other close friends Bob McIntyre and Gary Hocking, Jim Redman continued racing and captured both the 250cc and 350cc World Championships for Honda. He won six of the ten rounds in the 250cc series, finishing second in three others, and he won four rounds in succession out of the six-round 350cc series. In both classes he was supreme again in 1963. He was 350cc World Champion once more in 1964 and yet again in 1965, completing a remarkable record of four 350cc world titles in four years. In all, Jim Redman was World Champion six times in just four years, all on Honda bikes, and in a comparatively short grand prix career won forty-four World Championship races. His epic battles with Phil Read as Yamaha threw down the gauntlet to Honda in the 250cc class, are still remembered as some of the most thrilling races ever witnessed, and it was the challenge mounted by Yamaha through Read which denied Redman the distinction of equalling the record of John Surtees in becoming a double world title winner three years in succession.

There was a thrilling climax to the 1964 season. Redman had to win at Monza in the Italian Grand Prix and also in the last meeting of the season, at the Suzuka circuit in Japan, to retain his 250cc crown. The tension mounted as the Honda team captain opted to race a brand new Honda-6, introduced with typical cloak-and-dagger secrecy at Monza in an effort to gain a psychological advantage over the Yamaha camp. Redman knew about Honda's latest bike. It had been unveiled in Japan, for the benefit of privileged eyes only, as early as June, and after competing in the Finnish Grand Prix at Imatra a week or two before Monza, Redman had flown out to test-ride it.

The choice at Monza was now Redman's own. He could continue to race the Honda-4 or go for the faster, though as yet untried, Honda six-cylinder racer. Monza is a fast circuit which would give the advantage to the Yamaha which was faster than the previously raced Honda. Despite the new machine's suspect handling, Redman decided therefore to race the faster Honda-6, and with an advantage of three seconds at the end of the first lap it began to look as though he had made a wise choice. Phil Read made the chasing Yamaha an insistent challenge, however, and Redman had to push the new machine hard to keep ahead. In the high Italian temperatures the Honda began seriously to overheat. Redman kept it going but was reduced to three-quarters speed. Every time he opened the throttle wide, the machine automatically cut back, regaining momentum only when the throttle was eased down again. Even so, Redman was able to keep ahead of Read for some fourteen laps, by which time the Honda was becoming noticeably slower, Redman was powerless to improve the Honda's performance, and Read eventually moved ahead. In the end Redman was left to struggle unsuccessfully for second place, with Mike Duff, also on a Yamaha. Jim finished in third place.

Though Redman won the final round in Japan, he had already lost his title to Read and Yamaha. He finished the season just four points behind his main rival. In the 350cc class it was a totally different story. With no major factory challenge, Jim Redman swept from one grand prix success to another, finishing the season with a maximum eight wins and 40 points, against his nearest challenger, Bruce Beale, also on a Honda, with 24 points.

Redman was still Honda team captain when Mike Hailwood signed one of the biggest grand prix contracts ever to ride for the Japanese factory who had won virtually everything except the coveted 500cc World Championship. It was not a happy relationship, Redman undoubtedly keeping some 500cc rides for himself when perhaps Hailwood ought to have had them, and the most unhappy event of all during that season occurred when Redman took a tumble and damaged an arm. That injury, though it healed, combined with the retirement from racing of Honda shortly afterwards to signpost the end of Redman's racing career. He then left Britain for Rhodesia and thereafter settled in South Africa.

A stylish if at times an unexciting rider, Jim Redman was intelligent, shrewd, a hard negotiator and extremely astute. He ran the Honda team largely as he wanted and was adept at convincing the Honda bosses that his decisions were right for the factory. He was very much a family man. He neither courted nor enjoyed widespread public acclaim, and among his fellow riders Redman was known for his quiet skills and fierce independence.

Born in 1931 in Greenford, Middlesex, Redman went to stay with a friend in Rhodesia to help support his family after the death of his mother and father and there trained as a mechanic, sending money home to help sustain a sister and twin younger brothers. After going into partnership in a motor-cycle business with a friend and notable racing driver John Love, Redman began racing a Triumph 500cc 'special', then a Norton and an AJS. At twenty-six he became 350cc South African champion and at the end of 1957, now a naturalized Rhodesian, he travelled to Britain with ambitions to become a professional racing motor-cyclist. He quickly got noticed, racing second to the almost unbeatable Derek Minter at Brands Hatch in a race which also included such established riders as Mike Hailwood, Alistair King and Bob McIntyre. Despite his obvious talent, however, he made little impact that season and, frustrated and disillusioned, he packed his bags and returned to Rhodesia, intent on retirement. But his heart never left racing, and in 1960 he was back in Britain prepared to give it just one more chance. His ambition was to win a full-blown works contract. But roughing it as a privateer, putting up your own cash and scrambling to provide your own support services, was not for Redman. He tried hard to get into the MZ works team, but although racing boss Walter Kaaden professed interest, no definite offer ever emerged.

Redman's big chance came, as we have seen, when his friend Tom Phillis was sidelined with injury and he recommended Redman to Honda as a team replacement. Redman took his chance and then moved up to become team captain of the most powerful works team in the history of motor-cycle racing. He was a cautious and sensible rider, never travelling faster than was necessary to win, and a skilful tactician. He was also abrasive, and his rows with race organizers, often justified, were well known in the sport and reflected his tough, uncompromising attitude. You had to be a slick operator indeed to sidestep Redman, both on the track and off.

In the 1960s it was the ambition of every racer to gain a Honda contract. The factory dominated grand prix racing for much of the decade, and they were undoubtedly the most dynamic and successful racing factory in the history of the sport. Nothing before or since compares with their period of glory between, say, 1962 and 1966. Though many riders raced Hondas, no more than a handful signed a full works contract. Hailwood, of course, Redman, Phillis, Brown and also a remarkably successful racer from Switzerland called Luigi Taveri. He was already a veteran when he first rode for Honda, having been prominent in the 1950s. Riding MV, he finished in the top three places in the 125cc World Championship in 1955, 1956 and 1957, and yet again in 1958, this time on an Italian Ducati machine, having lost his place in the MV team. Good riding in 1959, however, earned him a recall by the Italian factory for 1960, and he repaid them by finishing in third position in the 250cc World Championship table. It looked to be bad news when MV Agusta quit the lightweight classes at the end of the season, but by now Honda were scouting for racing talent. They signed Taveri to join Redman and Phillis in the full-time racing squad. Riding the Honda in the 125cc series, he finished second to Hailwood on the Isle of Man, beat team-mates Phillis and Redman in Belgium, finished third in Italy and won again in Sweden, to end the season in third position.

The diminutive Taveri was a demon on lightweight machines, and when Honda decided to contest the new 50cc class in 1962, he was a natural choice, for both 50cc and 125cc rides. In the new class, however, the East German Ernst Degner, riding for Suzuki, was untouchable, though Taveri rode well to finish second on the Isle of Man, finishing third in the championship. He delighted Honda in the 125cc class by winning the World Championship with good wins on the Isle of Man, in Holland, Belgium, West Germany, Northern Ireland and East Germany. He collected 48 points against Redman's 38 and Tommy Robb's 30, both riding Honda machines. He was the first Swiss solo rider to gain a World Championship, and he continued to race Honda machinery until his retirement at the end of 1966, by which time Honda's big-spending race days were over. In 1964 Taveri, riding the new four-cylinder 125cc Honda, won five grands prix and finished in second place in four other world championship races to gain his second world title. He lost ground against the ultra-fast Suzuki and MZ teams in 1965, finishing fifth, but in 1966, with a new five-cylinder machine from Honda, he overcame a strong challenge from Bill Ivy on the two-stroke Yamaha, to secure his third World Championship.

Two other riders strongly associated with Honda were Irishmen Tommy Robb and Ralph Bryans. Robb was the older by some thirteen years, and as he was moving into his most successful year, Bryans had yet to make the breakthrough into the big time. Honda signed him to contest all four solo classes in 1962. Though he had good rides in both the 50cc and 125cc series, Tommy Robb's first grand prix win came, appropriately, in Northern Ireland, where he beat Jim Redman and Luigi Taveri to win the 250cc Ulster Grand Prix. He also came second to Taveri in the 125cc race at the same meeting. He ended the season in third place in both the 125cc and

350cc classes. But after that, as Tommy Robb's racing career began to dip in 1963, Ralph Bryans, the other Irishman, got his first big break, a contract with the Spanish Bultaco factory. No sooner had he begun celebrating than an even bigger opportunity arrived when Honda team captain Jim Redman came along with a much fatter contract and, to help Bryans, Bultaco sportingly stepped aside to enable the Irishman to sign for Honda. He won in Holland, Belgium, West Germany and Japan in 1964, his first year as a Honda works rider. These results gave him the runner-up position to Hugh Anderson in the 50cc World Championship. In 1965 he did even better and, considering his relative inexperience, for he did not know any of the classic circuits other than the Ulster and TT little more than a year before, his wins in Germany and France, on the Isle of Man and in Holland were remarkable against Hugh Anderson's Suzuki and Luigi Taveri's Honda. At only twenty-three he became the new 50cc World Champion. It was to be the Honda factory's only 50cc World Championship.

Tommy Robb, on the other hand, was never a World Champion, but he was a dedicated and enthusiastic rider, well liked by the crowds, particularly in Ireland. His career began in the 1950s when, at sixteen, he won his first race. As a road racer he won many events riding a 175cc MV and, later, Norton, Ducati and Matchless for a number of sponsors. His first appearance in the TT Races was in 1958, when he finished eighth in the Lightweight 250cc race on a NSU. He was a prolific Island performer, taking part in thirty-eight races between 1958 and his last race there in 1971. His best results were with Honda, but in 1967 he finished third in the Lightweight 50cc TT, riding a Suzuki machine. It was a good year for Robb because he also finished second in the production 250cc event riding Bultaco and seventh, also on Bultaco, in the Lightweight 125cc race.

Tommy Robb was born in 1935. Ralph Bryans was born in 1948 but, unlike the days when Robb was developing an interest in motor-cycle racing, Honda were already a big name when Bryans got the urge to race. He competed in almost all branches of the sport in his early days but switched to road racing seriously in 1962. A good performance that year was his ninth position in the Ulster Grand Prix. Again unlike Robb, Bryans signed for a major factory after a relatively brief apprenticeship. After his World Championship in 1965, Ralph Bryans looked set to repeat his success in 1966, despite the insistent challenge from the German rider Hans-Georg Anscheidt on Suzuki. Bryans was third in the opening round in Spain, Taveri winning the race and Anscheidt coming second, but he did better in the second round in West Germany. Anscheidt took the race, with Bryans second. The turn came on the Isle of Man, with Bryans gaining a vital win. He finished second in Holland and second again in Italy. All now depended on the final round in Japan, but Ralph Bryans was denied even the chance of going for the title. Honda refused to compete there, on the basis that the Fisco circuit was dangerous. A win in Japan would have given Bryans his second world title, but Anscheidt finished second there to Japan's Katayama and took the title by just three points. Even so, the season had its compensations for the Irishman. His performance on the Isle of Man went into the record books because his new lap speed record of 86.49 mph was to remain the best by a 50cc machine on the Isle of Man. The event was axed from the TT Races in 1968 without any improvement on Bryans' performance.

Once their Honda days were over, Tommy Robb and Ralph Bryans took different paths. Robb had a test ride for Yamaha but returned to Bultaco for factory rides, before competing on Yamahas, Aermacchis and Seeleys. It was on the big Seeley four-stroke that Robb finished fourth in the 500cc World Championship of 1960. He retired in 1973.

In contrast to Robb, who was racing for more than thirteen years, Ralph Bryans' career spanned no more than five or six years. When Honda dramatically announced their withdrawal from 50cc World Championship racing at the end of 1966, it was virtually the end of Bryans' career, although he continued to race Hondas in the 250cc class in 1967, finishing fourth in the table behind Hailwood, Read and Bill Ivy. Then he retired.

6. The Greatest of Them All

Motor-cycle racing was at its most compelling, exciting, stimulating and fashionable in the 1960s. Honda's commitment to the World Championships was the powerhouse. They grappled with Yamaha and Suzuki, also from Japan, for domination of the grand prix scene, in the process all of them spending huge sums of money until the inevitable occurred: the balloon burst and all three withdrew from racing towards the end of the decade.

While it lasted, it was a phenomenon. The Japanese involvement coincided with Britain's re-emergence as the mecca of the world in fashion, music and the modern lifestyle. It was the Swinging Sixties, with mini-skirts, the Beatles, Carnaby Street, Twiggy and, in motor-cycle racing, glamour riders such as Bill Ivy, Phil Read and Mike Hailwood, all from Britain. Motor-cycle racing was big box-office. Track stars had pop appeal and a lifestyle to match. They lived in West End luxury pads, had 'hang-on' girlfriends, jetted to Japan and back to test machines and discuss big-money contracts, enjoyed hectic parties, fast-moving cars and a contemporary lifestyle. In the era of flower-power and Beatle haircuts, British riders ruled the racing world.

The greatest of them all was Mike Hailwood. There was never any need for him to race motor-cycles for a living. His father was a millionaire. He could have become a professional playboy and lived a luxury life without lifting a finger. Perhaps it was because he did not have to make a living that he grew up with an ambition to make his own way, following his father's example in taking to motor-cycles. That he was able to live down his moneyed, privileged background in one of the toughest arenas it is possible to find and become arguably the most popular and respected motor-cycle racer of all time is to his immense credit. He was the golden boy with the natural talent and an instinctive flair not only in racing a motor-cycle but in expressing himself in a relaxed, easy-going, convincing manner. He was articulate and sharply in focus with a world which was becoming increasingly dominated by the media.

Hailwood was no fool. He didn't deny his father's help, insisting he came up the hard way — just for the sake of it. When Stan Hailwood said he would look after the organization so his son could concentrate on riding and racing, Mike was happy to let him do so. When old man Hailwood provided the opportunity for him to go to South Africa to gain important racing experience, Mike was only too happy to grasp the opportunity and benefit from it. Even before his name meant much in racing circles, his father had formed Ecurie Sportive, an off-track and tactical organization to make the opportunities for Mike and smooth his path on the way to the top. But all the money in the world will not win you friends or make you a champion. In the end you could not find a more popular racer than Mike Hailwood, and as for his talent — he won the World Championship six times in four years at the peak of his career. In the 1960s no racer was more successful or better known.

Stan Hailwood had been a motor-cycle enthusiast in the 1930s, riding a 500cc Cotton-powered sidecar in grass-track events in the south of England, and he nurtured the growing interest in motor-cycle racing he saw in his only son, Mike. Boss of a major motor-cycle dealership in Oxford, and extremely wealthy, he wanted the best for his son, so he sent the fourteen-year-old Mike for a private education to Pangbourne Naval College. Mike did not enjoy his time there and lived for weekends when he could get home to ride an old trials bike which his father had bought for him. After two years Mike was no more settled at Pangbourne than on the day he entered, so he talked his father into believing it was time for him to be making his own way in the world. He left prematurely and joined the Hailwood business, doing all the odd jobs a junior has to do. He moved then to Triumph, spending his weekends at scramble and trials meetings.

At seventeen Mike Hailwood became the youngest competitor to take part in the Scottish Six-Days Trial, but his heart was set on road racing. Family friend Bill Webster lent him a 125cc single overhead camshaft MV, and at Oulton Park Mike, left on the line, did so well to gain ground and so impressed with his enthusiastic style that Webster told Stan Hailwood later that he reckoned his lad was championship material. It was all the incentive old man Hailwood needed. He backed Mike by providing a 196cc MV, which was bored out to 240cc, and a 50cc Itom. In 1957, still only seventeen, Stanley Michael Bailey Hailwood won the 250cc event in Northern Ireland's Cookstown race, at record-breaking speed.

When racing finished in Britain that year, Mike continued to gain experience in South Africa, and on his return, in 1958, he quickly made an impact. His appetite for racing was undeniable. On the Isle of Man that year, while still only eighteen, he competed in all four solo classes, finishing third, seventh, twelfth and thirteenth. That same year he won three out of the four A-CU Road Racing Stars, forerunner of the British Championships. His first classic win came in 1959, when he was nineteen, the 125cc class of the Ulster Grand Prix, riding a Ducati, and in 1960 he became only the second rider, after Derek Minter, to lap the Isle of Man Mountain Course at over 100 mph on a single-cylinder machine.

In those days many talented riders, even if they had the ambition, did not have the chance to compete in grand prix events. Works contracts were hard to get; sponsorship, when negotiated, was seldom if ever sufficient to enable a rider to contest more than the isolated World Championship round, generally at circuits nearest to home, such as Holland and Belgium. A rider needed a lot of backing to become a member of the fabled 'Continental Circus', contesting the whole series of grand prix events. Most riders anyway could make more money riding at the short circuits in Britain, such as Brands Hatch and Mallory Park, which were easier to get to, which did not cost as much in terms of time, travelling and transport for rider, mechanic and bike, and where, if you could get among the winners, you could pick up useful money fairly regularly to keep you going until a bigger break came along.

But that was not for Mike Hailwood. His ambition from the beginning was to compete at the highest level, as the member of a highly paid works team, with all the glamour and recognition which a World Championship would bring him. While less fortunate riders stayed in Britain to be seen regularly at home circuits, thus gaining the loyalty of national crowds, Hailwood was seen only at selected important events in Britain, preferring to pick and choose the races which he considered would enhance his career. When he did arrive in the paddock at a domestic circuit, the gleaming transporter and the

Hailwood entourage were at times ludicrously in contrast to the primitive conditions which were the less fortunate lot of most other riders. On both counts Hailwood for a while lost his public image locally, though internationally and on the Isle of Man, which he never denounced as Sheene, Agostini, Read and others were to do later, his popularity gained momentum.

On an uncompetitive Ducati, Mike did well to finish in third place in the 125cc World Championship of 1959, but in 1961, while still only twenty-one, he became World Champion for the first time. That year saw him making history on the Isle of Man, where he became the first rider to win three TT races in a week. Through his father's influence he was loaned Honda entries in the 125cc and 250cc races, and Hailwood made no mistake. On the 125cc machine he smashed the lap record from a standing start first time round and kept the Honda going at maximum revs. His second lap was even faster, and he raced on to win from Honda official team riders Taveri and Phillis. The luck every champion needs came to Hailwood later that day. Bob McIntyre was always tough opposition on the Isle of Man and, riding a Honda-4, was favourite in the 250cc race. After putting in the fastest lap at 99.58 mph, he looked certain to win, but overheating problems forced his retirement on the last lap, and Mike was able to race through to win at an average speed of 98.38 mph.

Hailwood's ambition knew no bounds, and before racing began he had set his heart on capturing four TT trophies that year. His hopes were dashed when, in the Junior race, his AJS broke down fifteen miles from home. He made no mistake in the Senior TT, however, despite formidable opposition from Gary Hocking on the powerful works MV. By comparison, Hailwood's Bill Lacey-tuned Norton fell well short on outright speed, but Hocking had trouble with the Italian machine almost from the start, and when it finally died, Mike was left with a good ride home to win his third TT in a week, though even before Hocking's retirement, Hailwood's riding had been impressive.

Mike's loaned Hondas had come about only after his father had agreed to import Honda machines through his dealerships, but on the 250 machine, though lacking full works support from Japan, Mike astonishingly went on to take the 250cc World Championship from under the noses of Honda's contract riders, Tom Phillis and Jim Redman. He won in Holland, East Germany and Sweden and was placed second in France, Northern Ireland and Italy, to finish the season six points ahead of Phillis and eight points ahead of Redman.

By this time Hailwood was keen to concentrate on the bigger machines, and in particular the more prestigious 500s, but there had been few opportunities for works rides since the shock retirement at the end of 1957 of the Italian giants Gilera, Guzzi and Mondial. Since then MV Agusta had been left alone to dominate the class, but when his star rider, John Surtees, decided to retire at the end of the 1960 season, the autocratic Count Domenico Agusta, boss of MV, lost some of his natural enthusiasm and, not helped by falling sales at home and other problems, had only partially backed Rhodesia's Gary Hocking in the 1961 series. That year Hocking, despite lacking full works support, still managed to bring MV Agusta their fourth successive 500cc World Championship, but Hailwood was now poised to take over. Bill Webster, MV Agusta distributor in Britain, had recommended Hailwood to Count Agusta, who watched him in action on specially loaned MVs at Monza, towards the end of the season. Mike impressed, finishing second to Hocking in both the 350cc and 500cc races, and was signed to ride for MV in 1962.

The famous Italian factory was alone in supporting 500cc World Championship racing at that time and Hailwood had leapfrogged an enormous queue of riders hoping to attract Count Agusta's attention. Hocking felt threatened by Hailwood's arrival in the MV camp, but they rode in 1962 as team-mates — neither, however, giving an inch to the other, whatever racing instructions Count Agusta might have issued. Honda, having secured a firm base in the 125cc and 250cc classes, were contesting MV's, till then, unassailable position in 350cc racing with new, modified versions of their highly successful 250cc racer, and Count Agusta's main concern was to repel the challenge, by whom it did not much matter. Hocking's relationship with Hailwood did not improve, he rowed with Count Agusta, and his mind was made up when his good friend Tom Phillis was killed on the Isle of Man that year. It affected him deeply but he went out once more to race, won the Senior TT and then dramatically announced his retirement from racing. He returned to Rhodesia but tragically and ironically was killed in December that same year after being tempted back into racing, but this time in a Formula 1 car.

Hailwood on the MV then became the undisputed king of world-class 500cc racing. By huge points margins, he won the title in 1962, 1963, 1964 and 1965, but for 1966 he left the racing future of the famous MV factory in the hands of the emerging young and handsome Italian Giacomo Agostini and signed what was reputed to be one of the richest contracts ever in motor-cycle racing, to race in 1966 for Honda. The Japanese factory had won just about every honour in motor-cycle racing, except the 500cc World Championship. With their new machines and the finest and most successful rider in the business on their side, they reckoned they could overcome any challenge MV might produce and take the most famous title away from the Italian factory, which had by now taken the 500cc World Championship for the past eight years. Honda by this time, and in a mere five years, had amassed the astonishing total of eleven World Championships and twelve TT victories.

With golden boy Hailwood as the cornerstone of their team, and with insistent rumours that Honda would produce a new 500cc water-cooled V8 racer for the new season, 1966 was viewed with keen expectancy by all motor-bike race fans. The whole scene was interesting. Honda, in 1965, had cut back on their motor-cycle race programme in order to divert investment to car development and in consequence they had lost ground to challenges from both Yamaha and Suzuki. Bryans had managed to capture the 50cc title riding Honda, and Jim Redman was still the king of 350cc racing on the Honda, but by now Phil Read on the Yamaha was well entrenched in the 250cc class, taking his second title in two years, and Hailwood had continued the MV domination in the 500cc class.

The astute Redman had wanted Hailwood in the Honda team back in 1964, but the factory bosses did not respond. This was surprising considering Mike's winning rides on the loaned Hondas in 1961, but for 1966 each wanted the other: Honda wanted Hailwood to restore their flagging fortunes; Hailwood wanted Honda to break the tedium of riding a limited number of races on the MV and generally in races where there was no serious challenge. With Honda he would probably be competing in the 250cc, 350cc and 500cc Championships. His début at Barcelona in the Spanish Grand Prix was sensational. On a new 250cc six-cylinder, six-speed Honda, he won a superb race after Jim Redman's bike had caught fire on the first lap. In this class he became virtually unbeatable on the new machine all season. He won the next eight rounds, and won again in Italy, to romp home with 56 points, a massive 22 points ahead of his nearest rival, Phil Read, on the Yamaha. In the 350cc class, the handsome Agostini on the MV provided sterner opposition. Mike moved off to an optimistic start, winning the first and second rounds in West Germany and France. Agostini fought back strongly, beating Mike in his own backyard on the Isle of Man, when Hailwood had to retire. Mike won in Holland, Ago won again in East Germany, and although the Italian won in front of his home crowd once more at Monza, Hailwood's wins in Czechoslovakia, Finland and Northern Ireland were enough to give him the 350cc world title, by just six points.

It was by exactly that margin that he lost to Agostini in the major series, the 500cc World Championship. The frustrating (for Mike) side issue was that Hailwood might well have brought Honda the title they wanted most of all, had not team politics got in the way. By 1966 Jim Redman, sensing perhaps that his big-money days with Honda might be drawing to an end if the Japanese factory cut back their investment in racing, wanted desperately to win the 500cc world title. In the early rounds he rode the Honda 500cc himself when most observers had expected Mike to have prior claim. Despite their being team-mates, Redman was shrewd enough to see Hailwood as a potential rival and, certainly, a threat to his personal ambitions in certain circumstances. To reinforce his role as team captain he flew to Japan early in the year amid speculation that he had, surprisingly, not yet signed a new contract with Honda. He was in a strong negotiating position, and Honda were in something of a dilemma. He had brought the Japanese factory six of their eleven world titles, more than any other rider, and while he was perhaps moving towards the twilight of his career, that kind of record cannot be ignored, even by the independently minded Japanese. On the other hand, they did see in Hailwood their big chance of fulfilling their one remaining ambition in world-class racing, the 500cc World Championship.

Once Redman returned from Japan, having signed a contract for the new season, it was generally believed that he had been given what he wanted: reaffirmation of his role, not only as team captain but with total responsibility in all racing decisions.

Even so, had events not taken an odd turn and had Hailwood been given the opportunity of riding the 500cc machine from the beginning, Honda might still have won the all-important championship. The factory produced two machines, but the problem began when Redman smashed the gearbox of one while practising for the opening 500cc Grand Prix of the season at Hockenheim in West Germany. A further complication arose when it was realized that, should both Redman and Hailwood ride in the 250cc, 350cc and 500cc races, as intended, they would be exceeding the maximum daily mileage limit imposed by the FIM on riders in grand prix events. Permission for them to exceed the limit was refused, so both were forced to withdraw from one race. Yamaha were a major threat in the 250cc class so the combined might of Redman and Hailwood was required there. Redman then suggested that Hailwood was better equipped to counter the challenge of Agostini in the 350cc event, leaving him to take the 500cc machine. Hailwood, while acknowledging the strategy of the decision, nonetheless felt outmanoeuvred and the situation became so tense that the issue had to be referred to Japan. Honda chiefs felt obliged to support their captain so Redman took the 500 machine and Hailwood dutifully accepted the decision to ride in the 250cc and 350cc races. He won them both, and Honda must have been relieved when Redman outpaced Agostini on the MV to win the 500cc class. The new Honda proved exceptionally fast at Hockenheim, and Redman, rubbing salt into Hailwood's wound, dominated the race, setting a new lap record for the famous West German circuit of 112.99 mph.

At the next championship meeting, at Clermont-Ferrand in France, Hailwood rode superbly again, beating Redman to win the 250cc event and overcoming Agostini's challenge in the 350cc race. There was no 500cc event in France that year, so the next battle in that particular class was in Holland, racing on the Isle of Man in 1966 having been put back from June to September because of a seamen's strike. Hailwood again romped home in the 250cc class, beating Yamaha's Phil Read and Redman, and also in the 350cc race, where he was again superior to Agostini. Redman continued to show the Honda chiefs that the 500cc title was very much a possibility in his hands, and again he outpaced Agostini. Indeed, at this stage he had beaten the Italian rider on his factory MV in two races out of two, and was sixteen points ahead of his rival.

It was in Belgium, at the sensationally fast Francorchamps circuit at Spa, that the Honda dream faded. In the wet Redman's machine aquaplaned. He crashed, breaking his left forearm, and was out of action for six weeks, missing vital grand prix rounds in East Germany, Czechoslovakia and Finland. Only at this late stage in the season, with Redman out of action, was Hailwood now able to commandeer the superior bike and take up Honda's challenge. But he was a long way behind and, even accepting Hailwood's remarkable talent on a fast machine, it was asking much to expect him to make up lost ground and overhaul Agostini with just five rounds to go to the end of the season.

As crowds sensed the drama, every race was fought in an electric atmosphere as the Hailwood-Agostini battle was joined. In East Germany, Mike seemed certain to fall further behind as Ago set a blistering pace and, in an attempt to match him for speed, Hailwood's Honda yielded to the pressure, after just five laps. With Hailwood retired, Honda supporters agonized as Agostini maintained the pressure as, in an act of defiance and intent, he took the MV to a new absolute track record at Sachsenring of 107.77 mph, more than 3 mph faster than Hailwood's previous record, also set on an MV. But with only six miles to the chequered flag, Ago crashed and was unplaced in the race. In Czechoslovakia, in the next round, the Italian had not completely recovered from injury, though he raced. He could not match Hailwood on the day and, thus, in the fifth round and with only four more rounds to complete the season's programme, Hailwood registered his first win. It was one of those supreme Mike Hailwood moments, for he also beat Agostini in the 350cc round and Phil Read on the Yamaha to take the 250cc race, giving him three wins out of three races at the same circuit. In Finland, while Hailwood won the two other classes, Agostini consolidated his position in the 500cc Championship battle as Hailwood, struggling to control the unruly Honda, could only finish second.

At this point Jim Redman stepped back into the situation to complicate the issue. His early season successes had given him a good points advantage, and although his arm was still not completely mended, he knew he had to get back into the fight in the next round, the Ulster Grand Prix at the Dundrod circuit at Belfast, to stand any chance of achieving his one remaining racing ambition, the 500cc World Championship. In an eleventh-hour drama he cabled Japan for authorization and made a 6,000-mile dash from his home in Durban to Dundrod. He knew that to keep in the championship race he must finish in the first three in

Northern Ireland. On the other hand, a win in Northern Ireland would be enough to secure the title for Agostini. It looked at this stage, with Redman back in business, as if Mike Hailwood was once more out of the reckoning. Jim, however, was not back in business. His arm stiffened badly in practice, and reluctantly he had to withdraw. The battle between Agostini and Hailwood, MV and Honda, was now on again, and this time, despite a powerful machine whose handling characteristics made it hard to control at speed, Hailwood seized a dramatic victory, Ago finishing second.

After that, only two rounds remained, the rearranged TTs on the historic Isle of Man and at Monza, where Agostini, in the Italian Grand Prix, would be in front of his own fanatical supporters. Hailwood kept up the tension by scoring a resounding win on the Isle of Man. It was here that Redman, still bothered by his injured arm, accepted the inevitable and announced his retirement from racing. He never rode for Honda again. Hailwood and Agostini battled over the Mountain Course in sensational fashion, and Mike had to push the giant Honda to a new absolute lap record for the course of 107.07 mph to keep ahead of the dashing and insistent Italian. In the end it was Hailwood's race. He completed the 226½ miles just 2 minutes 38.8 seconds faster than Agostini.

Everything now depended on the final race in Italy. Against all odds Mike Hailwood had somehow managed to haul himself alongside Agostini. Only theoretically could he possibly have been given any chance after those early rounds, but so great were his talent and tenacity that he had turned theory into practice. The whole of racing saluted him as he lined up with Agostini at the famous Monza circuit in the last deciding round. Sadly, the drama and intense speculation were to be short-lived. Mike was forced to retire as the Honda's valves buckled, and Agostini raced ahead to take the flag and the 500cc World Championship — but only by six points.

Being 500cc World Champion was not an unknown experience for Hailwood. On an MV Agusta machine to which Agostini's 1966 championship model bore strong linear resemblance, Mike had taken the top title four years running, 1962 to 1965, an outstanding record in its own right. Even so, he made no secret of his ambition to win the title again on a Honda. Honda, on the other hand and while knowingly still keen to take the title from MV, seemed to self-destruct the possibility and Mike's ambition into the bargain, with their plans to cut back on racing. They pulled out of the 50cc and 125cc World Championships but agreed to support Hailwood and Ralph Bryans in the three bigger machine classes. Only Yamaha, of the Japanese 'big three', were prepared to increase their investment in racing.

For Hailwood, 1967 was to be a momentous season. In an extraordinary sequence of events he took the 350cc title with eight points more than Agostini, to continue Honda's domination of the class, while in the 250cc class he tied with Phil Read, ending the season with 50 points. The title went to Hailwood because he had won five rounds against Read's four. But the 500cc title yet again eluded him and, with astonishing coincidence, by the same yardstick used to decide the 250cc World Championship.

The 500cc class had been fiercely contested by Hailwood and Agostini all season, and racing could not have been closer. Agostini won in the opening round in West Germany. Hailwood then gained advantage with wins on the Isle of Man and in Holland. Ago fought back strongly, winning the Belgian Grand Prix and the East German Grand Prix. Further wins by the Italian in Finland and Italy and three more wins by Hailwood in Czechoslovakia, Northern Ireland and Canada, meant that when racing was done for the season both Hailwood and Agostini had 46 points each. Mike had won five grands prix. Ago, also, had won five grands prix. The title had to be resolved on the number of second places each had achieved. Mike's tally was two (Belgium and Italy), but Ago's was three (Holland, Czechoslovakia and Canada), so the Italian became the 1967 500cc World Champion.

There was no further chance for Mike Hailwood to gain the most coveted title once more, for Honda lost much of their interest in grand prix racing after 1967 and, after competing in a number of international races in 1968, Hailwood left the two-wheel scene to begin his distinguished career racing cars.

It must be accepted that in terms of results Honda's massive investment in 500cc bike racing at the highest level had failed. Research and development costs alone were massive, though never officially revealed. Back-up services, certainly in 1966, were prestigious. Hailwood's contract alone was the biggest ever paid up to that time and is probably still one of the biggest ever paid to a British rider in real terms.

The bike itself was enormously powerful and startlingly impressive.

Styled and finished to perfection, as by now one had come to expect of the Japanese, it was immaculate and phenomenally fast. When first wheeled out at the start of the season, it easily outpaced the MV of Agostini, but the Italians responded instantly and were soon back with a new and superior three-cylinder MV for the Dutch TT. It was so good that it shocked the Honda camp and forced Redman to comment: 'When the big Honda made its début at the West German Grand Prix I thought we'd have the fastest 500 for at least five years, but MV have shot that idea down in only six weeks.' It was certainly as fast as the Honda, but, more importantly, it was more reliable and its handling was superior. Hailwood complained bitterly at the time and also in later years, with the benefit of hindsight, that Honda's big mistake was in not listening to their riders enough. In their passion for results they insisted on increasing the power when their cause might well have been better served in making the machine more manageable.

Hailwood's loss to bike racing was mourned. Mass consensus reckoned the greatest career in motor-cycle racing was, sadly, at an end, but a decade later he came back for those emotion-packed 'token' rides on the Isle of Man in 1978 and 1979 and showed that the Hailwood magic was as sharp and as sparkling as it had ever been. His return was received with enormous enthusiasm. His success in the Formula 1 race in 1978 and in the Senior TT in 1979, on an 860cc Ducati and a 500cc Suzuki respectively, was a jewel of racing romance come to life and relished by fans everywhere. It completed his unprecedented record of fourteen wins on the Isle of Man, over the toughest racing circuit in the world.

Long before his retirement from motor-cycle racing Mike Hailwood had proved himself to the satisfaction of almost everyone in the sport to be one of the greatest riders of all time. Statistically his record was impressive. Between 1961 and 1967 he won nine World Championships and seventy-five grand prix races. In 1963 he broke every lap and race record except one in the entire 500cc World Championship series.

But Hailwood meant more than just records. He lived down his 'silver spoon' background to become one of the most respected, admired and best-loved characters in the business. Geoffrey Duke might have shown a more classic style. Yvon Duhamel might have been more breathtaking. Bill Ivy might have been more fearless and Phil Read more controversial, but if you pull together all the qualities which collectively make an outstanding, successful and memorable motor-cycle racing champion, you would probably find them all in greater abundance in Mike Hailwood than in any other rider. He was fast, consistent, shrewd, determined, skilful, stylish, with a fine sense of balance and a remarkable ability to read a race. His sense of humour and easy-going personality gave him a relaxed yet compelling presence. Any race programme that listed Mike Hailwood was certain to draw the crowds. He had an enormous international following and was a true Champion of Champions. His earlier playboy image was a natural response to the big-money contracts and the big-time bike-racing days of the 'Swinging Sixties'. Despite being caught up in the pranks and off-track parties of the 'Continental Circus', he rode seriously, diligently and with enormous concentration, and he did much to update the image of bike-racing which, until the emergence of 'Mike the Bike', had suffered from its lack of glamour. Yet he never lost that sense of quiet fun, nor the ability to keep both feet on the ground in the midst of success. His presence enriched the racing scene. After his glorious come-back rides on the Isle of Man he impishly told a television interviewer there: 'Basically I only wanted to come over here and probably do one class and have a good time, see my old pals and have a bit of a booze-up and leg-around, but of course it's all got out of hand and got terribly serious, which was not the object of the original exercise really, but there we are ...'

Not the least memorable of Mike Hailwood's achievements occurred on that day in 1964 when, in far-away Daytona, he captured the one-hour record. The record had stood since 1957 when the great Scottish rider Bob McIntyre had travelled to Monza and set a new time for the distance of 141 mph. Seven years later, after McIntyre had been killed while racing at Oulton Park in 1962, Mike's father, Stan Hailwood, very much involved with his son's racing at that time, said that they would have been happy for the record to remain in credit to 'Bob Mac' for all time as a permanent memorial, '... but I knew that one day it would be broken and had already heard rumours of an attempt by someone else.'

Mike was at the Daytona circuit preparing for the United States Grand Prix, and the entire project centred around whether he would be able to go for and take the world-record in the morning, for he would be racing in the World Championship event in the afternoon. Before leaving Britain for the United States, Mike and his father had been warned about the folly of such an attempt by Dickie Davies, the Dunlop competitions manager. A world-record attempt of that kind would need special track tyres, he said, which would take much more time than was available to prepare. You just could not go for something like that with ordinary tyres. Another setback was Count Agusta's downright refusal, for fear of failure and any possible prejudice the world-record attempt might have on the result of the day's grand prix, which he considered much more important. But Hailwood was keen to make the attempt, despite Count Agusta's attitude. He knew he had a good chance of gaining the record because he had lapped a Norton at Daytona at 139.6 mph a year before and the multi-cylinder MV was faster. The Daytona authorities also encouraged the attempt because of the prestige should a new world record be set at the track. They sent a cable to Italy asking Count Agusta to change his mind, but whether permission was ever granted was never revealed.

Meantime, Stan Hailwood's dilemma was whether to disregard the Count's initial refusal and run the risk of fouling up Mike's chances in the Grand Prix, or back his hunch, and Mike's confidence, that his son could go for the two — and be successful in both. The problem was that the Hailwood entourage had been supplied with just two MV Agustas, the race-prepared machine intended for the afternoon's race and a practice mount. It would be too risky to use the race machine for the world record attempt, because if anything went wrong there would be no hope that even Hailwood could win the Grand Prix on a practice bike; but was a practice bike, even a mighty MV, good enough to smash the world One Hour Record? Mike accepted the situation with customary calm, going to his hotel bed as usual the night before and leaving the decision to his father.

By dawn, after a restless night, Stan Hailwood had made up his mind. He would let Mike make the attempt on the practice bike. As Mike slept, Stan roused the MV mechanic and then sprint expert and British racing journalist Charlie Rous. The bike was fitted with a new fairing, tyres were changed and quickly the machine was made ready for the attempt. At 9 am Rous informed the FIM officials and timekeepers that Mike would be going for the record. Only then did old man Hailwood telephone his son and tell him the attempt was on and to get down to the track immediately.

Within a short time, Mike was waiting on the start line, astride the MV. It was to be a standing start with the engine running. Before a small group of officials, timekeepers, press, radio and television people, the Union flag was dropped and Mike was away. On the first lap Hailwood's speed was disappointing, only 136.5 mph, well short of McIntyre's record-breaking 141 mph. Easing more speed out of the MV, Mike pushed up his average after five laps to 141 mph, but his aim was 145 mph. After half an hour he was still falling short of his aim, and his pit began to signal frantically, urging him to go even faster than his lap average at that point of 146.5 mph. Another fifteen minutes of hard and nerve-racking riding and the record looked secure, but then his speed began to drop, by just a second or two on each lap. Success looked to be in doubt again, but then the time was up and victory was won: a new One Hour Record at the new speed of 142.2 mph, not all that much in excess of Bob McIntyre's record of seven years before, but enough all the same.

That very afternoon, Mike Hailwood took the other MV out in the United States Grand Prix and completed an astonishing day of bike-racing by winning the major 500cc event with new lap and race records. It was a remarkable achievement and so typical of the golden boy of racing, the most popular racer of all time.

Mike Hailwood was awarded the British Empire Medal in 1968 and the George Medal in 1973. After his retirement from all racing, his tragic death in 1981 in a domestic road accident, which also took the life of his young daughter, Michelle, shocked and numbed the entire nation. Britain's most popular motor-cycle road racer of all time was gone. He left behind a magnificent legacy of racing achievement.

7. How Many World Titles Do You Hold?

A contemporary of Mike Hailwood's with whom he shared bike-racing's top billing in the 1960s was the handsome Italian Giacomo Agostini. His flashing smile, wholesome good looks and that special Latin temperament gave him a pop-style image and made him a magnetic draw with race crowds all over the world. At home he was a national hero and his talent and success on a race bike enabled him to become the most successful World Champion of all time. In a phenomenal ten years he won no fewer than fifteen world titles. For five years running he was 350cc and 500cc double World Champion, and between 1966 and 1975 he won an impressive 124 grands prix.

In the World Championships Italy has a proud heritage. From the beginning in 1949 the country was strongly represented, in both riders and machinery. Nello Pagani, Bruno Ruffo, Dario Ambrosini and Umberto Masetti were legends in their own country, and riding those superbly engineered Mondial, Guzzi, Benelli and Gilera machines, they quickly made an impact on the early years of the post-war championships.

Probably Italy's greatest rider in the days before Agostini was the unassuming Carlo Ubbiali, a brilliant rider of lightweight machinery. Though World Champion nine times in as many years, Ubbiali did not enjoy the widespread recognition or the trackside fan-appeal of Agostini. One reason for this is that he rode in the days prior to the glamorization of the sport in the 1960s. For Ubbiali and his contemporaries there were no colourful leathers, space-age crash hats or lucrative contracts for a whole string of talented riders. Another unfortunate reason was that Carlo Ubbiali persisted in riding the smaller bikes. Not a very big man, his small stature enabled him to fit neatly and conveniently onto the smaller bikes, but there is no doubt that had he decided to move up into the 350cc and 500cc classes, his public recognition would have been much greater. As it is, he remains largely unknown except with the more serious followers of motor-cycle racing, among whom he is still acknowledged as one of the most skilful riders of any generation.

Similar comments are appropriate for the Spaniard Angel Nieto. In 1985 he had been bike-racing for almost twenty-five years, but include him in a list of champions alongside Hailwood, Agostini, Duke, Surtees, Sheene and the Americans Freddie Spencer and Kenny Roberts and many people would wonder how his name got there. Yet Nieto has won more World Championships than any rider other than Agostini. His comparative lack of recognition internationally arises because his outstanding record of thirteen World Championships has been recorded in 50cc and 125cc racing. It is likely that he would have become more widely known with two or three 500cc world titles to his credit. In his home country, however, Angel Nieto, like Agostini, in Italy, became a sporting hero not only for his World Championship successes but also because many of those successes were scored on Spanish machines. National pride is never greater than when a local lad makes good on locally built machinery. Nieto did it first as long ago as 1969, with a 50cc world title, riding a Derbi, but his latest achievement, some fifteen years later, brings his links with Agostini fractionally closer, for he won his latest 125cc World Championship in 1984 on an Italian Garelli machine.

Giacomo Agostini and Angel Nieto are the two most successful motor-cycle road racers of all time, in terms of World Championship results. While they are close to one another in age (Agostini born 1943, Nieto in 1947) and both were in the racing spotlight in the late 1960s and 1970s, Agostini retired from racing shortly after winning the 500cc world title in 1975 while Angel Nieto was still racing — and winning — in 1984.

Agostini, like Hailwood, grew up with the benefits of a wealthy parentage and at seventeen was already showing an interest in motor-bikes, riding a 175cc Morini in domestic road races and hill-climb events. On a borrowed works machine he entered his first major road race in 1943. A year later he not only became Morini's top works rider but beat the established professional Tarquinio Provini to win the 250cc Italian Championship. His astonishingly long and successful career with MV Agusta began when he was signed by the famous racing factory in 1965. Until then he had not raced any machine heavier than a 250cc, but he took naturally to the 350cc and 500cc rides he was given by MV. Honda and Yamaha were by now collectively fiercely contesting all except the 500cc and sidecar classes and in the 350cc class Agostini was lining up with Mike Hailwood, from within the MV camp, Honda team-leader Jim Redman and Phil Read on the fast Yamahas. Undaunted, the Italian caused a sensation by missing the world title by a whisker in a class which Honda had taken comfortably for the previous three seasons. He was helped considerably by a brand new three-cylinder racer, which replaced the massive MV-four for that season. It had improved handling and reduced frontal area for less wind resistance, and looked trim and workmanlike against the heavier, multi-cylinder Hondas.

Sensational wins in West Germany, Finland and Italy and good third-place finishes in Holland and on the Isle of Man put Agostini well in contention for the 350cc title at his first attempt. In the final grand prix of the season in Japan, he looked all set to astound the racing world as he held strongly to a commanding lead. Then disaster struck and a broken contact-breaker spring put him out of the running, so that he finished the season in second place to Jim Redman on the Honda. Nonetheless, the Japanese Grand Prix was a humiliating experience for the massive and prosperous Honda organization because, even with Agostini out of the running, Redman on the Honda still could not beat Hailwood on the second MV Agusta machine. In the 500cc class that year, there was no serious opposition to the MVs, and Hailwood once again took the championship with ease (48 points), with Agostini second (38) and Paddy Driver on a Matchless with 26 points.

Agostini's big chance came the next season, after Hailwood had left MV to ride for Honda. The epic battles between the two former team-mates, which in 1966 and 1967 ended in sensational cliff-hanger situations, have been described earlier, but thereafter, with Honda retired and most of the serious factory opposition in the 500cc class retired from racing, Agostini was left for a number of years to race against the clock and his own best performances. He captured his first world title in 1966 (500cc class) and repeated his success in the same class in 1967. In 1968 he achieved the first of his phenomenal record of five consecutive double 350cc and 500cc

World Championships.

As Agostini shattered all previous records by winning every round in both the 350cc and 500cc classes (a total of seventeen races), Angel Nieto was still racing largely unnoticed in the 50cc World Championship in the early stages of his international career, though he was already moving in among the results. The next year, as Agostini raced ahead once again to take two more world titles, Nieto registered his first grand prix win at the East German Grand Prix at Sachsenring and went on to take the 50cc title by the narrowest of margins from the Dutch ace Aalt Toersen on a Kreidler. As the Spaniard chalked up his first World Championship, Agostini was already well on his way to becoming the greatest grand prix racer of them all, for he had already won six World Championships.

Agostini's record-book statistics are sometimes coloured by the indisputable fact that the majority of his World Championships were won when there was hardly any factory opposition to the MVs. To push the pendulum too far over, however, would do the Italian an enormous injustice. It is to his credit that he often exceeded his previous best, and his concentration and consistency were almost always impressive. At speed on the classic MVs he was always great to watch, and he was able to steer it well round the demanding Mountain Course on the Isle of Man. In seven years he won ten TT races, a record which includes no fewer than four Senior/Junior TT doubles. He later, along with Phil Read and Barry Sheene, became a carping critic of the Mountain Course, part of a growing disillusionment among many riders which was ultimately responsible for the removal of the TT races from the grand prix programme.

This and his criticisms of Phil Read after the latter had found a place in the MV team while Agostini was left, mentally bruised and disillusioned, to seek solace in a short-term contract with Yamaha, were virtually the only disturbances in a career of surprising tranquillity and contentment. There were hardly any shocks, no outrages to speak of, but despite all that, there was nothing about Agostini which was mediocre. Like Hailwood, he was perhaps not the most exciting rider, nor the most dramatic or sensational, but his smooth style displayed no eccentricity and was always impressive. It was not surprising that his critics would make much of his 'easy' wins, but Agostini showed that, when it was needed, he could fight alongside the best. His record proved it.

After beating off the challenge from Hailwood on the Honda in 1966 and 1967, Agostini fought courageously when the Finnish sensation, Jarno Saarinen, burst like a firecracker on the grand prix scene in 1971 and 1972. He yet again showed character and courage when, his pride battered after Phil Read had robbed him of the 500cc world title in 1973 after winning it for seven consecutive years, he fought back with impressive dedication and determination to win it back again on the unfamiliar two-stroke Yamaha just two years later.

Though only 5 feet 5 inches tall, Agostini was a great charmer. He encouraged an enormous following with his charismatic personality. His female fans were legion. They would surge round him as he flashed that broad Latin smile and squeal delightedly as he casually ran a hand through that curly, dark hair. He was a leading figure, along with Hailwood, Phil Read, Bill Ivy and others, of the grand prix Continental Circus during its most exciting, sensational and glamorous days — and in terms of title-winning, he outlasted all the top riders from that scintillating era.

In 1974 Agostini was thirty-one. He had just been dislodged by MV and was still nursing an injury after crashing heavily while test riding in Italy. His career had slumped, and at Daytona, on the sweeping, banked circuit and against all the top American as well as European riders, he was set to race the Yamaha two-stroke after a lifetime of riding and racing four-stroke machinery. Among the formidable line-up was the hard-riding, fearless French-Canadian Yvon Duhamel, the all-American Gary Nixon, Britain's new golden boy, Barry Sheene, and the future World Champion, Kenny Roberts. All had raced at Daytona before. Agostini had not.

Casting aside all self-doubts, Agostini thrust the Yamaha into the lead from the start. Despite a hard challenge from the Yamaha-mounted Hideo Kanaya, which ended only after the Japanese rider overdid things on lap 5, his machine cartwheeling across the infield to cause something of a sensation, Agostini kept in front. Menacingly to the rear, however, Sheene led a group of riders who were now closing the gap. The Italian's hopes began to fade as Sheene surged ahead, and Roberts and Nixon were seen to be outriding him. Though both Sheene and Duhamel were to drop out with mechanical trouble, Agostini's chances did not look good, with less than half the race to run, for both Roberts and Nixon were ahead of him. Roberts, in the lead, slowed with machine problems and as Nixon surged ahead, Agostini hung on grimly. Temperatures were up into the nineties, and it was one of the most gruelling races Agostini had ever ridden. But luck was with the Italian. Nixon's machine began to have problems, and then, in an attempt to overtake a back marker, the American surged up the banking, lost control and in the crash so damaged his Suzuki that he was unable to continue. Determination had won the day, for Agostini now had a clear run to the line to win the race and the £6,500 prize money. He was so exhausted after the race that he was not able to go up to receive the Daytona Trophy for fully twenty minutes.

That year, on the Yamaha, he captured the 350cc world title, and in 1975 he re-established himself as the top 500cc rider in the world with wins in France, West Germany, Finland and Italy. With Phil Read on the MV, Barry Sheene riding Suzuki, and other riders of outstanding ability such as Lansivuori and Kanaya, it was a tough series, but Agostini finished six points ahead of Read to take his fifteenth World Championship, a magnificent record.

Agostini was a little unusual perhaps among World Champions in that he remained with one factory for a very long time. For eight years he was with MV, only in 1974 and 1975 riding for Yamaha. The stark reality of the situation is that there was little serious alternative for a number of years if he wanted to give himself the best chance of remaining a World Champion. There were just no other factories competing with any chance of seriously challenging the Italian factory, though Agostini always seemed to give the impression that he would not be in any hurry to change if there had been a choice. He seemed happy and contented to stay with MV Agusta. Only after Phil Read joined MV did he become disenchanted with Count Agusta, complaining that he was having to ride second-best machines while Read took the priority bike. That forced his split with MV and his move to Yamaha, a shift for which the fanatical and intensely patriotic Italian fans never really forgave their former hero. After his two World Championships on the Japanese machine he retired from motor-cycle racing, though he continued to keep close to the sport through the running of his own team with a series of sponsors.

Though Agostini and Angel Nieto share centre stage in terms of the most World Championships won, temperamentally they are very different. Agostini is not typically Italian, being generally calm and not given too easily to emotional outbursts. The little Spaniard, on the other hand, is characteristically Spanish, his flashes of temper and bad manners being put down charitably by friends in the race game as high spirits and a deeply rooted commitment to win races. With more experience and the passing of years, he mellowed considerably, however.

After starting racing when he was thirteen on a second-hand 50cc Derbi machine, it was typical of Nieto's determination to move into the sport professionally that he went to Spain's famous Bultaco factory and got himself a job in their racing department. When he saw that there was little chance of being given a racing opportunity, because Bultaco already had more riders on their books than they knew what to do with, he quit and moved to the racing department of the Derbi concern. This small factory, which had been established in 1951, was enterprising, with a keen sensitivity to the value of racing. They built mainly 49cc two-stroke machines and from these developed effective racing versions. It was on these machines that Nieto was to be so successful, building his international reputation. He was also to be successful on the 123cc racing versions which the factory developed from the basic concept and which were fitted with water-cooled two-stroke engines.

In 1968 the Madrid-born future racing star became determined to make a name for himself on the grand prix circuits. That year in the 50cc class he gave Suzuki's Hans-Georg Anscheidt a hard time, finishing second to the German before a delighted home crowd and notching a third place in Belgium at the ultra-fast Spa circuit. The very next year he was able to repay the faith Derbi had placed in him. In the 50cc Championship, he finished second in the opening encounter in Spain, was second again in the French Grand Prix and scored his first grand prix win at the East German Grand Prix at Sachsenring. Another victory in Northern Ireland and a further second place in the final round in Yugoslavia gave him his first World Championship. The following year, 1970, saw him totally in command, and he took his second 50cc world title in two years by a comfortable margin. Competing for the first time in the 125cc class, he managed to finish second to Dieter Braun of West Germany. He secured the 125cc championship again in 1971, when he finished second in the 50cc class, and in 1972 crowned a remarkable season of racing by becoming 50cc and 125cc double World Champion.

At the peak of his form, Angel Nieto was disappointingly left without a grand prix ride in 1973, Derbi being forced to withdraw from the expense of mounting a racing programme at the end of 1972, though the Spaniard continued to ride their machines in national events in Spain. With Derbi still out of racing, there followed a disastrous move to the Italian Morbidelli factory, with whom, in two years, he failed to win a single grand prix. Disappointed, frustrated and angry at his lack of success, Nieto thought for a time about shifting to motor-racing permanently, but in 1974 he was back racing on two wheels and on a Derbi managed to win two grands prix in the 50cc class that year.

At this point Angel Nieto had become totally bored with 50cc racing and, in the hope of moving up to ride 125cc and 250cc machines, said he was finished with 'tiddler' racing. Bultaco's racing come-back, to counter the all-conquering Morbidelli marque in the 125cc class, changed Nieto's plans, and in 1976 he found himself back on the racing 'fifties'. He won the title yet again and in the 125cc class finished second, despite a competitive machine becoming available to him for only the second half of the season. Disappointingly, Nieto's natural desire to succeed in 250cc racing never materialized, and his inability to race the bigger machines and win was proved conclusively when he attempted to move into 750cc racing on a Yamaha. But in the smaller classes, the world has not seen a greater exponent. He claimed another 50cc world title in 1977, finishing third in the 125cc class (both on Bultaco), and after moving to Minarelli he finished second in 125cc racing in 1978 and claimed that world crown again in 1979. In 1980 Angel Nieto was still racing, eleven years after winning his first world title and, though he finished third in the 125cc class that year, proved his ability yet again in 1981 when he secured the 125cc World Championship by a massive margin of 140 points against Reggiani of Italy, with 95.

By now the able Spaniard really had seen enough of 50cc racing and was concentrating on the 125cc class. In his mid-thirties and at a time when nobody would have been surprised had he decided to call it a day, Nieto, it seemed, was only just getting his second wind. He moved to the Italian Garelli factory and on their 125cc machines won the World Championship again in 1982, once more in 1983 and, almost unbelievably, yet again in 1984, to give him his longest run of four World Championship successes in his entire career.

A thirty-eighth birthday celebration in 1985 could be enough to prompt Angel Nieto, the Peter Pan of road racing, to accept that time and tide will not wait, not even for a racing Spaniard. If, however, he continues to race seriously in the mid-1980s and beyond, that once seemingly untouchable fifteen World Championships won by Giacomo Agostini, which put him at the time in a class totally apart from all other champions, could be in jeopardy. As the road-racing season emerged from hibernation once more in April 1985, Angel Nieto must have been thinking: just three more World Championships would do it, but to beat the time barrier he might well be forced into racing the 'tiddlers' yet again, now the 80cc World Championship. But even without another race, Angel Nieto fully deserved his close links with Agostini as one of motor-cycling's greatest-ever champions.

8. Champions Without a Title

World Champion titles are one thing, but they are not the total proof of talent. Certainly it would be difficult if not impossible to win a World Championship without the ability to ride a motor-cycle at speed successfully, but for all sorts of reasons there have been skilful, courageous, exciting and impressive motor-cyclists who, despite their obvious talent and outstanding ability, have failed to win a world title.

Bob McIntyre missed the accolade of winning a World Championship by a whisker. Illness prevented him from competing in the final grand prix of the season at Monza in 1957, and the 500cc World Championship which he looked certain to collect was lost forever.

Derek Minter was one of the most stylish riders of any generation. A tough, outspoken character, he missed the chance of works rides because too frequently he said what he felt, and on the Isle of Man in 1962 he committed the unpardonable sin of outriding the might of the Honda official works team, with the unforgiving Jim Redman as team captain, on a loaned Honda. The Honda officials never allowed him to forget his defiant gesture and continued to snub him when at times he was a natural and obvious choice to join the team.

There was no rider more courageous or who sought more passionately a world title than John Hartle. He rode with a flourish which often ended in serious injury, but so obsessed was he with bike-racing that he returned to the sport when often his career seemed to be at an end. Tragically, he was still without a world title when he crashed at Scarborough on the notorious Oliver's Mount circuit and was fatally injured.

McIntyre, Minter and Hartle could not earn a world title between them, but for all that, they were great riders, among the greatest ever produced by Britain. McIntyre gets into the record books because of his historic ride on the Isle of Man in 1957 when that elusive 100 mph lap of the tortuous 37¾-mile Mountain circuit was finally achieved. It was a milestone for the sport and a personal triumph for one of the most dedicated and respected riders ever to climb into a racing saddle. To put the record into perspective, we need to go back to those times and include some of the background and history of the famous races on the Island. Speed milestones, as we have already witnessed in earlier pages, had become the prerogative of the great Jimmy Simpson, who had been first to lap the famous circuit at 60, 70 and 80 mph. But in 'Bob Mac's' day the race was on to be the first to race a 'ton-up' lap — and in the late 1950s a number of riders were moving towards the target.

These were also the days of the great Geoffrey Duke, John Surtees and formidable riders of the calibre of Reg Armstrong, Bill Lomas, Cecil Sandford, Bob Brown and Keith Campbell. On a four-cylinder Gilera, Geoffrey Duke had come close in 1955 when his 99.97 mph was at first greeted as the first 100 mph lap on the Isle of Man, but amid howls of protest and desperate disappointment for Duke, confirming calculations revealed that his time of 22 minutes 39 seconds was just 99.97 mph. Simpson had set his earlier speed milestones on British machinery, but there was little hope in the mid-1950s that a British bike would claim the first 100 mph lap. Of the riders, Duke looked the best candidate. On those last racing Nortons he had pushed the figure to 93.33 mph in 1950 and 95.22 mph in 1951. It was Duke again in 1952 with a lower speed (94.88 mph), but then in 1953 and 1954 the new Norton team-leader, Ray Amm, came spectacularly into contention with a dazzling display which gave him figures of 97.41 mph in 1953 and, in the Junior TT (would you believe) the following year, 94.61 mph.

By 1955 Geoffrey Duke had 'gone foreign' and was riding the ultra-powerful Italian Gilera, and in 1956 John Surtees was riding the equally powerful Italian MV — both of which in terms of absolute speed were far superior to the British Nortons. Surtees had got close with 97.79 mph in the Senior event of 1956, but it would be appropriate if the following year the specific 100 mph lap landmark could be reached, for 1957 would be the fiftieth anniversary of the TT Races. Bob McIntyre, after being a member of the AJS works team in 1954, was now the Gilera team-leader. The talented Scot

Acknowledged by many as the greatest motor-cycle racer never to win a world title, Bob McIntyre went into the record books as being the first rider to complete a 100 mph lap of the famous Isle of Man Mountain Course. He is seen on the Gilera during one of his record-breaking laps in 1957.

There was no greater exponent of short-circuit racing in Britain in the 1960s than the outstanding King of Brands Hatch, Derek Minter. Here Derek, sporting his famous number 11, negotiates Druid's Bend at his beloved Kent circuit.

Grand Prix action as Phil Read and Jarno Saarinen, on MV and Yamaha respectively, battle for honours in the 500cc German Grand Prix in 1973. Read won the race and went on to take the 500cc World Championship that year.

Britain's first sidecar World Champion Eric Oliver during the French Grand Prix at Rouen in August 1953. With passenger Stan Dibben he won the race and the Sidecar World Championship for the fourth and last time in five years.

Pocket-sized dynamite racer Bill Ivy (5) is ahead of Mike Hailwood (2) as they crank over to take a bend during the 1967 Canadian Grand Prix. Ivy won the 125cc race, Hailwood the 250cc and 500cc events.

In startling contrast to Oliver's sidecar combination is the futuristically designed sidecar of racing ace Rolf Biland, with passenger Kurt Waltisperg, both of Switzerland. Rolf caused consternation among the FIM officials with his controversial outfit.

Gyon, Hungary, 19 April 1937 and Britain's Eric Fernihough, wearing spectacles near to the centre of the picture, poses with his team, observers and officials after claiming a new world speed record of 169.78 mph to beat the German, Henne's former record by a whisker. Eric's record stood until 21 October when Piero Taruffi raised it to 170.5 mph.

Racing sensation of the 1970s and the greatest road racer ever to come from Finland, Jarno Saarinen poses with the giant trophy after winning the famous Race of the Year at Mallory Park in 1972. Saarinen's enormous courage and fine sense of balance made him one of the most exciting racers of all time.

Born in Venezuela of Italian parents, Johnny Cecotto was at times a brilliant rider, but he suffered from inconsistency. He is seen riding the 500cc Yamaha in the Belgian Grand Prix of 1978. He was 350cc World Champion in 1975 and beat Kenny Roberts to the Formula 750 World Championship in 1978.

Powerhouse riding from the French Canadian Yvon Duhamel was a feature of Team Kawasaki in the 1970s. A courageous and mercurial rider, Duhamel was one of the most fearless racers of any generation.

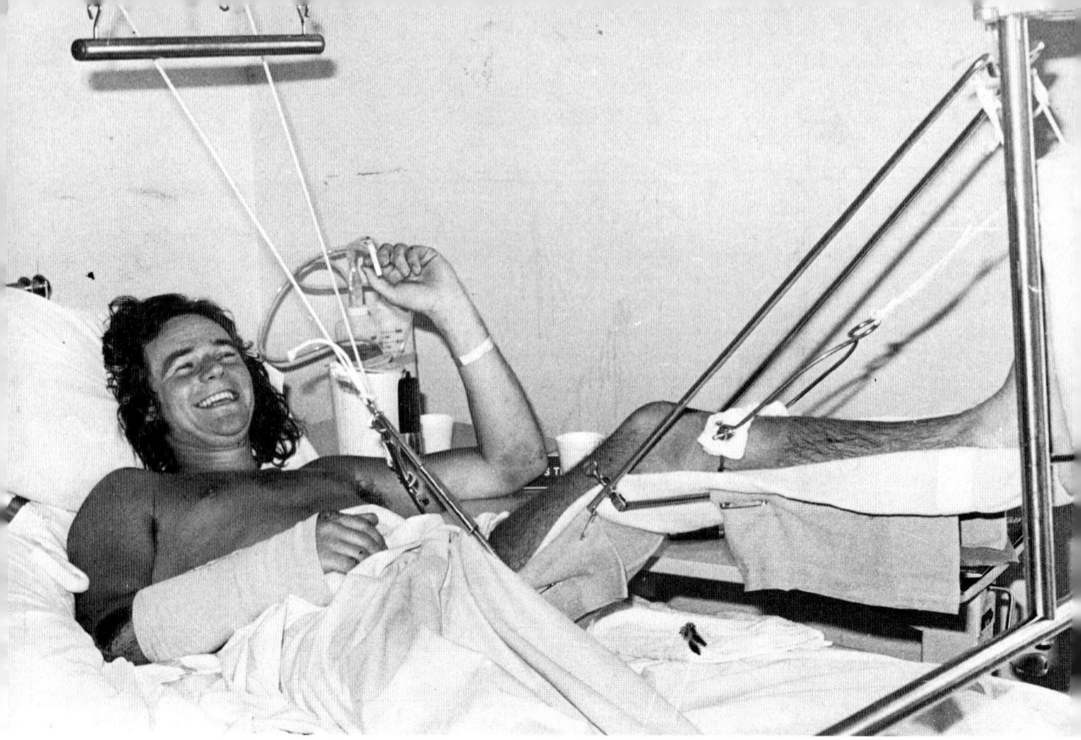

Still smiling, Barry Sheene seems not too disturbed by all the pulleys and
wires after his horrific crash at Daytona. Without doubt Barry has been
one of racing's all-time favourite riders, an outstanding media personality.

With his favourite Number 7 up front, Sheene gets his knee to the ground
and cranks the big Suzuki well over during the Spanish Grand Prix of
1978. After taking the 500cc World Championship in 1976 and 1977,
Barry finished second to Roberts in 1978.

Italian ace Marco Lucchinelli races round the Spa circuit in the 1983 Belgian Grand Prix. After winning the 500cc World Championship in 1981 he switched from Suzuki to Honda in one of the biggest cash deals ever negotiated in motor-cycle racing.

(*Left*) 'King Kenny' Roberts, tough, uncompromising American, delights the Brands Hatch crowd in 1980 with this all-action 'wheelie'. Riding Yamaha, he completed a consecutive trio of 500cc World Championships that year.

Randy Mamola marked his return to grand prix racing in 1984 by riding a Honda for the first time at the Jarama circuit in Spain. His spectacular cornering technique and forceful riding took him into second place behind Yamaha mounted Eddie Lawson.

Racing sensation of the 1980s, Freddie Spencer, moves the Honda at speed in the Yugoslavian Grand Prix at Rijeka in 1984. He went on to win the race from Mamola and Raymond Roche. Favourite to win the 500cc world title, he almost certainly would have done so, had not he been plagued by injury.

After playing second fiddle to Kenny Roberts, who won the world title three times, fellow American Eddie Lawson emerged a worthy World Champion. Riding Yamaha machinery, he successfully battled with Freddie Spencer to take the title for the first time in 1984. The Lawson style is seen at Jarama that year in the Spanish Grand Prix where he won the round and rode the fastest lap.

had been invited the previous year to join Geoffrey Duke in the Gilera team but, wishing to remain faithful to Britain for as long as possible, he turned down the offer. However, a year later it was obvious that if Bob wanted to win in international events, British machines were no longer good enough and he reluctantly joined Gilera. Duke was out of the 1957 TTs because of a dislocated shoulder sustained at Imola, leaving McIntyre Gilera's Number 1 rider. There was enormous interest and intense speculation about who would be the first rider to achieve the first 'ton' lap. The Senior TT had seventy-four entries, and many were in with a chance. World Champion John Surtees on the MV was a hot favourite. McIntyre was a possibility. Interest also centred on Dickie Dale when it was known that he would be mounted on the first eight-cylinder machine to be seen on the Island — the spectacular Guzzi V-8.

McIntyre, for all his greatness as a rider, was not particularly interested in records. His prior aim was to win the race. He made that clear before the start, as journalists speculated about the magic 'ton'. McIntyre's morale enjoyed a welcome boost when he won the earlier Junior event, setting new lap and race records on a machine which had definitely gone off song in the latter stages.

Friday 7 June 1957 turned out sunny with a clear sky, ideal conditions for the Golden Jubilee Senior TT Race, specially extended to eight laps to commemorate the occasion — more than three hundred miles of some of the hardest racing in the world. The atmosphere was highly charged as the starting maroon sounded and riders set off in pairs at ten-second intervals. Immediately Bob McIntyre showed his determination to win. On the brilliantly tuned, scarlet-painted four-cylinder Gilera, he set a cracking pace from the standing start and on the first lap came within a fraction of reaching the magic milestone. His speed of 99.99 mph sent a buzz round the crowd, for he had already smashed Geoff Duke's existing record. Bob said later that he knew nothing of his speed on the first lap, nor indeed how he was doing during the remainder of the race. He was concentrating on winning, and as the race developed he was concerned to make up time on John Surtees, who had started out two minutes ahead of him. The epic ride was on lap 2 when, with head down and hurling the handsome Gilera round the Mountain Course, drawing on all his reserves of skill and courage, Bob McIntyre cracked the TT's 'ton' barrier wide open — the very first rider ever to do so.

Five years later, in his autobiography, McIntyre remembered the lap like this:

Down the sharp slope of Bray Hill on full throttle at 140 mph ... swing right over Quarter Bridge ... through the S-bend at Braddan ... slow down to 80 for the right-and-left sweep at Union Mills ... open up for the Crosby Straight and on to Highlander, hitting its notorious bumps at 130 mph ... Ballacraine coming up, a medium-fast bend beginning one of the slowest and most taxing stretches ... down to first gear and 35 mph ... over Ballig Bridge, once humpbacked but now levelled, at close on 100 ... now begin to climb to Creg Willey's. To think riders walked up here in the first TT! ... then through the S-bend known as Handley's Cottage because Wal Handley, winner of four trophies, once crashed here. It has been eased slightly since his day.

Through the bend at Baaregarroo at over 100 mph and an exhilarating run downhill to the Thirteenth Milestone ... through Kirkmichael ... change down for Birkin's Bend, the right-hander where Archie Birkin was killed when he hit a van during practice for the 1927 races (the roads were not closed for practice until after this) ... throttle down to thirty to avoid leaping too high on the humpback bridge at Ballaugh ... a right-hand, left-hand follows immediately ... now I'm winding up for Sulby Straight, fastest stretch of the whole circuit and I must be clocking 160 mph ...

Ramsey — 24 miles from the start — and there is a huge crowd in Parliament Square urging me on ... out of Ramsey again and I am starting up the Mountain ... Gooseneck, a severe uphill right-hander where the mist always seems to hang ... down to first gear and 40 mph past the Guthrie Memorial, monument to Jimmy Guthrie, winner of six TT races ... on a clear day one can see Scotland, native land of both of us, from this point. No time for sight-seeing now though ... East Mountain Gate — and the worst part of the climb is over ... Here is the Verandah with the valley 800 feet below ... Windy Corner, where the wind always blows ... going down hill now ... thirty-third Milestone ... Kate's cottage and I'm doing over 100 again. Slow down for Creg-ny-Baa; another big crowd of spectators here ... down through the gears for Brandish Corner, named after Charlie Brandish who broke a leg here in 1923 ... Hillberry, the 100 mph-plus corner where I had my first Island spill on the Gold Star ... no stand to worry about now ...

Governor's Bridge, a hairpin, and dead slow for the last of the 200-odd bends ... accelerate again along Glencrutchery Road ... past the grandstands at near the maximum again ... look at my pit signals ...

Little wonder that, with so much to concentrate on, McIntyre was giving no heed to a 100 mph lap, but the crowds were now cheering wildly, for McIntyre had done it — the very first 100 mph lap on the historic TT course and after fifty years of racing; the official lap speed was 101.03 mph. Hardly had the crowd time to settle than McIntyre brought them to life once again, for on his third lap he averaged 100.54 mph and on the very next lap sent the crowd wild by cracking his own recently set record with a new average speed of 101.12 mph. What is more, he was at this point averaging over 100 mph for the whole distance! A stop for fuel and oil, and McIntyre once more surged off in pursuit of Surtees. A stone flying up from the rear wheel of a back marker's bike as he moved to overtake caught him through the narrow gap between his goggles and his crash helmet, but, as he said later, at more than 100 mph it felt the size of a brick. Though dazed and on the point of vomiting because of the pain, McIntyre somehow managed to keep going as the cold air clotted the blood pouring from the wound. With just three laps to go, McIntyre kept up the pressure, passing Surtees, and then on the sixth lap averaged more than 100 mph again. Thereafter the Scot eased back, the race won, and he and Surtees crossed the finishing line virtually together, McIntyre a clear winner by virtue of his later start.

It had been a momentous day for Bob McIntyre and indeed for motor-cycle racing. He became only the second rider in the TT's fifty years' history to win the Senior and Junior races in the same year, and had shattered the 100 mph barrier with laps at 101.03, 100.54, 101.12 and 100.35 mph. After the Isle of Man, he finished second in Holland and won at Monza in the 350cc series, but he was eight points behind Keith Campbell on the Guzzi at the end of the season, Campbell becoming 350cc World Champion. In the 500cc class that year McIntyre was leading the challenge as riders prepared for the Dutch TT at Assen. Straight from the success of his Isle of Man triumph, he was leading and pulling away when he had to stop to change an oiled plug. When he went out again, Surtees had surged ahead and McIntyre set after him. Bob said afterwards: 'I began making up ground. On the twenty-fourth lap of the thirty-lap race there was only Surtees ahead. I was catching him and should have passed him a couple of laps from the end, but I was trying too hard ... I left the road and went into the ditch. When John took the chequered flag I was on my way to hospital with concussion.' As a result he missed the Belgian Grand Prix and finished second in the Ulster Grand Prix, being sick after the race and suffering severe pain in his neck. Nonetheless, he went to Monza for the final race in the series, the Italian Grand Prix. He won the Junior race but was violently sick on the machine. Bob explained later: 'I was obviously ill and Mr Gilera packed me off to hospital, refusing to let me ride in the 500cc race. He was right. The doctors found I had broken a bone in my neck at the Dutch TT and my sickness at Monza had been caused by the jolting it had received.' So sadly he finished the series in second place to 500cc World Champion Libero Liberati.

Bob McIntyre was born in Glasgow in 1928 and after an apprenticeship in scrambling made his road-racing début in an amateur race on a 350cc BSA Gold Star. The Isle of Man was the magnet for all budding champions in those days, and McIntyre raced there in the Manx in 1952. A magnificent second place in the Junior TT of 1955, riding a Norton, gained him increasing attention. His career is well known for his successful association with ace tuner, entrant and sponsor Joe Potts. For Potts he rode AJS and Norton and moved to Gilera only when it was certain that there was no possibility of his gaining a world title on British machinery. A master of his craft, McIntyre was at home on both short and long circuits, and his following among dedicated followers of motor-cycle racing was immense. He rode as a factory rider for only three seasons of his ten years career. In 1954 he was with AJS, then in 1957 with Gilera. In 1962 he rode for Honda. He was unfortunate in that, not long after he had secured a place in the Gilera team, the Italian factory withdrew from racing at the end of 1957.

In November that year McIntyre took a 350cc Gilera-4 to Monza. Gilera's intention, as a final gesture, was for McIntyre to capture the One Hour Record, which had stood to the credit of Ray Amm since he completed 133 miles within the specified time on a 500cc Norton at Montlhéry, the French high-speed track, in 1953. Except for the sidecar springing with which McIntyre equipped the machine, because of the bumpy Monza circuit, it was virtually the standard bike on which he had been competing earlier that year in Junior events. Only once before had he used a banked circuit, but he set off, not at all confident that the 350cc machine would be capable of raising the record. Once in top gear and with the throttle fully opened, he said he left it like that and he was soon hitting the banking at 155 mph. The circuit was so bumpy that at times he had to stand up on the footrests, holding on to the handlebars for dear life. Then, after about fifteen minutes, the bike stopped. McIntyre was not altogether upset. Controlling the bike at that speed on such a bumpy circuit was not particularly comfortable, and he expected Gilera to call off the attempt. Instead they told him not to go away. They then loaded the machine onto a lorry and took it off to the Gilera factory only about five miles away. They fitted the bike with a new magneto and were back within a couple of hours.

A new start on the record was made, and this time the machine kept going. It was an enormous strain, but after the hour he was flagged in with a new record at 141 mph. The machine stood the strain well, but McIntyre finished the ride with his wrists swollen, his feet sore and the instep of one of his boots broken by the jarring of the footrest beneath it. He was so exhausted that the mechanics almost had to lift him from the machine. Later he called it his 'rodeo ride'.

A forceful and determined rider and by nature an individualist, Bob McIntyre found it hard to get a competitive ride after Gilera departed the racing scene. In 1961 he signed to ride the new Italian Bianchi twin in the 350cc World Championship and completed a similar arrangement, but this time with Reg Armstrong, who was then the Irish concessionaire for Honda, to ride a Honda 250cc. In the 500cc class he arranged to ride a Joe Potts Norton and Potts' 350cc AJS at home meetings. In the 250cc Championship he finished second on the Honda to Hailwood in Holland but won in Ulster, while on the 350cc Bianchi he finished second to Gary Hocking on the MV in Holland, and third in East Germany. On the Norton he was second to Hailwood, also on a Norton, in the Senior TT. The following year on the Honda he did well, running second to Jim Redman in the opening round in Spain, second to Redman again in France and second once more to Redman in Holland, but turning the tables he won from Redman in Belgium. He finished second yet again in the West German Grand Prix, but 1962 was to end in tragedy. Bob McIntyre crashed a five-speed experimental Norton at Oulton Park in August and died later from his injuries.

It was a tragic loss to motor-cycle racing, for Bob McIntyre was one of the most popular and respected of sportsmen, admired for his courage as well as his skill. Few people who were fortunate enough to see him in action, to witness his sensible yet exciting approach to bike-racing, would disagree that, if ever a rider ought to have been a World Champion, it was Bob McIntyre. Given more chances of riding competitive machinery as a full-blown member of a factory team, it is almost certain he would have won at least one world title. But it was not to be.

Another brilliant rider who also never became World Champion was 'the Kentish Flyer', Derek Minter. Four years younger than McIntyre, Minter (born 1932) was at his peak in the early 1960s, riding from one success to another at British circuits such as Oulton Park, Mallory Park, Snetterton and Brands Hatch, where he was undisputed 'King'. A superb stylist, he was simply the most outstanding short-circuit road racer of all time. Minter's career began during his National Service in the early 1950s when he competed in Trials. His first road races were sponsored by local garages near to his home close to Canterbury in Kent. He began to attract notice riding 350cc and 500cc Nortons at popular home circuits, and in 1958, after turning full-time professional, he had his first outings to the Continent, gaining commendable third and fourth places respectively in the Dutch TT and Belgian GP against tough international opposition. By 1960 he was acknowledged as Britain's leading 'privateer' and, affectionately known as 'The Mint', he dominated Britain's short circuits.

When John Surtees left motor-cycle racing to concentrate on car-racing, the enthusiastic Brands Hatch crowd, who had adopted Surtees as their 'king', bestowed the honour on Minter, and for many years he was their undoubted favourite. When the Brands Hatch authorities, seeing the commercial value in the unexploited 'King of Brands' name-tag, decided in 1965 to put the title up for grabs officially in a King of Brands race, it was surely the most popular win at any race meeting anywhere when Minter beat factory riders Mike Hailwood, Bill Ivy and Phil Read to win the title, underlying his authority by winning, in addition, the day's 350cc and 500cc races.

Nineteen-sixty-two was probably Derek Minter's best year. His record was exceptional. To the delight of his legion of fans at Brands Hatch, he dominated one particular meeting so profoundly that in one afternoon he entered five races, won all five and established five new records. He became British Champion for the third time, won Mallory Park's famous 1,000 guineas race, then the richest in Britain, and was voted Man of the Year in the national poll run by *Motor Cycle News*. He also that same year won the 250cc TT on the Isle of Man on a year-old, non-works Honda against the combined might of the official Honda works team.

His two most remembered triumphs took place on the Isle of Man. The first was in 1960 when he became the first man to lap the Mountain circuit at 100 mph on a single-cylinder machine. The year had started well for him, and over the Easter weekend he entered nine races, won eight at record speeds, was placed second in the ninth and registered nine lap records. Incidentally, it was Bob McIntyre who ran him into second place at the Easter Oulton Park meeting.

On the Isle of Man that year McIntyre and Minter set off together as rivals in the Senior TT, both riding Nortons. Minter was content to follow McIntyre round at the start of the first lap but passed him at the 33rd milestone. Minter's speed for the opening lap was 99.51 mph, and he said later that had he known he was so near he could have taken the record then, for he was riding with power to spare. He led at the start of the second lap and, applying the pressure, raced magnificently to finish with a lap speed of 101.05 mph. He was forced to retire with a split oil tank on the third lap, when he was handily placed in the race behind John Surtees and John Hartle, both on MVs. Before Minter's record lap on the single-cylinder Norton, only three other riders had cracked the TT ton in five years: McIntyre, of course, with his epic lap, back in 1957 and, since then, Hartle and Surtees — all of them on Italian multi-cylinder machines.

Minter's performance on the single-cylinder Norton was remarkable, only to be eclipsed perhaps by his TT Honda ride two years later. He was provided with a 250cc Honda by Hondis Ltd, who were then the official importers of Honda bikes in the UK, but against the power of the official works team led by Jim Redman, few observers gave him a chance, for Minter's Honda was a year old. McIntyre shot into the lead from the start and was soon all of thirty seconds up; obviously he was going to take a lot of catching. He pushed the Honda hard to record a first lap time of 99.06 mph, but when he was forced out of the race soon after with mechanical problems, the battle hotted up. Jim Redman, racing as the 250cc World Championship leader, took over after McIntyre's departure, but by the third lap Minter, who was making the older Honda fly, had raced into an almost unbelievable eleven-second lead. When Minter stopped to refuel, Redman once again took over, and on lap 5 there was little to choose between the two riders. But even before Redman was forced to make an unscheduled stop because of fuel-cap problems, Minter had virtually taken over, and he stormed ahead to finish the sixth and final lap in buccaneering style, claiming a magnificent victory.

It may well have been Derek Minter's finest hour, but the Honda officials were not amused. Though Minter had won on a Honda machine, it did their cause little good, in terms of commercial sales to the public or in amassing points towards the important World Championship, to see their factory-prepared, bang-up-to-date bikes ridden by their highly paid works aces unseated by a private rider on a one-year-old model who was not even contesting the World Championship rounds. Nor did it ultimately work to Minter's advantage. When he talked to me about the incident some ten years after the event, he said: 'When I look back I think I might have been given a warning, but I didn't realize it at the time. Before the race, as we were lining up for the start, the Honda team manager came over to me. We were about to push off. I remember him saying: "Don't forget, Jim's leading the World Championship." I didn't think anything of it at the time. I was too keyed up ready for the race. But I suppose it could have been meant as a warning that I had to let Jim Redman win.' Honda did not forget and Derek was never able to get a contract out of them, though at times no one was more qualified. Even if he had realized the significance of the words, it is hardly likely that Derek would have taken notice. As I said at the time: 'He didn't back pedal for anyone and "the Mint" in full flight was very much his own master. He picked his own races, negotiated his own fees, fought his own battles, and said what he felt' — and, sadly, paid the price.

For all that, Derek Minter was an outstanding character and an immaculate rider. He was sheer poetry in motion, and there was no greater thrill than to see him make one of his traditionally bad starts and then begin relentlessly to take on all opposition, surging through the field, moving into the lead on the last bend or the final straight to score a magnificent victory. Nobody had greater success at Brands Hatch, and his outstanding rides on the Isle of Man are still remembered with excitement, but for Derek himself his best rides were on the Gilera. At Monza he unofficially cracked John Surtees' lap record by more than 1.5 mph, with a lap at 120.75 mph and the following day, in practice, recorded 121 mph. His lap record of 90.34 mph on the difficult Brands Hatch circuit in 1963 was not improved upon for another five years, though his Gilera was powered by a five-year-old engine. It took other top riders six and seven years to better many of his short-circuit records. The familiar Number 11, which Minter always insisted on, quickly identified him from the pack and in the second official King of Brands race in 1966 it was the Number 11 machine which most of the partisan Brands Hatch crowd wanted to see once more storming to the front, but sadly, defending his crown, Derek had to retire with mechanical problems and pint-sized Bill Ivy took the title.

'The Mint's' best days were over. His final race was appropriately at Brands Hatch in October 1967 when he celebrated with champagne wins in the 350cc and 1,000cc events and a second place in the 500cc final. Now in his early fifties, Minter runs a successful haulage business and still lives close to Canterbury, with his wife Jenny, whom he first met when she was his most dedicated fan, and their two daughters Leanne and Michelle.

When Geoffrey Duke decided in 1963 to try to bring some of the competitive edge back to the 500cc World Championship series by persuading Gilera to let him have their old 1957 racers to challenge the factory MV Agustas ridden by Agostini, he immediately chose Derek Minter to spearhead the attack. Minter's team-mate on the unsuccessful challenge was John Hartle, a more obviously aggressive rider than Minter but one who, like Minter, never achieved his ambition of becoming a World Champion. His big-time début was at the Oliver's Mount circuit at Scarborough, and it was there that he lost his life fourteen years later. One of the most determined of racers, Hartle had made a poor start, but was making up ground well and had set the fastest lap at 66.94 mph. After negotiating the Mere hairpin and accelerating up the steep climb, it seems that John Blanchard, just ahead, struggling to negotiate second gear, decelerated just as Hartle began to gain speed. The two riders collided and were flung from their machines. Blanchard was unhurt, but Hartle crashed into the footbridge scaffolding at Quarry Hill and died. Until then John Hartle had shown an astonishing capacity for survival. An earlier crash at Scarborough kept him out of racing for two years, and a later crash at Imola put him out of action once again for a further two years.

John Hartle, from Chapel-en-le-Frith, was an enthusiastic TT rider and first rode on the Isle of Man in 1955 on a Norton, finishing sixth in the Junior event and thirteenth in the Senior race. He joined the Norton factory team in 1956 for what was to be their final year of racing. On the Isle of Man he finished second to John Surtees on the MV in the Senior and was third in the Junior event. He scored his first classic victory at the Ulster Grand Prix that year and finished a commendable third place in the 500cc World Championship. With Norton no longer racing, Hartle was forced to compete on his own privately entered Norton in 1957; he made little impression, but his style and racing ability impressed John Surtees, who suggested he be given a ride on a 250cc MV. He responded magnificently by winning the Belgian Grand Prix at record speed. His reward was a contract with MV Agusta for the following season.

The racing withdrawals of Gilera, Guzzi and Mondial gave MV Agusta a clear field in 1958, and John Hartle, riding alongside John Surtees, responded well. In five of the seven rounds in the 350cc class he finished second to Surtees and notched two second places and one third in the 500cc series, finishing the season as runner-up to World Champion Surtees in both classes. On the Isle of Man that year he went into the record books, along with Surtees, by lapping the TT course at more than 100 mph. Hartle's speed was 100.08 mph, and at the end of that year he was in distinguished company indeed, for he, McIntyre and Surtees were still the only riders to have reached the historic 100 mph lap milestone on the Isle of Man.

Hartle remained with MV until the end of 1959, but it was not altogether a happy relationship. Surtees' role as premier rider for MV unfortunately overshadowed some impressive performances by Hartle, but in too many races he was impeded and frustrated by crashes or mechanical breakdown. Even so, he finished second to Surtees for so long he finally decided to break away, and in 1960, with few if any works rides available, he was back again on his own Nortons. That year he won the 500cc Ulster Grand Prix, pushing Surtees into second place, and in 1963, during the Gilera come-back, he finished second to Mike Hailwood in the Senior TT after lapping at an astonishing 105.56 mph, and was second to Jim Redman on the Honda in the Junior event. He won in Holland and was second in Northern Ireland before the ill-fated Gilera come-back ran out of steam. Nonetheless, from just a few grand prix races, he finished third in the 500cc World Championship.

Despite horrendous crashes, John Hartle never lost his enthusiasm for racing. Everyone liked and admired him. A dour racer, he once demonstrated his keen sense of humour on the Isle of Man, after he had crashed twice, when somebody said he had chosen to fall off in two very funny places. He retorted: 'For only £15 start money I wasn't going to do it in front of the grandstand.'

To look at the record books and see that John Hartle was never a World Champion is to do his outstanding talent gross injustice. As with McIntyre and Minter, had fate been a little kinder and circumstances a little different, John Hartle could have taken his place alongside Bob and Derek in a much changed riders' World Championships table. Despite their absence in the listings, all three were great motor-cycle riders and well worth their place in this book along with the more successful grand prix racers.

9. Yamaha's Dynamic Duo

In the mid-1960s motor-cycle racing was desperately in need of a stimulant, a re-awakening. MV Agusta's predictable if impressive domination of the 500cc class looked never-ending and had robbed what was traditionally the most important series of much of its appeal. In the sidecar class, Germany's Max Deubel's skill had combined with the reliability of the BMW outfit to bring him the title for the past four years. Suzuki had made 50cc racing their own since the tiddler class was started in 1962. Honda, with Jim Redman particularly dominant, were supreme in 250cc and 350cc racing. Only in the 125cc class was there any real competition, as Suzuki, with the New Zealander Hugh Anderson, tried to consolidate the inroads they were making against Honda.

The spark which was to put fire back into the championship was provided by Yamaha, who, first through Phil Read and later Bill Ivy, set their sights firmly on the 125cc and 250cc world titles. Their assault was mounted with such style and carried through with such flourish and energy that, for once, the focus of World Championship racing shifted from the 500cc class to the all-action 125cc and 250cc classes. Read and Ivy, themselves among the most charismatic characters both on and off the track, became racing's new 'golden greats' as Read sensationally won the 250cc crown from Jim Redman in 1964, and in 1967 Ivy brought Yamaha their first-ever 125cc World Championship. But all this paled against the startling events of 1968 when, with Yamaha dominating both classes and to a background of torrid racing, the once firm friendship between Read and Ivy was shattered and ended in a feud which left the racing world shocked and divided.

Phil Read, born in Luton in 1939, had been in motor-cycle racing since 1956, when at only seventeen he raced at Mallory Park. He had been taken as a small boy to Silverstone by his father and was so impressed that by the time he was thirteen he owned a 250cc side-valve Matchless. His first race was on a 350cc BSA Gold Star which made way for a 350cc Norton, on which he won his first race. He went to the TTs for the first time in 1961, retiring in both Senior and Lightweight 125cc events, but on a Bill Lacey Norton he won the Junior race at an average 95.10 mph, beating Gary Hocking on the powerful MV. That same year he first experienced grand prix racing on the Continent. Always a colourful character, with a one-track determination to get what he wanted, Phil's move into the big-time came when Derek Minter crashed when riding for Geoffrey Duke's Gilera come-back team, alongside John Hartle. Phil was brought in for the injured Minter and had his first experience of riding a multi-cylinder machine. It was not a happy link. The Gilera took a lot of getting used to, and Read had bad moments in his début ride in the 350cc West German Grand Prix and took a nasty fall in the Ulster Grand Prix. Second places in Holland and Belgium meant he finished the season in fourth place in the World Championship, behind Hailwood, Alan Shepherd and Hartle. At home, success at Scarborough on the Gilera was a considerable boost, for Read shortly afterwards received a telegram from Yamaha inviting him to ride their 250cc twin in the Japanese Grand Prix at the end of 1963.

Yamaha, who began life making reed organs in 1887 and then pianos two years later, had since diversified into aircraft propeller production. Now they were following Honda's example and moving into motor-cycles strongly. In just five years, when the British industry had just about wound itself down, Yamaha motor-cycle production had surged from 27,000 in 1958 to 167,000 in 1963, and they now sought racing success to further their commercial sales. It was an incredible break for Phil Read. In the early stages of the race in Japan he was in front of Redman on the Honda, but he could not hold the lead, finishing in third position behind Redman and Ito on the Yamaha. The factory bosses obviously liked Read's style, and he became the first European to sign a racing contract with them.

The battle lines were drawn in 1964 as Yamaha made their first full-scale assault on the 250cc world title. Jim Redman, it should be remembered, had won the title in 1962 and 1963 and was determined to make it three in a row. However, in typically forthright style, he missed the opening round at Daytona in the United States because of an argument he had with organizers over expenses. Read's curtain-raiser though was a bitter disappointment. He failed to take advantage of Redman's absence, plug problems on the Yamaha keeping him out of the running. In Spain, in the second round, Tarquinio Provini on the Benelli was untouchable and won, with Redman second and Read third. By now Read was becoming more used to riding the Yamaha, and his confidence was boosted while preparing for the third round in France by being fastest in practice. It was a searing race, Read and Redman battling it out almost shoulder to shoulder. First Read would take the lead, then Redman, after clinging like a limpet, would surge ahead. This was racing at its best, and as they both left the remainder of the field well behind, they each clipped Gary Hocking's old record. At the halfway stage it seemed that Redman would do it. He was in the lead again and, perhaps, pulling away, but then the Honda went onto two cylinders, and Read was able to surge ahead to win, with Redman out of the points.

Redman turned the tables on the Isle of Man, with Read right out of the running, and he won again in Holland, with Read second. But there was no more than a wheel in it. Redman collected a second place in Belgium, with Read not in the listings, and at this point it would have been hard to find anyone willing to put a lot of money on Phil Read becoming World Champion. But the Luton lad was determined. A big bonus would be his reward for lifting the championship, and he was determined to win it. The tide turned in the West German Grand Prix. Read raced cleverly, following Redman for the first ten laps, but on the final lap, knowing he had the more powerful bike, he raced out of Redman's slipstream on the back straight and sped for the line, winning with new lap and race records of 99.37 mph and 97 mph.

In the following East German Grand Prix Read found himself battling with Mike Hailwood, the latter riding the local factory's MZ machine. The local vast crowd were in a frenzy of excitement as Hailwood went ahead of Read, setting a new lap record of 102.06 mph. Meantime, Redman was ahead of both of them, and it began to look grim for Read. Then Mike crashed in the centre of Hohenstein-Ernstthal, a town which was included in the Sachsenring circuit, and was out of the race. Miraculously, Read missed the falling Hailwood and recovered to chase and overtake Redman to gain a remarkable victory.

The Ulster Grand Prix was held in blinding rain, but Read and Redman renewed the battle at a critical stage in the championship. Phil had now won three rounds to Jim's two. In a close race Phil in the end won by a minute, and now he only needed to win the next round at Monza in Italy to make the title certain.

Quietly, however, Honda had been concerned at the progress being made by Read on the Yamaha and had secretly been working round the clock on a new 250 six-cylinder model. Read said when he was told about it he wouldn't believe it, but he went along to see and there it was, though disguised as a 350. It was too late for any counter-measures, and it would have been difficult to know what Yamaha might have done in response, so Phil took the only course open to him. He decided to go all out from the start, then pull into Jim's slipstream and make a break for it at the right moment. But, as recorded elsewhere, Jim's choice of the new six-cylinder machine instead of the earlier model worked against him. After setting a searing pace from the off, leaving Phil as he later put it, 'like a jet aircraft', the new Honda began to slow. Read caught him at about half distance and raced on to win at a record race speed of 113.91 mph. The title had been won and lost, for although there was the last round still to be raced, in Japan, Redman needed to win in Italy and Japan to retain the title. Phil Read became World Champion in his first full season with Yamaha, beating Jim Redman on the Honda by just four points.

Phil Read took the title again the following year, with his Yamaha team-mate Mike Duff in second place and Redman down to third. But in 1966 and 1967 Mike Hailwood, who in the meantime had been signed by Honda to capture the 500cc Championship and to consolidate their effort in 250cc and 350cc racing, re-established the Honda superiority, Read finishing runner-up in both years. Meantime, Yamaha had also set their sights on the 125cc crown. They had looked tentatively at the title as early as 1963, and in 1964 Read had an outing on the Yamaha 125 when he finished second to Redman in Holland. It was the following year that Bill Ivy had his first championship rides for Yamaha.

Born in Kent in 1942, Ivy started racing as a grass-track rider in 1958, when he was sponsored by Frank Sheene (father of Barry) as well as by Geoff Monty and Tom Kirby. He was only 5 feet 3 inches tall, but he was soon displaying an amazing capacity for handling bigger bikes. He did well on try-out rides in the 1965 TTs, and this led to a full-blown works contract for 1966. He had already made his mark on the British short circuits, taking the British Championship in 1965. With wins in the opening round of the 125cc World Championship in Spain, on the Isle of Man and in Holland and Japan (a result which particularly delighted Yamaha, who enjoyed being seen to do well in front of a home crowd), he finished the season second to Luigi Taveri on the Honda. In a remarkable display of riding, he consolidated his position in the Yamaha team in 1967, bringing them the 125cc world title with stirring wins in Spain, France, East Germany, Czechoslovakia, Northern Ireland, Italy, Canada and Japan. His astonishing will to win had beaten off formidable challenges, not only from top Suzuki riders such as Graham, Anscheidt and Katayama but from his team-mate Phil Read on the Yamaha. Read was runner-up in the class, but sixteen points behind. Ivy had also made considerable impact on the 250cc Yamaha. Wins in France and Belgium and second places at no fewer than five other grands prix had taken him into third place in the World Championship, behind Mike Hailwood, who took the title for Honda, and Phil Read, but Ivy was only four points adrift at the end of the season.

Read's performance, incidentally, was extraordinary. Riding the 250cc four-cylinder racer which had taken over from the twin-cylinder Yamahas which he and Mike Duff had raced earlier, he provided a formidable challenge to the six-cylinder Honda of Mike Hailwood. Both Phil and Mike ended the season with 50 points but, with five wins to Read's four, Hailwood took the title by the slimmest of margins. The 125cc and 250cc classes were now bristling with excitement and drama, with Phil Read, Bill Ivy and Mike Hailwood all competing with one another on the 250s.

When both Honda and Suzuki pulled out of the classics, 1968 had all the signs of being a very tame affair, but Yamaha continued racing and, with Read and Ivy still holding factory contracts, it turned into racing's most sensational year. The public has the greatest difficulty accepting that at times works riders have to conform to team orders, and although it was not then generally known, Yamaha's plan, with no racing opposition to speak of, was for Bill Ivy to take the 250cc World Championship and Phil Read to take the 125cc title. But, to appreciate subsequent events, it should be realized that the one immediate ambition of Read was to regain the 250cc crown which Hailwood had taken from him the year before.

Racing to team orders or not, Phil Read and Bill Ivy produced some of the most spectacular racing ever witnessed. Both strong-willed, both enormously talented racers, their efforts were affected by machine breakdowns, complicating Yamaha's pre-season race pattern. At the opening round in West Germany, however, the results sorted themselves out. After establishing a new lap record in the 125cc race, Ivy's Yamaha suffered a broken crankshaft and he was out of the race, leaving Read to win from Anscheidt on the Suzuki. In brilliant form, Ivy set new lap and race records in the 250cc event and charged ahead to win from Ginger Molloy on the Bultaco, while Read's challenge evaporated when he had trouble with the radiator on the Yamaha. In Spain, once more, events ruled. Bill retired in both races, and Phil also retired with engine problems on the 125cc machine. He was left to uphold Yamaha's interest in the 250cc race, which he did convincingly, also riding the fastest lap.

By this time the motor-cycle press had been openly speculating about Yamaha's racing plans, but so far no one could complain about the quality of the racing. It was every bit as nail-biting as the Hailwood-Agostini duels for Honda and MV, or the Hailwood-Hocking encounters earlier. And the pace of the racing and the excitement was well maintained.

On the Isle of Man, in the next round, both riders were in storming form. At a race average of 99.12 mph, Read won his third 125cc event in four years, with Bill Ivy finishing second. Bill also, sensationally, established the fastest lap at 100.32 mph to become the first rider in TT history to race a 125cc machine round the tough Mountain Course at 100 mph. It was an incredible performance from Ivy, and the outstanding feature of both Read's and Ivy's racing during 1968 was that, with little serious opposition, they did not have to produce such superlative riding to win their races. It was to their enormous credit that they did. Ivy was no less sensational in the 250cc race. His record lap of 105.51 mph from a standing start was a remarkable achievement, and he won despite some machine problems and a damaged foot.

The 'battle' continued in Holland and Belgium. In Holland,

according to plan, Read won the 125cc race and Ivy the 250, but the competitive edge between the two riders appeared to be getting keener as the season progressed. Their racing was fast and furious, and the sporting rivalry seemed hardly compatible with simply putting on a show for the grand prix crowds. There was no 125cc event in Belgium, so both Read and Ivy lined up for the 250cc race. Phil admitted later that he was determined to win the race, despite Yamaha's instructions, but fate played into his hands. After Bill charged to the front, Phil was plagued with a first-lap plug change, which cost him valuable time, but as he howled off in pursuit it was Ivy's turn to run into trouble — and his mechanical problems were more serious, putting him out of the race. Read was left to uphold Yamaha's prestige, and he scorched after race leaders Rosner and Gould, thundering into the lead just before the finish. This left Read only four points behind Ivy in the 250cc Championship and, of course, as planned, he was well ahead in the 125cc series. In the next round, in East Germany, Phil won the 125cc race, with Bill in second place, and in the 250cc event Bill won, with Phil in second place.

Now came the turning-point. Phil said later that he and Bill knew that the next round, in Czechoslovakia, was to be the last to be financed by Yamaha. They would withdraw from the World Championships there, leaving Phil and Bill to race out the remainder of the season on their own, financing their own entries but sticking to the Yamaha plan. Phil found the temptation too great. If he won the 250cc race in Czechoslovakia, Bill would still be two points ahead, assuming he came second, and Read considered that still left Ivy a fair challenge, for there were races in Finland, Northern Ireland and Italy to come.

It was raining hard at the start of the 125cc race. In difficult conditions Bill took a tumble and was out of the running. Phil went on to win. Bill, though suffering somewhat from the effects of the fall, was able to line up for the crucial 250cc race. Phil had virtually made certain of the 125cc Championship, and the 250cc world title was now dangling tantalizingly before him. They were side by side on the starting grid, and according to Phil, he looked across at Bill and said: 'Bill — you know you're going to have to race for this one.' Phil said that Bill understood the position. Then the race was on, and on drying roads Read hit the front, with Ivy racing hard behind. With Ivy gaining on Read, Phil decided that he must go all out to win. He did, and Ivy finished second. Bill was furious and afterwards stormed at Read. The two friends were friends no more.

The bitter feud lasted until the end of the season, and others became involved. The Yamaha officials back in Japan threatened to take Phil's works machines from him after he had sent telegrams stating his intention of racing to win in the remaining rounds in the hope of lifting the 250cc title. He said he would only relent if they gave him an assurance that he would be given the opportunity on works Yamahas to win back the title in 1969. But with a double World Championship virtually assured as a swansong, they were not prepared to give that assurance, and, to complete the scenario, they did not return to racing in 1969.

Meantime the Read-Ivy feud was the talking-point of motorcycle racing, as the FIM became involved, threatening Read with disciplinary action to make sure that he, and indeed Ivy for that matter, did not deliberately forfeit a race. Phil became branded a rebel, while Bill attracted much public sympathy. His many fans, while perhaps not agreeing with the principle of riding to team instructions, felt that he had been outwitted by Read, whether or not that was so. From then to the end of the season, Phil Read and Bill Ivy operated as separate units, with their own mechanics working on their own machines. With both factions sharing the same garage facilities, the atmosphere was tense. As the so-called innocent party, Ivy had at least a clear mandate for the remainder of the season to win, as and when he could. Read faced a dilemma. Yamaha were insisting that he continue to ride to the original plan, while he was being told by the FIM that he must not intentionally forfeit a race. The remaining rounds were highly charged with tension and expectancy. The crowds turned out in their thousands to see the now open rivalry between the two star riders.

The opening exchanges went to Phil Read. In the 125cc race in Finland he sped into the lead with Ivy close behind. Bill continued in Phil's slipstream, but then had to ride into the pits with brake problems. Though he rejoined the race, he could not make up the lost time and finished second to Phil's first place. A sudden shower before the 250cc event made the track difficult, but both Read and Ivy put caution behind them. Ivy was powering his way through and led convincingly until Read slipped ahead, outbraking Ivy on a bend. Bill thundered after Phil and finally overdid it, being flung over the handlebars to be taken away on a stretcher, though he was not badly injured.

Two races now remained, and Ivy had to win both to make the 250cc title his. The tension was unrelenting. Responding magnificently to the situation, Bill Ivy scored a resounding triumph in Northern Ireland. In the 125cc race Bill's own lap record was shattered by both riders many times, and in the end Ivy surged ahead to win by almost three seconds at a race average which was quicker than his previous lap record. Now came the big one, the 250cc race. Before an enormous crowd, and in wet conditions, Read took the lead, going like a bullet from the line, but Ivy was right there behind him. Bill clung to Phil as closely as if they were joined together, but as the track began to dry out, Ivy shot ahead in a breathtaking surge, to reverse the order. He was still in front when Read, with an engine badly overheating, had to retire. This was pint-sized Billy at his best, his greatest. He was now two points in the lead, with the final round in Italy to decide the championship. Phil led for most of the way in the 125cc event at the Monza circuit, but Bill managed to go ahead just two laps from home and held on to win, for Read, in a brave effort to keep in touch, came off. Even so, he remounted and finished second. In the deciding 250cc race, Phil Read moved into the lead, with Bill Ivy immediately behind him, and the race developed into one of high drama. Trying to overtake on a bend, Ivy slid into a broadside and only just recovered control. Then Phil's Yamaha developed problems, but it kept going. Bill's machine also went sick, and he finally had trouble making second place, but Read had won the race and the title.

But had he? Both riders had 52 points. Both riders had won five races. Both riders had two second places, so times in the four races where they were both placed decided the championship. Phil Read won by just 2 minutes 5.3 seconds.

There had never been a season like it for high drama, controversy and glorious racing. It was hard not to feel a sense of injustice for Bill, for, as Phil took both 125cc and 250cc World Championships, he was left with nothing. In the former he was just six points adrift at the end of the season.

Phil Read went on for a number of seasons and gained two more World Championships, in 1973 and 1974, maintaining his abrasive image in arguments with Giacomo Agostini after Phil had been recruited by MV to contest the 350cc and 500cc series.

Bill Ivy, disillusioned and desperately disappointed, announced his retirement from racing, but a contract to ride Jawa machinery for 1969 tempted him back to the grand prix circuit. His old magic was there as he fought a tremendous battle with Agostini in the 350cc Dutch TT. But tragically, while practising for the East German Grand Prix less than a month later, he crashed and was killed, on 12 July 1969. A product of the Swinging Sixties, Bill typified his age of free living, free thinking. He was one of motor-cycling's early jet-setters, and he lived life to the full — his long hair, rip-roaring, fun-loving lifestyle, and passion for fast cars girls, smart clothes and good food fitting in well with his trendy image. Yet he was devoted to his family.

One disappointing outcome to the sensations of the 1968 Yamaha season is that, as time goes on, it tends to be the squabbles and clashes which are remembered more than the ability of the two riders who gave motor-cycling some of its most outstanding moments.

10. Bike Racers With a Difference

Not all the great motor-cycle riders found their fame on the grand prix circuit. Some preferred to ride in long-distance races, measuring their skills and physical and psychological strengths against extreme standards of endurance, courage and personal determination. Others found it more challenging to race against the clock, setting new records in a lonely quest which, if successful, would stamp them forever at that particular time as the fastest man in the world on two wheels. Even on the road-race circuits, not all riders chose to ride solo. There were a number who opted for sidecar-racing and became famous for it.

The history of all three categories highlights outstanding talent, but favourites are often based on subjective judgements and are perhaps no less authentic because of it. For what possible yardstick can be applied to compare the qualities of Eric Oliver, for example, the Sidecar Champion in the immediate years after the Second World War, with Rolf Biland, Switzerland's four-times Sidecar World Champion in the 1970s and 1980s? Or world motor-cycle speed record-holders Jake de Rosier (1911), Eric Fernihough (1937) and Don Vesco, top speed man of the 1970s.

In endurance racing my choice is taken from the mid-1970s when the classic Bol d'Or twenty-four-hour marathon was probably at its peak and when Kawasaki, sometimes underrated in terms of its contribution to international motor-cycling, won the prestigious long-distance road race for the first time. The year was 1974. Honda had dominated the long-distance scene, but for 1974 the successful marathon partnership of Georges Godier, a Frenchman living in Switzerland, and Alain Genoud, a barman with a profound interest in motor-cycles, decided to switch from Honda to Kawasaki. The common link was a special frame designed by Fritz Egli, a former Swiss national hill-climb champion with a formidable reputation as a skilful·designer of racing frames. In 1974 Godier and Genoud stayed faithful to the Egli frame but preferred the Kawasaki power unit to the Honda one, and at the famous Bol d'Or that year they scored a significant win before a massive crowd of more than 100,000. For Kawasaki, it was a day to remember, and particularly for the Japanese factory's French importer, who saw his Kawasaki machines take three of the top four places.

At the start Genoud trailed the BMW of Hubert Rigal and Jacques Luc by more than a hundred yards, but after about an hour the Yoshimura Kawasaki ridden by Yvon Duhamel was leading, with Genoud now some twelve seconds behind. Two more hours into the race and Honda had taken the lead, but Godier and Genoud were only two seconds behind. As night came, so did torrential rain, adding to the problems of all riders as oil from a damaged machine settled on the track. The Yoshimura Kawasaki of Christian Leon suffered particularly badly — even to the extent of catching fire in the pits! — and eventually retired with a dropped valve. Godier and Genoud also had their problems, being forced into the pits three times for machine attention. At one point they were all of seven laps behind the leaders. But, as daylight came to mark the second day of racing, the Godier/Genoud Kawasaki was making good progress, running well and lapping six seconds faster than its nearest rivals. With just two hours to go, they were nicely placed in second position and set for a final speed battle with the Rigal/Luc BMW, but when the latter suffered machine problems and was forced into the pits, the Kawasaki was ridden comfortably to victory in glorious sunshine.

Sidecar-racing not only provides variety at a race meeting but produces a kind of racing magic all its own. In forty years outfits have changed out of all recognition. When Eric Oliver won that first World Championship for Britain in 1949, the combination was made up of two separate units, a bike and a sidecar, easily identifiable as such and simply joined together. In the 1980s the winning outfits are gleaming, all-enclosed, scientifically designed, and they look more like inter-planetary modules from a space-age movie than a racing motor-cycle combination.

Eric Oliver rode solo bikes before concentrating on sidecar events after the Second World War. A tough, cheerful individual, he paid enormous attention to detail when racing, studying the opposition, practising his starts and racing techniques and giving minute attention to the preparation of his highly successful Norton-Watsonian combination. He was a colourful character and a fearless competitor. He first entered the TT Races in 1937, but that year in the Senior event, and in 1938 in both the Senior and Junior, he retired. His best solo performance on the Isle of Man was in 1948 when, on a Velocette, he finished eighth in the Junior race.

A devout sidecar traveller by the time the new World Championship series was inaugurated in 1949, Oliver and passenger Denis Jenkinson, with wins in Belgium and Switzerland, won the first ever Sidecar World Championship. In 1950 and this time with Italy's Lorenzo Dobelli as passenger, Oliver kept a Gilera challenge at bay, winning all three sidecar championship races to become World Champion for the second time in two years in a devastating season. All three wins were at record speeds, and during the season he swept the opposition aside to win sixteen times in top races. Again with Dobelli, Oliver took the title for the third time running in 1951 and might have done it yet again the following year but a fall while racing in France, and machine problems, put him out of the running. Britain's other sidecar specialist at that time, Cyril Smith, provided Oliver's major competition in 1953. This time partnered by Stanley Dibben, Oliver won in Belgium, France, Switzerland and Italy to take the world title for the fourth time by six points from Cyril Smith.

A sidecar TT was reintroduced into the Isle of Man racing festival in 1954, and although Oliver beat the new challenge from BMW in the form of Hillebrand and Grunwald from Germany, and in spite of winning also in Northern Ireland and Belgium, the German team of Noll and Cron took the World Championship that year, with Oliver trailing just four points behind. Eric Oliver, Britain's first international sidecar champion and to this day perhaps the best exponent of this specialized form of racing in the UK, retired from active sport in 1955 and died in 1981.

There have been other impressive sidecar world champions, but the most successful in recent years, and certainly the most controversial, has been Switzerland's Rolf Biland. His Yamaha-powered Beo outfit created a storm when it emerged in 1978 because it contravened some of the established principles of sidecar racing and was felt by some to be outside the accepted spirit of the sport. Yet it was within the rules set by the FIM, and that was the problem. Biland's revolutionary design was impressive to look at, costly to build and extremely innovative. It had twin-driven wheels with the engine mounted between them, and although the outfit offered a number of advantages over more conventional sidecars, it was not the easiest thing to drive. Although some of Biland's main contenders for the title objected to it, no one suggested that Biland was not perhaps the world's best sidecar driver when he took the title for the first time in 1978. The FIM, in a dilemma over Rolf's creation, reacted sharply by banning the outfit 'on the grounds of safety', but within weeks the ban was lifted, the FIM at an extraordinary general meeting having decided to run two Sidecar World Championships in 1979, one for traditional outfits and the other for those exotic designs which incorporated such innovations as sidecar wheel steering and hub centre steering. Rolf Biland won the class title again that year, after which the idea of two classes was abandoned. Biland took the title again in 1981 and once more in 1983.

In sidecar World Championship racing, however, Germany's Klaus Enders has been the most successful. Born in 1937, this West German's brilliance took him to a world title for the first time in 1967, after former champion Fritz Scheidegger had been killed while racing at Mallory Park and Max Deubel had retired. He and passenger Ralf Englehardt won five of the eight events. He won the title again in 1969, 1970, 1972, 1973 and 1974, in 1970 with Wolfgang Kallaugh.

Racing against the clock and not other riders is what sprinting is all about. British national records are set over a number of distances and in a number of machine cubic-capacity classifications. Hobbs, Lecoq, Heckle, Sullivan, Hyde, MacPhail and Windross are names familiar to all sprinting enthusiasts, but from earlier times Fred Cooper, Alf Hagon and George Brown, the father-figure of British sprinting, are the most remembered.

Brown, who died in 1979, was a racer of outstanding courage and determination and on his fabled Vincent-powered machines, Nero and Super Nero, was for a time virtually invincible. Developing a passion for motor-bikes while still at school, he progressed to trials riding and grass-track racing. His early ambition to become a solicitor was abandoned after a meeting with the legendary Philip

Vincent, following which George took a job at Vincent's small factory. An outgoing character, George Brown was soon doing a lot of high-speed testing, for the factory and for his own excitement, and after trying for a long time to persuade Philip Vincent to let him do some all-out racing on the Vincent machinery, he finally got his way. At Brooklands he clocked 113 mph and also entered quite a number of road-race meetings, but Vincent felt he was too useful a member of his technical staff to take the risks of racing regularly. His road-racing career was effectively ended on the Isle of Man in 1953 when, racing down Bray Hill, he crashed into the wreckage of the MV on which Les Graham lost his life. He later suffered serious facial injuries in crashes at Cadwell Park and Eppynt, from which he was lucky to survive. He then began to concentrate on hill climbs, sprints and other speed events.

After leaving Vincents, where his brother Cliff had also worked, the Brown brothers, along with close aides, worked on Nero and Super Nero. George, by then proprietor of a motor-cycle shop in Stevenage, Hertfordshire, concentrated on sprinting with remarkable results. On Nero, Brown captured his first world record in 1960, when the machine was timed at 187 mph. Although he held countless records, some of them for years, his ultimate ambition was to be denied him. He wanted to become the fastest man in the world on two wheels, and he wanted it as much for Britain as for himself.

One man who did achieve that ultimate ambition was Eric Fernihough, the last British rider to hold the title, who also died in an attempt to regain the record for Britain. Fernihough's days were the bustling, barnstorming 1930s, leading up to the outbreak of the Second World War. Through such racers as Freddie Dixon, Bert Le Vack, Claude Temple, Oliver Baldwin and Joe Wright, Britain had held the outright world speed record for most of the 1920s, indeed almost going back to the days of Collier and George from 1909, but in 1930 there was a tremendous battle between Ernst Henne of Germany on a BMW machine and Joe Wright of Great Britain on his OEC-Temple. Henne had held the record in 1929 but Wright snatched it away in 1930 with a speed of 137.32 mph, against Henne's previous record of 134.68 mph. Henne responded with 137.66 mph, but then Joe Wright looked to have settled the issue, and indeed he had for two years, with a commanding speed of 150.70 mph. Henne, a determined and formidable competitor, showed he was not finished when, in 1932, he pushed the record to 151.86 mph. It was Henne in 1934, Henne again in 1935 and Henne once more in 1936 with speeds of 152.90 mph, 159.01 mph and 169.00 mph.

Onto the scene now steps Eric Fernihough with his Brough Superior JAP. In 1937 he went to Gyon in Hungary and rode his powerful machine to a new record of 169.78 mph. Taken by the way Henne had used streamlining on the record-breaking BMW, Fernihough had also virtually enclosed the Brough Superior, but once in Hungary he decided to run the machine almost totally naked, dispensing with the fairing. Within six months his magnificent record had gone, this time captured by Italy's Piero Taruffi on a Gilera, who clocked 170.5 mph. This latest record was itself beaten very quickly by Henne once more with 173.67 mph. And that was the target when in 1938 Eric Fernihough set off again for Gyon.

'Ferni' was a slim man who wore spectacles, not the sort you would identify as a speed record-breaker, but he had in 1935 been a sensation at Brooklands when, in his first season on a supercharged Brough twin, he smashed the outer-circuit lap record with an outstanding 123.58 mph. As a machine-tuner and development engineer he was exceptional and, for all his physical appearance, he had tremendous skill on a speed machine and enormous personal courage. Unable to attract much support from the motor-cycle industry in Britain, Fernihough was compelled to make his bids without specialist help and with limited facilities, putting him at a gross disadvantage against foreign competitors. But at Gyon the Brough Superior was going well. Then, at an estimated 180 mph, the machine veered off course. Somehow 'Ferni' stayed on for some 200 yards, but the Brough struck an intersecting track, and in the crash the gallant record-breaker was killed.

In contrast to Fernihough's unsponsored attempts more than forty years before, America's Don Vesco's record-breaking runs on Yamaha and Kawasaki machinery in the 1970s were so advanced as to bear little resemblance. Now the venue was the vast Bonneville Salt Flats in Utah and the amounts of money invested in the projects were prodigious. A fully enclosed projectile, very long and very low, had replaced the traditional-looking motor-bike in these now highly sophisticated days of record-breaking, and Vesco's race special was fitted with two 1,000cc four-cylinder Kawasaki engines and had turbo-charging. From the mid-1970s to 1978 Don Vesco pushed the ultimate speed record for a motor-cycle from 281.71 mph to 318.6 mph, a magnificent achievement. Even so, the days of Eric Fernihough seemed to have something special about them, certainly for British enthusiasts.

11. Racing Legends

Racing legends can materialize in an instant. It does not need years of riding and a whole series of wins for a name to live on. One incident is sometimes all it takes. Or a few races won in spectacular style. Much depends on timing, atmosphere, incident, the emotion and circumstances of the moment. Jarno Saarinen proved that motor-cycle racing can produce an instant hero. His impact was enormous. He arrived when world-class racing, with Hailwood's and Agostini's best years over, was looking for a new hero. And he fitted the bill perfectly. He was good-looking, young, brave, dashing and sheer dynamite as a racer. His meteoric rise to stardom brought him a World Championship in only his second year of grand prix racing.

Saarinen, born in the Finnish port of Turku in 1945, turned to motor-cycle road racing after an impressive career on dirt and ice in his native land and winning the Finnish ice-race championship in 1965. Two years later, thirsting for his next challenge, he was riding a 125cc Puch, moderately sedate by his standards, turning to his own Yamaha in 1968. As a privateer he contested the grand prix circuit for the first time in 1971, riding his own Yamahas in the 250cc and 350cc classes. Victory in Spain in the former and in Czechoslovakia in the latter, plus some sizzling placings on both bikes behind formidable opposition (which included Phil Read, Paul Smart, Rodney Gould and Tepi Lansivuori, (also from Finland) took him to second place in the championship tables in both categories, an outstanding exhibition of riding. Yamaha's Finnish importer provided Saarinen with rides in 1972, and on a new water-cooled version of the former air-cooled racers he performed brilliantly. Four impressive wins in the latter half of the programme brought him the 250cc World Championship at his first serious attempt. In the 350cc series he started the season in devastating form, winning the first and second rounds at the Nurburgring and Clermont-Ferrand in direct competition with Agostini. The Italian, on the MV, had made this class all his own for the previous four years, and so worried were MV by Saarinen's performance on the new Yamaha that they quickly introduced a new four-cylinder 350 and switched Phil Read from the 500cc class to support Agostini in a joint counter to the menace of the Finn.

Saarinen was the first rider for five years to beat the Italian in championship racing. A little more luck and he might well have taken away Agostini's 350cc title. The Swedish Grand Prix at Anderstorp was the crucial round. Saarinen maintained the pressure on Agostini, and it seemed that either could win, but then gearbox trouble on the Yamaha allowed the MV to move ahead, and Jarno was later overtaken by Phil Read to finish third. Although Agostini took the title for the fifth time in as many years, Saarinen actually won three rounds.

For Yamaha, Jarno Saarinen had come along at precisely the right time. They were expanding their range of road-going bikes into the bigger capacities, and road-racing success in the 500cc class would give them the boost they needed. More than anything, a strong challenge to Agostini and MV would show the public they could make successful 500s, as well as successful smaller machines. When pre-season rumours were confirmed, fans were more excited than they had been for years. Yamaha would step up their effort. Their intention was to continue to compete in the 250cc class. In the 350cc division they would give support to the other Finnish road racer, Tepi Lansivuori, but the real excitement was centred around the startling news that, with a newly developed water-cooled, four-cylinder two-stroke, they would make a serious attempt to break Agostini's stranglehold on the 500cc class. Saarinen was signed to a full-scale works contract, and he and the Japanese rider Hideo Kanaya, would lead the assault.

MV had already seen enough of Saarinen to take the challenge seriously. They had won the 500cc World Championship for the past fifteen years and had no intention of surrendering their title to Yamaha. Count Agusta signed Phil Read to ride alongside Agostini and rushed along a new and potentially faster four-cylinder, developed from the well-proved MV-3s. Major pre-championship races created a sensation. At the prestigious Daytona meeting in America, Saarinen became the first European rider to win the major 200 race, and in the Imola 200 he moved into the lead on the second lap and was uncatchable for the remaining thirty-one laps of the first leg and for the entire second leg.

In the opening round of the 1973 World Championship at the new Paul Ricard circuit in France, Saarinen's riding was devastating. Fastest in practice, the Finn took the new 500cc Yamaha to an outstanding victory, dominating the race and winning by sixteen seconds from Read on the MV, with Kanaya in third position. Agostini, who had decided to race the well-tried older MV rather than the new and as yet untried four-cylinder machine, was in contention at the start, but as Saarinen began to pull away he overdid things, trying desperately to keep up, and came off. With Saarinen and Kanaya finishing one and two in the 250cc series, the results in France were an enormous psychological boost for Yamaha. The second grand prix in Austria was even more of a humiliation for the, until then, all-conquering Agostini/MV combination. Before Saarinen's win in France, Agostini and MV had won forty-nine of the last fifty-seven races in the 500cc World Championship, but in the second round in 1973 Saarinen refused to be intimidated by the reputation of the Italian, or his famous factory machine. The Finn was fastest in practice, with Kanaya second and Agostini down in third position. Even so, Agostini elected once again to ride the MV-3, but the Italian champion never looked like getting in touch with the leaders.

After only a few laps he was 25 seconds adrift and more than nine seconds behind Kanaya, in second place behind an inspired Saarinen. It was left to Phil Read to provide the MV challenge. He raced away into the lead from the start and held grimly to it for two laps, before Saarinen moved to the front. Read was not beaten. He kept in touch and, on a damp Salzburgring made treacherous by persistent drizzle, made a monumental effort. Speeding through the 150 mph section, Read is said to have got so close to Saarinen that their machines came into contact, and in a situation of high drama at the end of the race Read condemned Saarinen for cutting into him to force him from taking the best line into the corner, while Saarinen complained that, if he had not braked hard Read would have forced him off the track and into the straw bales.

It was a rare battle, but the game was up when Read's MV began to suffer machine problems, and in the end he had to retire. Kanaya finished second, to complete a welcome Yamaha double. But that was not all: in the 250cc class at the Salzburgring, Yamaha machines finished in the first six places, with Saarinen and Kanaya first and second.

At this point in the championship Saarinen and Kanaya were leading the 500cc table, and the highest-placed MV rider was Phil Read, way down in fifth position. It was almost too long ago for anyone to remember when such a phenomenon had taken place in 500cc Championship racing. MV had earlier responded to the Yamaha threat and had been working on a full 500cc version of the 432cc four-cylinder racer which they had introduced at the start of the season. It was ready for the next round in West Germany. But that was not the only sensation. When in the 350cc race both MVs broke down with valve problems, there rapidly developed strong rumours that Count Agusta was on the verge of pulling his team out of the championships altogether. In the 250cc class at West Germany's Hockenheim track there was nothing to stop Saarinen and Kanaya, who again finished first and second. Then Count Agusta dropped his bombshell. He gave Read the new 500cc to race instead of his golden boy, Agostini. Phil proved the decision right. Riding in spectacular fashion, he moved into Saarinen's slipstream as they raced into the first right-hander away from the grandstand and some moments later brought the crowd to their feet as the early rider came into view at the end of the first lap, for Read was now in the lead. Saarinen put the British rider under continuous pressure, but the MV stayed in front and Read scored a magnificent victory. The dying minutes were an anticlimax as Saarinen petered to a standstill, his chain broken.

Not for years had there been anything to compare with the spectacular success of Jarno Saarinen, notwithstanding his first defeat of the season. In both the 250cc and 500cc championships the talented Finn led the world, but MV were determined to make a fight of it. With MV improving their machines still further and with nine rounds still to be run, it was the most spectacular and tension-packed season in prospect for more than a decade. The Italian Grand Prix at Monza was the next round, and MV were more confident. Team-manager Arturo Magni had missed the Hockenheim meeting in order to prepare a second new MV for Agostini. At Hockenheim, Read had proved that the new machine could really go, and he claimed that it was faster than the Yamaha on the straight. In the 350cc round Agostini restored some of MV's flagging fortunes and boosted his own confidence, battling courageously with team-mate Read and then Lansivuori. When that challenge was overcome, he took on Renzo Pasolini on a Harley-Davidson and finally raced home to a well-deserved win. The 100,000 crowd went wild in support of the 'home' victory, but Agostini's victory only served to fuel pre-match rumours that he was to leave MV for Honda, though the Italian racer later denied it.

Tragically the battle of the giants, MV versus Yamaha, Read and Agostini against Saarinen and Kanaya, did not materialize. In an appalling accident at the start of the 250cc race at Monza, fifteen machines were brought down and Jarno Saarinen and Renzo Pasolini were killed. Such was the horror of the disaster that the 500cc event was struck from the programme. On the day of Saarinen's funeral in his home town of Turku, Yamaha announced, as a mark of respect, that they would not officially take part in any further grands prix that year. The historic machines on which Saarinen had made such an impact were flown back to Japan, and MV were left to take the title once more unhindered.

Saarinen's superb balance on a racing motor-cycle was developed from his earlier experience on ice, and he was without doubt the most exciting road racer to emerge in years. He was a vivid personality and a brilliant rider, but lack of financial support in the early days almost brought a premature end to his racing career. Among a number of outstanding rides in Britain was his performance at Silverstone in 1972 when he became the fastest short-circuit racer, with a new lap record of 106.65 mph. He was the first Finnish rider to become a road-racing World Champion, though his sole title gives no accurate indication of his enormous ability.

Another racer of outstanding skill, but who unfortunately became known more for the off-track drama with which he was involved, was the East German Ernst Degner. He won the first-ever 50cc World Championship in 1962, becoming also the first rider to win a World Championship on a Suzuki machine.

Degner was born in Silesia in 1931 and on an East German MZ finished third in the 125cc World Championship of 1960. In the same class he finished second in a year when, if circumstances had been different, he might well have gained his first world title.

Despite Honda's formidable challenge in 1961, Degner finished second in Spain, France and Northern Ireland and scored convincing wins in West Germany, East Germany and Italy, but the drama that came in Sweden was unique in motor-cycle history. At the time Degner led the 125cc class, but with just one grand prix to be raced, in Argentina, he scuttled his chances of taking the title. In a dramatic move he defected from East Germany in favour of life in the West. The successful East German MZ bike was immediately denied him, but he borrowed an EMC bike from the famous engine-designer Dr Joe Ehrlich for the final grand prix in Buenos Aires. The EMC was similar to the famous MZ, though water-cooled, but unfortunately for Degner, it broke down in Argentina. Honda-riders filled the top five places, with Tom Phillis leading them home to win the race and become 125cc World Champion. Only six points separated Degner from Phillis at the end of the season.

Though Ernst Degner missed the title by the slimmest of margins, he had shown himself to be an extremely able rider and, on the smaller machines, one of the best in the world. Suzuki were among those who appreciated his skills. The second Japanese factory to take an interest in motor-cycle racing, Suzuki entered classic competition for the first time in 1960 with 125cc twins which were well outclassed. In the meantime they had studied closely the successful MZ racers, but in 1961, with new versions which bore a striking design resemblance to the East Germany factory machines, they were hardly more successful. Their problem was that MZ, in the meantime, had improved their machines sufficiently to keep them ahead. Suzuki seized their chance, however, deciding to support the 50cc World Championship when it was introduced into the World Championship series in 1962.

Before the season opened, Degner had been lured from West Germany to Japan and once there had joined the Suzuki organization as an engineer and rider. He scored his first victory on the Japanese machines on the Isle of Man, beating Taveri on the Honda. Suzuki had made a good job of their 50cc machines, using a single-cylinder two-stroke engine which was said to produce 10 bhp at 11,000 rpm, giving a top speed in excess of 90 mph. Riding with impressive dexterity, Degner dominated the class, racing to superb consecutive wins in Holland, Belgium and West Germany. A second place in the final round, again in Argentina, was enough to give him the title by just five points from Anscheidt on the Kreidler and, seven more points adrift, Taveri on the Honda. Although Degner competed in one or two 125cc rounds that year, Honda dominated the class in a year in which they won World Championships in three of the five solo classes.

Degner had been a respected engineer as well as a rider at the MZ factory, and his technical expertise was put to good use at Suzuki. He helped the Japanese factory to produce later versions of Suzuki's first World Championship lightweight machines which were ridden with devastating effect by the New Zealander Hugh Anderson. He, along with Degner and Frank Perris, spearheaded Suzuki's onslaught in the 50cc and 125cc classes in 1963. Degner won the 50cc Dutch TT and was second in France, Belgium and Argentina, but Anderson took the title with 34 points. Degner finished the season with 30 points, in third place, with Anscheidt on the Kreidler with 32 points in second position. In the 125cc class Degner made little impact, though Suzuki were happy as Hugh Anderson romped home to secure a magnificent double World Championship. Degner, however, beat his Suzuki team-mate to win in West Germany, and he also finished third on the Isle of Man and in the final round in Japan. It was not an altogether happy year for the East German though, for in Japan, in the final round of the 50cc Championship, he crashed and was badly burned.

After being out of action for a while, it took Degner some time to regain his form, but in the penultimate round of the 125cc 1964 World Championship he finished in third position, after Taveri on the Honda and Anderson on the Suzuki, and followed this encouraging performance with a convincing win in the final round in Japan. At thirty-four, Ernst Degner was approaching the end of his racing days in 1965, but that season he scored good wins at Daytona and at Spa in Belgium. He finished in fourth position in the 50cc and 125cc World Championships. He retired at the end of 1965 but made a token return to the Isle of Man in 1966 to race in the last 50cc TT, finishing fourth behind Ralph Bryans, Luigi Taveri, both on Hondas, and Hugh Anderson on the Suzuki.

Being a rider of lightweight machinery, Degner did not make the impact he would have done had he chosen to race 350cc and 500cc machinery. On the other hand, for French-Canadian Yvon Duhamel the reason he did not become more widely acclaimed internationally was simply that he had too few Grand Prix rides. Yet he was one of the most dynamic racers of all time. Disappointingly from a European point of view, he spent too much time riding around the American circuits. Known as the wild man of American road racing, Duhamel was only 5 feet 1 inch tall, but his gallantry and devastating style on a race machine quickly became legendary. He was frantically fast, seemingly totally without fear and excitingly spectacular. He often crashed, ignored the damage he did to his body and continued to the end of his extraordinary career to ride too close to the limits for comfort. It was appropriate that he built his reputation on Kawasaki, for at that time in the 1970s they were making an impact commercially with their big bike by selling a 'performance' image. He dovetailed ideally with their approach.

Born in Quebec in 1941, Duhamel gained early experience racing round the half-mile dirt tracks of North America. He appeared at Daytona for the first time in 1966, and in 1968 finished eighth there on a 500cc BSA and won the 250cc event. He also became the world's snowmobile champion. He was able to combine both sports for a time and in doing so became one of the highest earners in motor-cycle road racing at the peak of his career. It was said that his take from Kawasaki alone was in the region of $90,000. In the early 1970s Kawasaki were desperately trying to emulate Honda, Suzuki and Yamaha by building a world reputation for motor-cycle manufacture. They signed Duhamel to spearhead their drive for road-racing success, but their machines were hardly competitive, though 'Superfrog', as he became known because of his French background, carried them forward in sensational style, making those early 'green meanie' machines from Kawasaki look better than they were. He rapidly established his enormous reputation on such circuits as Talladega and Ontario, thrusting caution aside and, at Talladega, giving Kawasaki their first victory in an AMA National Championship race. He beat fancied entries from BSA and Triumph to win the famous 200 race there by almost 80 seconds at a near-record average speed of 108.46 mph.

Duhamel had already built a mighty reputation when he first raced in Britain at Mallory Park's 1970 Race of the Year, when he finished tenth riding a 350cc Yamaha. In the Anglo-American Match Race Series he was highest scorer, along with Peter Williams, in 1973 and a year later captained the American team. By that time his reputation had preceded him to Europe, for in 1972 he had returned to Talladega to win the 200 at a new record average speed of 110 mph — and on a standard frame model Kawasaki. That same year Duhamel won both 125-mile races to gain outright victory in the important Champion Spark Plug Classic at Ontario, for good measure smashing every motor-cycle record for the circuit and winning £10,000 in prize and bonus money.

When Kawasaki in America cut back their racing programme for 1974, they retained only one full works rider, Yvon Duhamel. At Daytona he was once more up among the leaders, but then went out with gearbox trouble, and in the Talladega 200 there were amazing scenes. Yamaha's Kenny Roberts and Don Castro moved into an early lead, but the focus of the race then switched as Duhamel came storming through the field like an express train. On the powerful 750cc Kawasaki, he committed himself completely in typical style and, in striving to overtake Roberts and Castro on the high-speed section, crashed at 130 mph. The machine was battered out of recognizable shape, and Yvon was hurled from the bike, rolling over and over, but he simply got to his feet and walked away.

Duhamel also featured strongly for a spell in long-distance events and in Formula 750 Championship racing, particularly in 1975, but the French-Canadian is not remembered for results. He was known as the hard man of racing and loved for his total commitment. He was such a competitive rider that his technique, particularly his cornering, caused consternation among other riders and delighted crowds. He seemed to spend almost as long recovering from crashes as he did racing. It is interesting to speculate how much more successful Yvon Duhamel might have been if he had tempered his enormous courage and outstanding ability with a little more science and discretion. But then results are not everything, and most of those who saw him in action would much prefer to remember him as he was, because there was no more exciting spectacle than Yvon Duhamel in full flight. When Kawasaki's interest in racing dwindled, his factory contract expired and his top racing days were over. By 1978 the then thirty-nine-year-old racer was turning more to his numerous business interests, but his relatively short yet spectacular career in racing made a welcome and glorious contribution to the world of motor-cycling.

Kawasaki, for whom Yvon Duhamel rode almost exclusively, would have made greater impact in top-class road racing but for their policy of racing basically road-going machines. They made their mark in the longer-distance road races in North America and in marathon events, but for a long time they ignored the grand prix scene. When British rider Dave Simmonds captured the 125cc World Championship for Kawasaki in 1969, he received little help from Japan, other than the loan of a machine. His operational headquarters were the awning of his caravan which doubled as a workshop, where he would work late into the night. At other times Simmonds and a number of other riders tried to persuade Kawasaki to commit themselves more fully to a full racing policy, but without success. When interest in 750cc competition grew to the extent of the series gaining full World status in 1977, Kawasaki could have claimed that their policy was correct, but the interest was short-lived, and when the 750s quickly lost their new-found status, the focus of the racing season switched once more to the traditional grand prix classes.

Only when Kawasaki moved into the production of 250cc and 350cc machines did they begin to accept the value of grand prix racing, and for a while, through such riders as Kork Ballington, Anton Mang and Gregg Hansford, they made a sparkling contribution to the racing scene. Kawasaki technology was never in doubt, and in the short bursts, when factory policy permitted them to make a grand prix challenge, they proved themselves worthy participants. Through Ballington and the German rider Anton Mang, they took the 250cc World Championship four years running, from 1978, and the 350cc World Championship, again through Ballington in 1978 and 1979 and Anton Mang in 1981 and 1982, before the class was withdrawn from the World Championship calendar.

It was the American rider Gary Nixon, however, who first shot Kawasaki into the world racing headlines in the 750cc series, in 1976, the year before it gained World status. One of the most popular and successful of American road racers, Nixon began his career with Harley-Davidson, but while competing in drag races he achieved his first significant win on a British 650cc Triumph. He scored impressive success with factory 500cc Triumphs in the early 1960s and in 1967 and 1968 was America's number-one rider. In 1968 he became the first rider to win both the 200-mile race at Daytona and the 100-mile lightweight event in the same year. Nixon had mixed fortunes on Kawasaki, but he surged into prominence in 1976 when he decided to compete in the Formula 750 Championship, though Kawasaki had cut back their racing programme substantially. Nixon bought a 1975 factory Kawasaki and immediately set about showing the world how competitive he and the bike were.

At the opening round at the famous Daytona circuit he fought magnificently, climbing up the field and thrilling the crowd with a spirited duel with Barry Sheene on the Suzuki. In the end Nixon finished second to Johnny Cecotto to gain twelve championship points. The second round, the Venezuelan 200-miler, was badly organized, and workmen were still busy on the circuit with just three days to go to the race. Cecotto proved fastest in practice, but in the race it was Gregg Hansford on his Kawasaki who captured attention as he rocketed ahead of the field. Cecotto and Sheene moved to the front as Hansford's machine failed, but a second-lap drama centred around Victor Palomo on the Yamaha and Gary Nixon on the Kawasaki. It began when Steve Baker pulled his Yamaha into the pits to have his carburettor adjusted. He restarted quickly, but in Nixon's calculation he was now one lap behind. When Baker moved back onto the road, Nixon made no attempt to challenge him, on the assumption that he, Nixon, was now a lap ahead. The timekeepers obviously shared Nixon's view because at the end of the first leg of the race Cecotto was declared the winner, with Nixon second and Baker down in fifth position. When Baker discovered when lining up for the second leg that he had been given fifth position in the first leg, he protested, claiming his rightful position to be second.

It was in this confusion that the second heat was flagged away. Under the scorching South American sun, local hero Johnny Cecotto seemed certain to win the second leg, but then, with only a few laps remaining, he pulled into the pits suffering from heat exhaustion. Steve Baker went ahead to win the second leg, with Gary Nixon finishing second. Now it was 'make your mind up' time, and the judge declared in favour of Nixon as the outright winner; the Kawasaki rider was presented with the winner's trophy. Baker, however, lodged an official protest and, unbelievably, with the riders now back in their hotel, Nixon's victory was withdrawn and Baker declared the winner. Gary Nixon now protested and the argument within the authorities went on for the remainder of the season. In the end the decision was left until the FIM Congress took place in Belgium in October.

Meantime the series continued. In the third round at Imola Nixon was unplaced, and he missed the fourth round at Jarama in Spain because of poor start money. The Spanish rider Victor Palomo did ride, however, and finished second, a significant result as it turned out, because Palomo, a virtual no-hoper for the championship at the start of the season, was to emerge as a serious contender as the season developed. In the fifth round at Nivelles in Belgium in May, Nixon was supreme. He won the first leg conclusively and was second to Mick Grant, also on a Kawasaki, in the second leg, the two Kawasaki riders sharing the fastest lap at 94.663 mph. At this stage Gary Nixon was placed second in the table, behind Michel Rougerie on the Yamaha, but the next three rounds were to prove crucial for the American. He finished fourth at Nogaro in France and was unplaced at Silverstone. It was here that Palomo began seriously to threaten Nixon's championship hopes. Though Steve Baker won the first heat and Mick Grant the second heat, Palomo's fifth and second positions were enough to make him winner overall.

With just two rounds remaining, Nixon went to Assen in Holland still with a strong chance of taking the title. Rain in the first heat, when Gary was riding on dry-weather slicks, put him out of the running, and further misfortune in the second heat, when he suffered mechanical problems, made it a dismal meeting for him. He finished in seventeenth position overall, all the more disappointing when compared with Victor Palomo's first position, resulting from a third place in the first leg and a fourth place in the second. The championship now rested on the outcome of the final round at Hockenheim in West Germany, though the position was confused. There was talk that the results of the round in Spain might not count, because there had been only six finishers, and the Venezuelan controversy still remained unresolved, but assuming the Spanish round results stood, Nixon was leading with 47 points against Palomo's 46. Nixon did well in the early stages of the first leg at Hockenheim but lost time in the pits when petrol was accidentally sprayed over his visor, and he eventually finished in seventh position. Palomo did better, ending the first leg in fourth position. In the second heat Gary Nixon had a storming race, disputing the lead with John Newbold and then with Palomo, the Spaniard at one point closing to within a few seconds, but Nixon rode on to win a magnificent race, with Palomo second. The overall result was Palomo first, with Nixon in second position.

But who had won the championship series? Palomo claimed the

title on the basis of the results as they stood at that time. No one could dispute it, but Nixon pinned his faith on the FIM committee meeting in October reversing the judgement made at Venezuela all those months before. On that basis Nixon would be the champion. Unable to make any sense out of the results from the Venezuelan meeting, the road-race committee of the FIM Congress finally decided to delete the results, and that meant that Victor Palomo was the winner, with Gary Nixon in second position. It was a disappointing outcome for the likeable American.

Nixon was a rider of great character and one of the most popular Americans to ride on European circuits. Born in Oklahoma in 1941, he turned professional in 1962 and became one of the best paid and, say some, one of the unluckiest riders in motor-cycling. After winning at Daytona in 1967, he was set for a factory Yamaha, but at the last moment officials changed their minds because he still had his hand in plaster from a crash which, incidentally, had not prevented his winning the American title. Though small in stature, he was a tough racer and after breaking a thigh in 1970 continued to race with plates and pins holding his leg together. Only a year before, he had been on the verge of having a leg amputated following a crash. Another crash spoiled his chances of riding a new four-cylinder Suzuki in 1974. A legend in America, Gary Nixon is remembered most for his association with Kawasaki, though he was with them for only two seasons.

Kawasaki's more profound heroes, however, were the grand prix racing trio of Kork Ballington, Gregg Hansford and Anton Mang. Collectively they brought Kawasaki a cluster of world titles and sufficient recognition to carry them forward as a significant force in grand prix road racing in the late 1970s and early 1980s.

Ballington, a Southern Rhodesian, competed successfully there and in South Africa before moving to Britain to try his luck in Europe. He was not an instant success. An unspectacular rider, his stylish consistent form gradually attracted attention, and after winning numerous British national races and attaining a good position in the national Superbike Championship, Kawasaki's UK team-manager Stan Shenton paired him with Barry Ditchburn in the long-distance Thruxton event. But with Mick Grant and Barry Ditchburn established members of the Kawasaki team, there was no room for a regular place for Ballington.

The break he so well merited took a long time coming, but a

shake-up at Kawasaki saw both Grant and Ditchburn depart and the welcome mat offered at last to Ballington. He repaid their confidence handsomely. In 1978 he brought Kawasaki a double World Championship, winning the 350cc and 250cc titles. He dominated the 350cc series, winning in Austria, Italy, Holland, Finland, Great Britain and Czechoslovakia to amass 134 points against nearest rival Takazumi Katayama's 77. In the 250cc class he had a tougher battle, but from his Kawasaki team-mate Gregg Hansford. Kork finished on top with 124 points to Hansford's 118. To prove his form was no fluke, he repeated his staggering performance in 1979. Other Kawasaki riders provided tough opposition in the 350cc class, with Hansford finishing third and Anton Mang fourth, but Kork took the title with 99 points from Patrick Fernandez on the Yamaha with just 90 points. In the 250cc class Ballington's riding was little short of brilliant. With seven wins from twelve rounds he totalled 141 points against his nearest rival, Gregg Hansford with 81 points.

Hugh Neville Ballington was now considered among the élite of grand prix racers. He was totally professional in his approach and mixed fast and accurate riding with discipline, style and safety. Within just two years he had climbed up alongside motor-cycling giants Mike Hailwood and Jim Redman as only the third racer to be double World Champion two years running. His unhurried, seemingly effortless riding was deceptive, and although his switch to 500cc racing on the Kawasaki was a courageous move, he was never able to duplicate the success he achieved on lower-capacity machines. Fighting Yamaha and Suzuki in the top-class of motor-cycle racing was a confrontation which Kawasaki were not really up to, but in spite of having less competitive machinery, Ballington was still tipped as a 500cc World Champion on a new Kawasaki 500 expected for 1982. But a season is a lifetime in motor-cycle racing, and when Kork switched from the 250cc and 350cc classes his best days were over. He finished twelfth in the 500cc championship race in 1980, eighth in 1981, ninth in 1982 — not bad results on machinery which was hardly competitive in the toughest sphere of motor-cycle racing.

Gregg Hansford was another particularly exciting Kawasaki rider. This blond, handsome Aussie blazed the Kawasaki trail in his homeland before venturing to Europe for the first time in 1978. Riding works machines meticulously prepared by notable Kawasaki backroom expert Neville Doyle, he rode with outstanding success and brilliant style over several seasons in Australia, New Zealand and the Far East. He performed .well at Daytona and scored a sensational victory over the fancied Steve Baker at Mosport in Canada in the 1977 Formula 750cc World Championship. A scintillating, exciting rider, Gregg's only problem was finding the consistency necessary to win a World Championship. For three years running, from 1977, the highly respected publication *Motocourse* put him in the world's top ten riders, praising his outstanding technique on the corners and his exceptional qualities in outbraking opponents, and claiming that, 'On a tight track on a fast bike, no one in the world could count on beating him.' Editor Barry Coleman reckoned him the 'best braker in the business'. Statistically, Gregg had to contend with Ballington in racing the smaller Kawasakis, and Kork, being smaller, had a natural advantage. But Hansford did well all the same. He finished second in the 250cc class and third in the 350cc class in 1978 and 1979, but in 1980 it was the turn of the German rider Anton Mang to uphold the winning tradition of Kawasaki in these classes.

Germany has no impressive reputation for producing solo bike world-beaters, but Mang dramatically changed all that as he rode Kawasaki machines to grand prix success in the early 1980s. A modest and charming character, Mang was born in 1949 and had been in the business of racing for some time when he secured his first World Championship in 1980. He romped the 250cc class, amassing 128 points to runner-up Kork Ballington's 87, and was only three points short of World Champion Jon Ekerold in the 350 cc class. He might well have taken that title also, but for a crash on the first bend in the first round at Misano in Italy. His riding for the remainder of the season, in both classes, was virtually faultless.

In both classes in 1981 he was supreme, never faltering. He won fifteen grands prix to finish way ahead of the opposition in both classes. In the 250cc class his form was sensational, winning ten of the twelve rounds and finishing the season with a massive tally of 160 points, against Jean-François Balde, also on a Kawasaki, in second place with 95 points. In the 350cc class he achieved a personal ambition, proving to himself conclusively that he could beat the impressive Jon Ekerold on the Yamaha, even though the latter was injured trying to keep in front at an international meeting. But by then Tony Mang had beaten Jon in open combat in

Austria and Yugoslavia. Mang finished a massive 51 points ahead of his traditional rival and hardly put a foot wrong all season.

In 1982 Mang could have hoped for more factory support in a season which saw the Kawasakis struggling against increasingly potent opposition. Even so he again took the 350cc title comfortably, scoring 81 points against his nearest challenger, Didier de Radigues on the Chevallier, with 64 points. A depressing mix-up in France in the opening round was to cost Mang the 250cc title. Bad organization and the poor condition of the circuit at Nogaro raised a storm of protests among the riders. The situation worsened and became increasingly confusing as a wholesale walk-out of riders threatened. Mang, convinced that the boycott by the top riders would materialize, left the meeting — prematurely, as events were to prove, for in the end many more of the star riders lined up for the race than had at first been expected. While Mang forfeited the chance of gaining important championship points because of his walk-out, France's Jean-Louis Tournadre, riding a Yamaha, won the race, collected a maximum fifteen points and went on to sneak the world title from under Mang's nose, for the German was just one point behind the Frenchman at the end of the season.

Kawasaki, whose reputation had been built on a performance image, had in Ballington, Hansford and Mang riders who reflected that image. Hansford particularly was exciting to watch and had that special charisma which thrilled the fans and made him a special attraction whatever circuit he visited.

A World Champion of a different kind, but no less deserving, was the quiet, unassuming Walter Villa, an Italian born in Modena. Villa is known from the record books for being the first, and only, rider in the thirty-six years of the World Championship series up to and including 1984 to win the 250cc title three years running, and to win a road-racing World Championship on a Harley-Davidson machine. The likeable Italian crowned three years of superb riding by adding the 350cc crown in 1976 to become a double World Champion that year.

Walter was born in 1944 and began racing in 1962. He won a number of Italian national championships before venturing on to the grand prix circuits. He rode a 350cc Yamaha in 1973 with limited success, but in 1974, having switched to Harley-Davidson, he was brilliantly successful, sweeping aside a strong Yamaha challenge from riders of such outstanding merit as Kent Andersson, Patrick Pons and Kenny Roberts to win the 250cc World Championship for the first time, with wins in Finland, Holland, Italy and Czechoslovakia. A serious illness threatened to keep him from racing in 1975, but he recovered sufficiently not only to compete but to dominate the class once more, with wins in West Germany, Spain, Italy, Holland and Sweden. He collected 77 championship points — West Germany's Dieter Braun was closest to him with 58 points. His double World Championship in 1976 crowned a superb three years of riding. In the highly competitive 250cc series he claimed the title with wins in seven of the eleven rounds, and in the 350cc class he won in France, Finland, Czechoslovakia and West Germany.

A remarkable aspect of Villa's success was that he never had a full works contract from Harley-Davidson, despite his achievements, but he was a very good rider indeed. Though a quiet, unfussy individual, Walter Villa had enormous strength of character. Many accused him of causing the appalling crash in 1973 which took the lives of Saarinen and Pasolini, because it was claimed that the oil on the track which resulted in the fatal pile-up had been dropped by Villa's Benelli-4. Villa himself was badly injured in the crash, but accepting the inquiry's judgement that the multiple pile-up was not his fault and had been caused when Pasolini's Harley-Davidson seized, he put aside the horrors of that moment and regained his confidence, composure and self-respect. Ironically, Villa took over from Pasolini on the Harley-Davidson machines, and no rider deserved his success more.

World Champions come in all shapes and sizes, but one of the most youthful, exciting, flamboyant and charismatic was the Venezuelan teenager Alberto 'Johnny' Cecotto who, at nineteen, became the youngest rider ever to win a road-racing world title. The explosive nature of his impact on motor-cycle racing came straight out of the story books and was perhaps only equalled by his similarly sudden demise.

Born in far-away Caracas in 1956, Cecotto gained instant attention when first competing in the grand prix because it is not every day that a new world-class rider is Venezuelan — and because of his sensational début. He pushed all other riders out of the headlines when, in the opening round of the World Championships of 1975 at the Paul Ricard circuit in France, he won both the 250cc and

350cc races. Against the likes of Agostini, Pons, Villa and Kanaya, the tousled-haired youngster set about proving that his début success was no fluke. Further wins in Italy, West Germany and Finland were enough for him to take the 350cc World Championship from Agostini at his first attempt — and Agostini had won the title for the previous seven years. Cecotto's winning margin was an impressive nineteen points. Another win in Belgium and second places in Finland and Italy gave him fourth place in the 250cc World Championship.

Despite his youth Cecotto was a local hero before moving into world competition, becoming his country's 1,000cc champion in 1973 and 1974. A student of mechanical engineering, he gave up studying to become a professional racing motor-cyclist. Johnny competed at Daytona for the first time in 1974, finishing 35th, but just two years later he was at twenty the youngest-ever winner of the Daytona 200, at a record speed of 108.77 mph, lapping all his rivals.

After receiving support and sponsorship from the Venezuelan importer of Yamaha machines, Andres Ippolito, who became his manager, Cecotto was given official support by the Japanese factory, and at the start of 1976 there was no hotter property in grand prix racing. But in the end his indifferent form, inconsistency and a tendency to crash made it a disappointing season. Certainly, his machines could have been better, but at the core of the problem was probably the unsettling effect of tempting offers which, it was rumoured, were on the verge of being made by Ferrari for Cecotto to turn to Formula 1 car-racing. He made no secret of his desire to race cars, but the start of 1977 saw him once more Yamaha mounted, and he started well with victory in the 350cc race in the opening round in Venezuela. Then came the disaster at the Salzburgring when, on the eighth lap of the 350cc Austrian Grand Prix, he became the innocent victim of a five-rider pile-up. He was out of racing for several months with a badly broken arm, but when he returned towards the end of the season he was calmer, had a better mental approach and seemed renewed in spirit and enthusiasm.

In Sweden, Finland and Czechoslovakia, the latter where he won the 350cc race in convincing style, he showed flashes of his old brilliance, so that when he announced his intention of competing in the 500cc class in 1978, along with riders like Kenny Roberts, Barry Sheene, Wil Hartog, Pat Hennen and Steve Baker, his fans' excitement knew no bounds. But unfortunately it was the adventurous

Cecotto back at his most capricious. His talent was never in question and he rode some stunning rides, but his inconsistency was agonizing. In all too brief snatches he fed crowds the idea that, if not the most classical rider around, he was the most manful and was capable of taking the 500cc title with ease. Unfortunately, brilliance would be followed by indifference, though at the end of the year, despite his lamentable lapses, he still managed to finish in third place behind Roberts and Sheene. In the Formula 750cc World Championship, however, Cecotto roared to glorious victory and finished ahead of a highly competitive field led by Kenny Roberts, Steve Baker, Gregg Hansford, Christian Sarron, Gianfranco Bonera and Patrick Pons, to snatch the title from the favourite, Roberts.

The final round at Mosport Park in Canada was the decider. Roberts needed to win, and if Cecotto finished outside the top seven places the American would claim the title. Roberts on the day was not prepared to match the speed of Mike Baldwin, who won both legs, so race positions put Roberts in second place, with Cecotto, by no means on his best form, down in fifth. Just five points gave the Venezuelan the championship at the end of the ten rounds. He finished third in the Formula 750cc World Championship in 1979, the last year in which Formula 750cc racing had World status, and with the demise of the class, Johnny Cecotto faded also.

He returned to grand prix racing in 1980, finishing sixth in the 500cc series and fourth in the 350cc class, but lack of success sapped his interest and he quickly disappeared from the scene in favour of motor-racing. His loss was much regretted. Johnny Cecotto was a colourful personality, both on and off the track, an exciting racer who, whatever his form, had the ability to draw the crowds and glamorize the sport.

12. Racing to the Top in the 1980s

For almost thirty years World Championship racing had to get along without the Americans. As early as the 1920s the national body for motor-cycle racing in the United States had broken away from the FIM, and for some forty years the sport in America and in Europe developed along different lines. For a long time a British rider risked suspension by competing in America, and there was no place for American riders in European events run under the auspices of the FIM. Not until the 1960s, when in America and Europe motor-cycle racing was enjoying an enormous boom, largely through the influence of the Japanese, did the obvious advantages of a reconciliation between the American Motorcyclists Association and the Fédération Internationale Motocycliste take on a positive, defined meaning. In the late 1960s the AMA was re-admitted into the FIM, and the way was then clear for transatlantic competition. This led to the Anglo-American Match Race Series, held for the first time in 1971, and the FIM Formula 750 Prize Winners Championship in 1973, this latter competition being awarded World Championship status for the first time in 1977.

The fascination in all this for the average race fan was how, in open competition, the top European riders would fare against their American rivals. It is true that the British riders did not see themselves under any serious threat. After all, they were specialists in road racing, used to competing week after week on the natural road and specially created European circuits with their wide range of corners and faster straight sections. The American riders, in contrast, had been forced into developing more all-round skills, through having to compete in the National Championships in dirt-track racing, run over loose surface circuits of half a mile and a mile, more traditional road racing and American-style TT racing, a combination of motocross and dirt-track racing. In addition, their background was firmly in 750cc and 1,000cc racing, specialist machines of lower capacity becoming significant in America only in the 1960s.

Legendary names of North American racing were now seen in Britain for the first time: Dick Mann, Cal Rayborn, Yvon Duhamel, Gene Romero, Gary Fisher, Art Baumann, Gary Nixon, Dave Aldana and Kenny Roberts among them. In the Match Race Series, comprising teams of American and British riders competing against each other over three meetings held during the Easter weekend, Rayborn particularly showed the standard of American riding, even on the unfamiliar short circuits of the UK, by winning three of the six races in the 1972 competition to become the top individual rider, though Britain as a team won the series. It was the first serious indication that British riders dismissed the American challenge at their peril. For a time, however, American racers were not particularly attracted to World Championship racing. Among the first to contest the grand prix series seriously were Pat Hennen, who finished third on a Suzuki in the 1976 500cc World Championship, and Steve Baker, a dynamic young rider who, though frail-looking and bespectacled, was probably the first American to make a major impact on European racing.

The year of Steve Baker was 1977, when he became the first-ever Formula 750 World Champion and finished in second place in the 500cc World Championship. The run-up began in 1976 when the modest, good-humoured Baker, admired for his personal qualities as well as his riding ability, scored heavily with British fans. Had he contested more 750cc rounds he would almost certainly have ended that season with the 750cc Prize, but he outrode the majority of high-ranking competitors to become, for many fans, the road-racing personality of the year — after Barry Sheene, that is, who won the 500cc World Championship in 1976. But Baker was devastating in the Anglo-American Match Races and at Silverstone, making him a man to watch in 1977. Though positionally he was superior in 1977, his performance overall was perhaps slightly less impressive. He fell off too often and was short on that chilling consistency which devastates opponents and can make a rider a World Champion. Nonetheless, Baker was seen as one of the most exciting of a new crop of road racers to emerge in the 1970s. With maximum points from rounds in the United States, Spain, Great Britain, Austria and Belgium, he romped away with the Formula 750 World Championship with a total of 131 points, against runner-up Christian Sarron's 55 and Giacomo Agostini in third place with 45 points.

Baker made no secret, however, of his disappointment in missing the 500cc World Championship. For a while he ran Barry Sheene close. In the opening round in Venezuela, he finished second to Barry and shared with him the fastest lap at 96.55 mph. In the second round in Austria, both Sheene and Baker were among the top riders who boycotted the 500cc race following the multiple pile-up in the 350cc event and subsequent confrontation between the riders and the organizers, the former alleging ineptitude and gross inability by officials to handle the situation following the crash. So no points for either rider there. Although in the next round in West Germany Sheene finished first and Baker third, at this point only eight championship points separated the two riders. Fourth fastest in practice, despite falling, Steve lost ground in the fourth round in Italy. His anticipated challenge to Sheene did not materialize in the race. In the early stages, though Virginio Ferrari had moved off the line and into the lead, Baker was running fourth, while Sheene, battling to make amends for a dreadful start, was down in fourteenth position. Barry moved steadily through the field and overtook all opposition to win and gain a maximum 15 points while Steve finished in fourth position, adding just eight points to his total.

In France, in the next round, Baker finished third to stay loosely in touch with Barry, who won yet again, but from then the championship moved away from him. Sheene won again in Belgium and Sweden to finish the season with 107 points. Baker's final tally was 80 points. He finished fifth in Holland, second in Belgium, third in Sweden, twelfth in Finland. He was forced out with mechanical trouble in Czechoslovakia and finished second to fellow-American Pat Hennen in the British Grand Prix at Silverstone to round off the season.

On a good day Steve Baker was very impressive. Back in 1976 he won five of his six races in the Britain versus America series, and a convincing victory at Imola got everybody thinking he was a future World Champion. He was, in terms of 750cc racing, but he did not achieve his real ambition of becoming 500cc champion of the world.

Born in Washington State in 1952, Steve Baker was 5 feet 6 inches tall and weighed 9 stone four pounds. He made his racing début in America on quarter-mile dirt tracks with a 100cc Suzuki. As a professional he rode Yamaha machinery, but after 1977 his career declined. In 1978 he finished sixth in the 750cc series and seventh in the 500cc World Championship, but disappointingly we had seen the best of Steve Baker and after a series of crashes he left racing, which was all the less exciting for his departure.

But Baker's form and style, not to mention his winning of the Formula 750 World Championship at his first attempt, underlined what British and Continental riders had by now begun to believe. Through the vanguard of Dick Mann, who won once in Britain in 1971, Cal Rayborn, who won three races in one weekend in 1972, the compelling performance of Pat Hennen in grand prix racing and Gary Nixon in Formula 750cc racing, they could no longer look disdainfully at the American riders who, on strange circuits in a foreign country and in a branch of motor-cycle racing which was unfamiliar to them, had begun to show British riders the way home. Steve Baker at his best proved conclusively that the vision of American riders being crude and undisciplined exponents, only at home when riding unsophisticated big machines over rough ground, was ludicrously wide of the mark.

The American invasion, plus the soaring impact of a new generation of road racers from Italy, France and Germany, would soon, in the 1980s, relegate Britain to a secondary power. The old country went down under an onslaught of foreign talent — Randy Mamola, Kenny Roberts, Eddie Lawson and Freddie Spencer from the United States; Marco Lucchinelli, Franco Uncini, Virginio Ferrari, Eugenio Lazzarini and Pierpaolo Bianchi from Italy; Raymond Roche, Christian Sarron, Jean-François Balde and Guy Bertin of France; and Anton Mang and Martin Wimmer from West Germany. The lone British star left to ride the grand prix range and uphold a once proud tradition was Barry Sheene.

Barry, to become a sterling millionaire from racing motor-bikes and from sundry commercial spin-offs, was Britain's golden gift to road racing in the late 1970s and early 1980s. His devastating crashes at Daytona and Silverstone (which shattered his lean body yet were unsuccessful in taking the smile from his face or blunting his chirpy Cockney spirit) shot him into the headlines all over the world and made him everybody's hero. Immodest, frank, uninhibited, yet with a candour and impish sense of fun which were difficult to resist, Barry became the most popular motor-cycle racer Britain has ever produced. Taking little from the past and expecting no free rides from the future, he simply got on with the business of racing motor-cycles — professionally, confidently, outspokenly and successfully. Though Barry Sheene's two World Championships were won in 1976 and 1977, he remained a champion in many devoted fans' hearts well into the 1980s, and it was a sad day indeed for British racing when he announced, with his usual philosophical and sensible matter-of-factness, his retirement from the sport in January 1985. For British motor-cycle racing it was a great disappointment, for there was no other British rider on the horizon ready to take his place as an international attraction on the grand prix circuit.

Barry was born in London in 1950, taking after his father in developing a passion for racing motor-cycles. Frank Sheene was a former rider, and, incidentally, Barry's brother-in-law, Paul Smart, became a works rider for a number of factories. Sheene made his racing début in 1968, showing immediate promise. He won the 125cc British Championship in 1970, and the very next year, at his first attempt, he caused a sensation by missing the 125cc World Championship by just eight points, on a privately entered Suzuki twin. Yamaha stepped in, signing him for their factory team in 1972, but it was an unhappy and unsuccessful experience. He joined Suzuki GB in 1973. Among his successes that year were the Formula 750cc Championship and the *Motor Cycle News* Superbike Championship. Barry enjoyed riding the big 750cc so much that he was sure that his days of riding the lighter machinery were over. His achievement in winning the 750cc Championship at his first attempt and against an array of formidable opposition was disappointingly undervalued, however. It was the first year of superbike racing at this level, and the formula was not due to gain official World status for another four years. While he had still to make his mark in the World Championships with the more powerful machinery, at home circuits he was a live wire, clinching the King of Brands title.

By now Barry Sheene was being tipped as the next Hailwood, and in 1974 his progress to the top continued. Suzuki moved back into grand prix racing with a new 500cc two-stroke, water-cooled, four-cylinder machine. He started well, riding second to Phil Read in the opening round in France, but injuries at Imola and in Sweden put paid to any hopes he might have had for World Championship honours that year. But at home he won the important Race of the Year at Mallory Park and was once more the MCN Superbike Champion. His prospects for 1975 were excellent, and by now his pop-style image was paying off financially through off-track merchandizing deals; such was his appeal that Thames Television planned an hour-long documentary on him.

His new-season Suzuki was in fine fettle, and Barry was confident of his chances for the season as he hurtled his machine round the impressive Daytona circuit in the United States, practising for the famous early-season Daytona 200. In his last private practice session before the race, using the eighteen-degree banking to the full, Barry was clocking almost 180 mph when the rear wheel suddenly locked solid and the appalling and, by now, historic crash occurred. Barry was catapulted over the handlebars and along the track, bones being broken and flesh being painfully ripped off in the process. Miraculously he survived and, thanks to his enormous courage and the dedication of doctors, surgeons and medical staff in America and Britain, he was back racing in just seven weeks. The crash made worldwide headlines, and anyone who did not know Barry Sheene before for his racing ability knew him now as the survivor of the most horrendous crash. What heightened the drama was that a camera crew was filming Barry at the time, and the camera was kept running to record the full horror of the disaster. He began racing again with a metal pin holding one of his legs together.

His other black moment came seven years later, this time at the famous Silverstone circuit in Britain and once again during practice. With his gaze focused on the *Daily Express* bridge, he crested the oncoming blind rise to be confronted by the bike of a crashed rider strewn across the circuit right in his path. Observers reckoned Sheene had darted a glance behind him to see how close a pursuing rider was to him. He crashed straight into the stricken bike. Other riders were hurt, but Barry's injuries, once again, were nauseating. Witnesses said he was hurtled 30 feet into the air before crashing to the ground 100 yards away, to be carried forward by the momentum for another 200 yards. He lay motionless. Colleagues thought he was dead. Yet the indestructibility of the man was evident when, just a few days later and recovering in a small private room in Northampton General Hospital, Barry was condemning the authorities for allowing bikes of different capacities to practise at the same time. Cheerful, but in great pain, he told *Motor Cycle Weekly*'s Nick Harris: 'I said somebody could get killed out there, but little did I realize at the time it was so nearly going to be me.'

Barry subsequently recovered to ride and race again, but in the meantime the X-ray plates showing the pins which held his limbs together became almost as famous and easily recognizable as Barry himself, since then often referred to as the 'nuts and bolts man.'

As a motor-cycle racer Barry Sheene's best years were 1976 and 1977 when, riding Suzuki, he captured the coveted 500cc World Championship against a formidable American challenge. In 1977, with wins in six out of the eleven grands prix, he finished the season with 107 points. Steve Baker was second with 80 and Pat Hennen third with 67. Barry was by this time considered, almost without argument, the best motor-cycle rider in the world and one of the sport's outstanding ambassadors. For a while in 1978 the Yamahas of Kenny Roberts and Pat Hennen, not to mention the emergence of the Americans as world-class riders, put Barry at a disadvantage. Even when Suzuki produced a faster and better bike for him partway through the season, he was still unable to make the impact he was looking for to gain a third world title. His early season riding also suffered because he was not 100 per cent well and in the later stages he did not always seem mentally prepared for battle. With two wins, in Venezuela and Sweden, and good placings in Austria, France, Holland, Belgium and Great Britain, Barry surrendered the title to Kenny Roberts by a margin of ten points.

If his World Championship riding was disappointing, Sheene proved himself, on form, to be a magnificent rider still, with an exciting display against Kenny Roberts at Donington Park, and he emphasized his place in British racing, even allowing something for the superiority of Sheene's machinery, by taking his fifth Superbike Championship in six years. Barry battled on in 1979, and although he gained maximum points in three rounds, his five no-scoring rounds were enough to drop him down to third place in the World Championship table behind Roberts and Virginio Ferrari. He then switched to Yamaha, but 1980 was unproductive in terms of World Championship results. In 1981, however, with a new square-four Yamaha, the Londoner proved he could not be discounted, climbing up to finish in fourth position behind Marco Lucchinelli,

Randy Mamola and Kenny Roberts.

In 1982 he proved the importance of consistent riding, for although he did not win a grand prix all season and did not score points in six rounds, he still managed to finish joint fourth with Kenny Roberts. Barry had developed the new OW61 V four Yamaha so successfully, and he was racing so well, that he was a threat in every grand prix he raced. Some commentators believe that, but for the serious injuries he sustained in the appalling practice crash at Silverstone prior to the ninth round in the twelve-round series, he could well have taken the title. When he travelled to Silverstone, he was in joint second position with Roberts, Franco Uncini holding top position.

In 1984 Barry Sheene was still racing, arguably as well as ever. Despite his horrific crashes, uncompetitive machinery, millionaire status and security, and advancing years (for a racing motor-cyclist), he still found the motivation to race in the World Championships. Back on Suzuki machinery, he finished his final grand prix season in sixth position. Then, early in 1985, came the expected announcement of his retirement. From Barry there were no regrets. He would miss it, of course, he said, but by now his great passion was piloting his private helicopter and looking after his interests in a number of business directorships. These were to be his new challenges — with truck-racing just for fun.

Barry Sheene's loss to motor-cycle racing was monumental. For the circuit fans he was a great rider. He rode fast, his line was exemplary, he could outbrake most other riders, and he applied intelligence and astute thinking to the way he rode races, making him an excellent tactician. He was outspoken, and his career was punctuated with outbursts against what he considered to be the injustices and ineptitudes of the A-CU and the FIM. He campaigned courageously and passionately for greater track safety for riders and was not afraid to refuse to ride or boycott an event if the standards did not satisfy him. For his wider circle of fans, he never lost his boyish charm, his impish appeal, his Cockney chirpiness. He spoke with candour and honesty about his likes and dislikes and made new rules as he went along. He shunned dinners where he would have to wear a dinner jacket and would not go to restaurants if they would not permit him to wear jeans. Only once did he relax his principles against humbug and formality: he wore a suit and a tie when he went to collect his MBE from the Queen at

Buckingham Palace in 1977. His love-life confessions and racy lifestyle raised a few eyebrows, and the way he and former model Stephanie McLean lived together openly while she was still married was not to everyone's taste. It was not so much a condemnation of what had happened but the almost brazen and uncompromising expression of their relationship. They found excitement, pleasure and comfort in one another, and were more than happy for the world to know about it. Later they got married and had a daughter.

Barry spoke his mind and acted in his own way. He had a public personality which clicked on television and radio. He was easy, casual, finely tuned in to the media generation. His racing and commercial spin-offs have made him, he says, the biggest earner ever in motor-cycle racing. He now has a thirty-three-roomed Elizabethan manor house standing in twenty-two acres, close to Gatwick Airport, his own helicopter, expensive car and numerous business interests. He has learned a lot about wine, become a television celebrity as the co-presenter of a popular programme, is a shrewd businessman with an appetite to learn more (he claimed *The Money Programme* was his favourite on television), defies the health advocates by smoking Gitanes openly and, when he chose to announce to the world that he would retire from motor-cycle racing, he did so in style at London's exclusive Mayfair Hotel. A far cry indeed for the man who was born in Gray's Inn Road, suffered from asthma as a child and left school at fourteen.

Above all perhaps, Barry Sheene has always been a man determined to get what he wanted in life, and in motor-cycle racing he must surely have realized most of his ambitions. He admits, however, that the Silverstone crash destroyed his racing career. While acknowledging the support he received from Heron Suzuki in Great Britain in 1983 and 1984, he still felt at the time of his retirement announcement that he was good enough to win the world title. He is confident he would have won it in 1982, if the Silverstone crash had not happened, but when Suzuki Japan pulled out of racing at the end of 1983, the machinery available to him just was not up to winning a World Championship. Indeed, it was the lack of competitive machinery available to him which made him quit when he did.

A natural showman with a keen sense of fun, Sheene will also be remembered for his television 'Wheelies' and for his cheeky and irreverent V-sign to Kenny Roberts during their television race duel in 1979.

Barry was the last of the great British riders. In the 1980s the Italians and the Americans had taken over the 500cc World Championship. His immediate successor to the title was the hard-riding, tough-talking Californian Kenny Roberts. Kenny and Barry had been activists in the unsuccessful attempt in 1980 to form a breakaway World Series, but without the support of the FIM it was doomed, and their efforts for riders to have a greater say in the running of races and, in particular in the elimination of circuits which were not prepared to meet certain safety standards, failed. They were racing buddies, each holding the other in great esteem, and when Barry tried unsuccessfully to make it three 500cc World Championships in a row, it was Kenny who stepped in to win his first title in 1978. If never a great favourite with the British racing public, Roberts was certainly a golden boy in the estimation of Yamaha. His loyalty to the one factory was unusual in motor-cycle racing, and when he and Sheene rode Yamahas together, it was Kenny who was rewarded when Yamaha brought out a new model in 1981 by being the rider chosen to develop it.

Like many champions Kenny Roberts was riding motor-cycles early in life, and while still in his teens was making a name for himself in the amateur ranks. His ambition was strong and he developed a talent that matched it. Within four years of entering his first professional race, he was America's National Champion. At twenty-two, in 1973, he became the youngest rider to win that championship. Calculating and analytical in his approach to racing, Roberts rode very hard indeed and fought equally hard for the shabby treatment he claimed riders were often subjected to in Europe. He was too intense and resolute to win many British hearts, and he did not seem to smile very much, but, on some of the best machines around at the time, he rode brilliantly to take the World Championship from Sheene in 1978. He won it again in 1979 and yet again in 1980. This latter year he fought off an insistent challenge from Suzuki in the form of Randy Mamola and the Italian aces Lucchinelli and Uncini, but three wins in the first three rounds gave him a breakaway start which enabled him to claim a fairly comfortably won championship.

In 1981 the Suzuki challenge became a serious threat. Roberts' earlier Yamaha was replaced by a new square-four model, and while he spent the season trying to sort it out, particularly its deficient handling, the brilliant Marco Lucchinelli moved up to take the title. Roberts continued to have problems throughout 1982, and by now the fast-talking, hard-hitting Kenny was making no secret of his lack of enthusiasm for the World Championships. He had little respect for the FIM and little patience with more compromising riders, but he wanted to turn his back on Europe with the world title once more firmly in his grasp. A young American, in character and personality totally different from Roberts, got in the way, and after a gruelling series in which the quiet, gentlemanly Freddie Spencer won six rounds and Kenny Roberts also won six, the twenty-one-year-old took the title by just two points to become the youngest 500cc World Champion in history. It was a classic battle, with Roberts and Spencer the only two racers in with any real chance. With the battle lost, 'King Kenny' Roberts did not return to World Championship racing in 1984, the fight becoming much closer and the title going to another American, Eddie Lawson, with Randy Mamola in second position.

With three World Championships to his credit, it would be a miracle if Kenny Roberts came back into grand prix racing now. In 1983 he opened a Yamaha dealership in the United States to which he gave increasing attention. Sheene fans did not take to the American, because he deposed their champion hero when taking the title for the first time in 1978, but a less biased assessment will put Kenny Roberts up among the greatest of champions. He displayed a raw talent which was exceptional, and although he riled many fans because of his fiercely outspoken comments and the emphasis he gave to the money-making side of racing, this rugged-jawed rider of extraordinary talent, with his fast, knee-to-the-ground style, was exciting to watch and had an uncanny magic which made every meeting he attended bristle with expectancy. When Roberts took the 500cc World Championship from Sheene, it seemed to herald a period of American domination, but a couple of Italian riders stepped in after Roberts had departed to give their country the title for the first time since Agostini's last success in 1975.

Marco Lucchinelli was looking very much a future champion in 1980 when, despite being let down frequently by machinery break-downs, he still managed to finish in third place behind Roberts and Mamola. The good-tempered Italian had been knocking lightly on the door for some years. When Sheene won his first World

Championship in 1976, Lucchinelli finished in fourth place, riding Suzuki, but he slumped to eleventh the following year and was only marginally better at ninth in 1978. In 1979 he was eclipsed by his fellow Italian rider, the outstanding Virginio Ferrari, who finished second to Roberts, with Marco down at eighteenth. A little more luck in 1980 and he would have been a serious challenger to Roberts and Mamola, but the promise was definitely there and he was showing outstanding style and attack.

In 1981 that extra bit of maturity which comes from experience was enough to bring the likeable Italian the title. At times he showed flashes of real brilliance, and in the end, though both Kenny Roberts and Randy Mamola, not to mention Sheene and the talented New Zealander Graeme Crosby, were all going hard for the title, Marco beat them fair and square, and his championship was very well deserved. His riding was controlled but aggressive, and he showed his mastery of many different types of circuit. After falling in the first grand prix of the season in Austria, he was third in West Germany and fifth in Italy before winning in France to collect maximum points in the fourth round. He was second in Yugoslavia, but magnificent results in Holland, Belgium and San Remo meant he led Mamola at that point in the championship by sixteen points. It was now a battle between the two of them, and at Silverstone the American climbed closer, finishing in third place to gain ten points, while Lucchinelli failed to score. Now only eight points separated the two, but Marco opened the gap in Finland, finishing ahead of the field with a devastating exhibition of front riding. He stormed into the lead from the start and in fiercely determined mood, was never caught. Mamola finished fourth. It had been a magnificent battle, and the tension was maintained to the end.

As they lined up for the final round in Sweden, Lucchinelli had 103 points, Mamola 94. If the American won and Marco failed to win any points, Randy would take the title. Mamola moved off to a good start along with Ballington and Crosby, with Marco and Sheene leading the rest of the field. Lucchinelli, so afraid of falling off and ruining his chances of a world title, was riding with extreme caution, but Mamola kept up his challenge, until the weather stepped in to take a hand. Rain before the start had set all riders wondering about their choice of tyres, but when it started to rain again, Randy's hopes faded. With the circuit getting wetter, he dropped down the field, finishing the race at a bitterly disappointing thirteenth, gaining no additional World Championship points. Marco Lucchinelli's equally dismal ninth position was enough to give him two extra points, so the Italian became World Champion by a margin of eleven points.

Even with Roberts, Mamola and Sheene as contemporaries, Marco Lucchinelli now carried enormous impact, and his standing soared even higher when he was offered a massive £700,000 contract spread over two years to ride new Honda machinery in the 1982 series of 500cc World Championship events. It was reputed to be easily the biggest deal ever made to a motor-cycle rider and far beyond anything Suzuki could offer in an effort to keep the twenty-seven-year-old World Champion riding their machines. Marco reckoned that with luck he had another three years riding at the top and until Honda came along he had not been in the really big money. But now, with extra start money from riding as World Champion, and being free, despite the Honda offer, to negotiate additional sponsorships with helmet and racing-leathers companies, he had every prospect of becoming a millionaire within the next couple of years. Moreover, he would have the exciting Freddie Spencer as a team-mate, for in 1982 the young American would contest the World Championships seriously for the first time. Marco's other Honda teamster would be Takazumi Katayama. There was speculation as to whether the Italian had done the right thing in moving to Honda — not financially, that could never be in doubt, but in terms of retaining his world title. There were many experts who fancied that the new three-cylinder, reed-valve two-stroke machines just would not have the power to stay with the Suzukis and Yamahas of Uncini, Roberts, Sheene, Crosby and Mamola, not to mention the Kawasaki of Ballington.

In the opening round, in Argentina, Marco stayed with the leading pack for a number of laps, but when his Honda began to overheat, he had to drop back and finished in fifth position, with Roberts, Sheene and Spencer occupying the first three places. In the second round, in Austria, an outstanding battle developed between Lucchinelli and his talented fellow-Italian, Franco Uncini, riding Suzuki. They raced well ahead of the field, and in a magnificent spell of riding Marco broke the lap record alternately with Uncini. An all-action final lap kept the crowd at fever-pitch excitement as the two Italians fought fiercely, clashing fairings as they raced into corners side by side. Lucchinelli had led into the last lap, but only a few moments later, in a desperate effort to overhaul Uncini's challenge, he ran out of road and onto the grass. At that speed there was no possibility of his staying with the machine but the crash, thankfully, was not as bad as it looked, though Lucchinelli suffered a couple of broken bones in his foot.

The next grand prix, at the Nogaro circuit in France, was a fiasco. Bad organization and severe overcrowding in the paddock had already put the top riders in a bad mood, and they came in from unofficial practice expressing disbelief at the state of the circuit. Some said it was so bumpy it was more like a motocross track. Others went so far as to say it was virtually unrideable. Aggravating an obviously difficult situation was that Nogaro had been condemned a couple of seasons before when riders had given an ultimatum about not riding there again without significant improvements being made to the surface. This time all the top 500cc works riders refused to race.

The next round, in Spain, did not improve Marco's chances of retaining the title. He finished in fifth position, the same position he had achieved in Italy. At this stage Roberts and Uncini were leading the championship table with 48 points each, followed by Sheene, Crosby, Spencer and then Lucchinelli, in sixth position Good rides in the remainder of the season and the Italian could still retain his world title. But with no points from the Dutch TT, only five from Belgium and three from Yugoslavia, the position now looked grim, for he was still down in sixth position. The outcome of the British Grand Prix at Silverstone was crucial. The race was marred by the horrific practice crash of Barry Sheene, who broke both legs and an arm, and an early casualty in the race itself was Kenny Roberts, who crashed out of the race at Copse Corner on the first lap. Lucchinelli made a pitiful start and never really got to grips with the opposition, finishing well down in seventeenth position. He was not now in the running to retain his title.

While Marco was left to contemplate a miserable and disappointing season, his fellow-countryman, Franco Uncini, was systematically surging forward. His win at Silverstone made his gross points tally an impressive 103. Roberts and Sheene were the nearest, with 68 points each. Marco's luck did not improve and he ended the season in eighth position. The man who took over as World Champion, Franco Uncini, was also destined for a short spell at the top. By 1983 both Lucchinelli and Uncini had been eclipsed, and the 500cc World Championship was dominated by the Americans, who filled the first four places at the end of the season, with the three main factories — Honda, Yamaha and Suzuki — sharing the spoils.

The new hero was the quiet, religious, youthful Freddie Spencer. At twenty-one, he became the youngest-ever 500cc World Champion. Spencer is a worthy champion because he had to crush the likes of topliners Kenny Roberts, Randy Mamola and Eddie Lawson to finish top of the 500cc table, by just two points. Nor did Spencer's Honda have the gut power of Roberts' Yamaha, so it was left to the youngster to exploit the Honda's lightness and greater flexibility in outmanoeuvring the three-times champion.

Freddie is a popular racer. He is not a hell-raiser. He is not controversial. He wins friends quietly with his gentle smile and calm personality. He is not in the least aggressive, in many ways undemonstrative, and when riding he is smoother than Roberts. Yet it would be wrong to underestimate his determination, for he is fiercely competitive, a trait which becomes obvious when finding his line on corners. Once there, he takes a lot of shifting, but on the straight, when overtaking for instance, he can alter his line with a degree of positiveness that makes the competition think twice about taking liberties. He has proved himself a fine tactician, but once on a winning streak he sticks with it. He once told *Motor Cycle Weekly*'s Peter Clifford: 'It was something I learned in high school basketball. If you are leading by thirty points, don't throw away the game plan that gave you the thirty point lead.'

'Fast Freddie' was born in Shreveport, Louisiana, and began racing the dirt-tracks in America when he was only six. It was not until he was eleven, in 1973, that he began to do some road racing, and the conversion was a steady process, gaining ground in 1977 when he won four Western Road Race Association national championships. His first contact with European racers came in 1974 when he rode in the amateur 125cc race at Daytona. It was his first visit to the famous speed circuit, and he saw Agostini score his victory in the historic 200 race there. His first major impact on British fans was his triumph in the transatlantic series when, as a member of the triumphant American team and still only eighteen, he thrashed superstars Roberts, Mamola, Sheene and others to win both legs at Brands Hatch on the Honda 750.

In the 1983 fight for the World Championship, Spencer moved

off to a fine start, winning the first three rounds in South Africa, France and Italy, his nearest rivals at this stage being Roberts and Britain's Ron Haslam. Not until the fourth round in West Germany did Kenny Roberts begin to threaten. Easily fastest in practice, Spencer seemed set for a convincing win when he took an early lead in the race and put a considerable distance between himself and Roberts by the end of the third lap. But after three more laps Freddie's Honda sounded very sick and he began to lose power. On the eighth lap he was having to nurse the machine along to gain a place, and Roberts surged ahead to win from Katayama, with Spencer finishing in fourth position. In Spain Spencer and Roberts produced a fine, race-long classic battle with no one else in with a chance. Spencer collected the maximum fifteen points while Roberts' second place gave him twelve valuable points to add to his total. The championship literally cracked back into life in the next round in Austria. At the end of lap 12, as Freddie raced the Honda past the pits, there was an enormous bang and he was out of the race with a broken crankshaft, leaving Roberts to score maximum points. Now Kenny was only four points adrift in the race to the championship. Six rounds remained and Roberts made a tremendous fight of it. He won in Holland, Belgium, Great Britain and San Marino, but it just was not enough. Though Freddie managed to win only two of the remaining six grands prix, in Yugoslavia and Sweden, his three second places and one third piled up enough additional points to bring him the World Championship.

He responded to his success typically, with a calm philosophical acceptance, his attitude also when he is beaten in a race — and when he is beaten to the championship, as he was in 1984 by fellow American Eddie Lawson. That year he missed five grand prix rounds because of injury and still brought the Honda home to finish fourth in the table. But Freddie Spencer is not the kind of man you expect as a motor-cycling World Champion. Sports writer Malcolm Folley described him as about as threatening as a choirboy, adding: 'But don't be fooled by the clean-cut Freddie Spencer — on the track he is the leader of the pack.' Freddie admits he is different. He enjoyed a private education, says that religion helps him in his personal life as well as when racing, and is more concerned with making money than spending it on a lavish lifestyle.

That Freddie Spencer is capable of winning many more World

Championships there is no doubt. He is young enough to be riding at the top level for another six or seven years at least and, barring serious injury, given a fair share of luck, the right machinery and the motivation necessary to pound the grand prix trail, you could put money on it. Except perhaps for that motivation. World Championships seldom come easily, and whether Spencer will have the passion and the monomania to stay grand prix racing, whatever the circumstances, is perhaps another matter.

If not, who will take over? That is the fascination and the excitement of motor-cycle racing. Generations mourn the passing of their favourites, claiming there can never be anyone to replace them. The doubts and the uncertainty are the lifeblood of racing, but one thing is certain: great motor-cycle riders will emerge in the future, as in the past and present, and, whether World Champions or not, will claim their place in the history of the sport.

World Championship Results 1949-1984 Inclusive

1949

125cc
1 Nello Pagani, Italy (Mondial) 27
2 R. Magi, Italy (Morini) 14
3 Umberto Masetti, Italy (Morini) 13

250cc
1 Bruno Ruffo, Italy (Guzzi) 24
2 Dario Ambrosini, Italy (Benelli) 19
3 R. Mead, GB (Mead Norton) 13

350cc
1 Freddie Frith, GB (Velocette) 33
2 Reg Armstrong, Ireland (AJS) 18
3 Albert Foster, GB (Velocette) 16

500cc
1 Les Graham, GB (AJS) 30
2 Nello Pagani, Italy (Gilera) 29
3 A. Artesiani, Italy (Gilera) 25

Sidecar
1 Eric Oliver, GB (Norton) 26
2 Ercole Frigerio, Italy (Gilera) 18
3 F. Vanderschrick, Belgium
  (Norton) 16

1950

125cc
1 Bruno Ruffo, Italy (Mondial) 17
2 G. Leoni, Italy (Mondial) 14
3 Carlo Ubbiali, Italy (Mondial) 14

250cc
1 Dario Ambrosini, Italy (Benelli) 30
2 Maurice Cann, GB (Guzzi) 14
3 Fergus Anderson, GB (Guzzi) 6

350cc
1 Bob Foster, GB (Velocette) 30
2 Geoffrey Duke, GB (Norton) 24
3 Les Graham, GB (AJS) 17

500cc
1 Umberto Masetti, Italy (Gilera) 28
2 Geoffrey Duke, GB (Norton) 27
3 Les Graham, GB (AJS) 17

Sidecar
1 Eric Oliver, GB (Norton) 24
2 Ercole Frigerio, Italy (Gilera) 18
3 Hans Haldemann, Switzerland
  (Norton) 8

1951

125cc
1 Carlo Ubbiali, Italy (Mondial) 20
2 G. Leoni, Italy (Mondial) 12
3 Bill McCandless, Ireland
  (Mondial) 11

250cc
1 Bruno Ruffo, Italy (Guzzi) 26
2 Tommy Wood, GB (Guzzi) 21
3 Dario Ambrosini, Italy (Benelli) 14

350cc
1 Geoffrey Duke, GB (Norton) 40
2 Johnny Lockett, GB (Norton) 19
3 Bill Doran, GB (AJS) 19

500cc
1 Geoffrey Duke, GB (Norton) 35
2 Alfredo Milani, Italy (Gilera) 31
3 Umberto Masetti, Italy (Gilera) 21

Sidecar
1 Eric Oliver, GB (Norton) 30
2 Ercole Frigerio, Italy (Gilera) 26
3 Albino Milani, Italy (Gilera) 19

1952

125cc
1 Cecil Sandford, GB (MV) 28
2 Carlo Ubbiali, Italy (Mondial) 24
3 E. Mendogni, Italy (Morini) 16

250cc
1 Enrico Lorenzetti, Italy (Guzzi) 28
2 Fergus Anderson, GB (Guzzi) 24
3 Les Graham, GB (Velocette) 11

350cc
1 Geoffrey Duke, GB (Norton) 32
2 Reg Armstrong, Ireland
(Norton) 24
3 Ray Amm, Rhodesia (Norton) 21

500cc
1 Umberto Masetti, Italy (Gilera) 28
2 Les Graham, GB (MV) 25
3 Reg Armstrong, Ireland
(Norton) 22

Sidecar
1 Cyril Smith, GB (Norton) 24
2 Albino Milani, Italy (Gilera) 18
3 Jacques Drion, France (Norton) 17

1953

125cc
1 Werner Haas, W. Germany
(NSU) 30
2 Cecil Sandford, GB (MV) 20
3 Carlo Ubbiali, Italy (MV) 18

250cc
1 Werner Haas, W. Germany
(NSU) 30
2 Reg Armstrong, Ireland (NSU) 23
3 Fergus Anderson, GB (Guzzi) 22

350cc
1 Fergus Anderson, GB (Guzzi) 30
2 Enrico Lorenzetti, Italy (Guzzi) 26
3 Ray Amm, Rhodesia (Norton) 18

500cc
1 Geoffrey Duke, GB (Gilera) 38
2 Reg Armstrong, Ireland (Gilera) 18
3 Alfredo Milani, Italy (Gilera) 18

Sidecar
1 Eric Oliver, GB (Norton) 32
2 Cyril Smith, GB (Norton) 26
3 Hans Haldemann, Switzerland
(Norton) 12

1954

125cc
1 Ruppert Hollaus, Austria (NSU) 32
2 Carlo Ubbiali, Italy (MV) 18
3 Herman Müller, W. Germany
(NSU) 15

250cc
1 Werner Haas, W. Germany
(NSU) 32
2 Ruppert Hollaus, Austria (NSU) 26
3 Herman Müller, W. Germany
(NSU) 17

350cc
1 Fergus Anderson, GB (Guzzi) 32
2 Ray Amm, Rhodesia (Norton) 22
3 Rod Coleman, New Zealand
(AJS) 20

500cc
1 Geoffrey Duke, GB (Gilera) 32
2 Ray Amm, Rhodesia (Norton) 20
3 Ken Kavanagh, Australia
(Norton) 16

Sidecar
1 Wilhelm Noll, W. Germany
(BMW) 30
2 Eric Oliver, GB (Norton) 26
3 Cyril Smith, GB (Norton) 22

1955

125cc
1 Carlo Ubbiali, Italy (MV) 32
2 Luigi Taveri, Switzerland (MV) 26
3 Remo Venturi, Italy (MV) 16

250cc
1 Herman Müller, W. Germany
(NSU) 19
2 Cecil Sandford, GB (Guzzi) 14
3 Bill Lomas, GB (MV) 13

350cc
1 Bill Lomas, GB (Guzzi) 30
2 Dickie Dale, GB (Guzzi) 18
3 A. Hobl, W. Germany (DKW) 17

500cc
1 Geoffrey Duke, GB (Gilera) 32
2 Reg Armstrong, Ireland (Gilera) 26
3 Umberto Masetti, Italy (MV) 19

Sidecar
1 Willy Faust, W. Germany
  (BMW) 30
2 Wilhelm Noll, W. Germany
  (BMW) 28
3 Walter Schneider, W. Germany
  (BMW) 22

1956

125cc
1 Carlo Ubbiali, Italy (MV) 32
2 R. Ferri, Italy (Gilera) 14
3 Luigi Taveri, Switzerland
  (MV) 12

250cc
1 Carlo Ubbiali, Italy (MV) 32
2 Luigi Taveri, Switzerland
  (MV) 26
3 Enrico Lorenzetti, Italy (Guzzi) 10

350cc
1 Bill Lomas, GB (Guzzi) 24
2 A. Hobl, W. Germany (DKW) 17
3 Dickie Dale, GB (Guzzi) 17

500cc
1 John Surtees, GB (MV) 24
2 Walter Zeller, W. Germany
  (BMW) 16
3 John Hartle, GB (Norton) 14

Sidecar
1 Wilhelm Noll, W. Germany
  (BMW) 30
2 Fritz Hillebrand, W. Germany
  (BMW) 26
3 Pip Harris, GB (Norton) 24

1957

125cc
1 Tarquinio Provini, Italy
  (Mondial) 30
2 Luigi Taveri, Switzerland (MV) 22
3 Carlo Ubbiali, Italy (MV) 22

250cc
1 Cecil Sandford, GB (Mondial) 26
2 Tarquinio Provini, Italy
  (Mondial) 16
3 Sammy Miller, Ireland
  (Mondial) 14

350cc
1 Keith Campbell, Australia
  (Guzzi) 30
2 Bob McIntyre, Scotland (Gilera) 22
3 Libero Liberati, Italy (Gilera) 22

500cc
1 Libero Liberati, Italy (Gilera) 32
2 Bob McIntyre, Scotland (Gilera) 20
3 John Surtees, GB (MV) 17

Sidecar
1 Fritz Hillebrand, W. Germany
  (BMW) 28
2 Walter Schneider, W. Germany
  (BMW) 20
3 Florian Camathias, Switzerland
  (BMW) 17

1958

125cc
1 Carlo Ubbiali, Italy (MV) 32
2 A. Gandossi, Italy (Ducati) 25
3 Luigi Taveri, Switzerland
  (Ducati) 20

250cc
1 Tarquinio Provini, Italy (MV) 32
2 H. Fugner, E. Germany (MZ) 25
3 Carlo Ubbiali, Italy (MV) 16

350cc
1 John Surtees, GB (MV) 32
2 John Hartle, GB (MV) 24
3 Geoffrey Duke, GB (Norton) 17

500cc
1 John Surtees, GB (MV) 32
2 John Hartle, GB (MV) 20
3 Dickie Dale, GB (BMW) 13

Sidecar
1 Walter Schneider, W. Germany
  (BMW) 30
2 Florian Camathias, Switzerland
  (BMW) 26
3 Helmut Fath, W. Germany
  (BMW) 8

1959

125cc
1 Carlo Ubbiali, Italy (MV) 30
2 Tarquinio Provini, Italy (MV) 28
3 Mike Hailwood, GB (Ducati) 20

250cc
1 Carlo Ubbiali, Italy (MV) 28
2 Tarquinio Provini, Italy (MV) 16
3 Gary Hocking, Rhodesia (MZ) 16
350cc
1 John Surtees, GB (MV) 32
2 John Hartle, GB (MV) 16
3 Bob Brown, Australia (Norton) 14
500cc
1 John Surtees, GB (MV) 32
2 Remo Venturi, Italy (MV) 22
3 Bob Brown, Australia (Norton) 17
Sidecar
1 Walter Schneider, W. Germany
   (BMW) 22
2 Florian Camathias, Switzerland
   (BMW) 22
3 Fritz Scheidegger, Switzerland
   (BMW) 16

1960

125cc
1 Carlo Ubbiali, Italy (MV) 24
2 Gary Hocking, Rhodesia (MV) 18
3 Ernst Degner, E. Germany
   (MZ) 16

250cc
1 Carlo Ubbiali, Italy (MV) 32
2 Gary Hocking, Rhodesia (MV) 28
3 Luigi Taveri, Switzerland (MV) 11
350cc
1 John Surtees, GB (MV) 32
2 Gary Hocking, Rhodesia (MV) 26
3 John Hartle, GB (MV/Norton) 18
500cc
1 John Surtees, GB (MV) 32
2 Remo Venturi, Italy (MV) 26
3 John Hartle, GB (Norton/MV) 16
Sidecar
1 Helmut Fath, W. Germany
   (BMW) 24
2 Fritz Scheidegger, Switzerland
   (BMW) 16
3 Pip Harris, GB (BMW) 14

1961

125cc
1 Tom Phillis, Australia (Honda) 48
2 Ernst Degner, E. Germany
   (MZ) 42
3 Luigi Taveri, Switzerland
   (Honda) 30

250cc
1 Mike Hailwood, GB (Honda) 44
2 Tom Phillis, Australia (Honda) 38
3 Jim Redman, Rhodesia (Honda) 36
350cc
1 Gary Hocking, Rhodesia (MV) 38
2 Frantisek Stastny, Czechoslovakia
   (Jawa) 30
3 G. Havel, Czechoslovakia
   (Jawa) 19
500cc
1 Gary Hocking, Rhodesia (MV) 48
2 Mike Hailwood, GB
   (Norton/MV) 40
3 Frank Perris, GB (Norton) 16
Sidecar
1 Max Deubel, W. Germany
   (BMW) 30
2 Fritz Scheidegger, Switzerland
   (BMW) 28
3 E. Strub, Switzerland (BMW) 14

1962

50cc
1 Ernst Degner, W. Germany
   (Suzuki) 41
2 Hans-Georg Anscheidt,
   W. Germany (Kreidler) 36
3 Luigi Taveri, Switzerland
   (Honda) 29
125cc
1 Luigi Taveri, Switzerland
   (Honda) 48
2 Jim Redman, Rhodesia (Honda) 38
3 Tommy Robb, Ireland (Honda) 30
250cc
1 Jim Redman, Rhodesia (Honda) 48
2 Bob McIntyre, Scotland
   (Honda) 32
3 A. Wheeler, GB (Guzzi) 19
350cc
1 Jim Redman, Rhodesia (Honda) 32
2 Mike Hailwood, GB (MV) 20
3 Tommy Robb, Ireland (Honda) 18
500cc
1 Mike Hailwood, GB (MV) 40
2 Alan Shepherd, GB (Matchless) 29
3 Phil Read, GB (Norton) 11

Sidecar
1 Max Deubel, W. Germany
  (BMW) 30
2 Florian Camathias, Switzerland
  (BMW) 26
3 Fritz Scheidegger, Switzerland
  (BMW) 18

1963

50cc
1 Hugh Anderson, New Zealand
  (Suzuki) 34
2 Hans-Georg Anscheidt,
  W. Germany (Kreidler) 32
3 Ernst Degner, W. Germany
  (Suzuki) 30

125cc
1 Hugh Anderson, New Zealand
  (Suzuki) 54
2 Luigi Taveri, Switzerland
  (Honda) 38
3 Jim Redman, Rhodesia (Honda) 35

250cc
1 Jim Redman, Rhodesia (Honda) 44
2 Tarquinio Provini, Italy
  (Morini) 42
3 Fumio Ito, Japan (Yamaha) 26

350cc
1 Jim Redman, Rhodesia (Honda) 32
2 Mike Hailwood, GB (MV) 28
3 Luigi Taveri, Switzerland
  (Honda) 16

500cc
1 Mike Hailwood, GB (MV) 20
2 Alan Shepherd, GB (Matchless) 21
3 John Hartle, GB (Gilera) 20

Sidecar
1 Max Deubel, W. Germany
  (BMW) 22
2 Florian Camathias, Switzerland
  (BMW) 20
3 Fritz Scheidegger, Switzerland
  (BMW) 20

1964

50cc
1 Hugh Anderson, New Zealand
  (Suzuki) 38
2 Ralph Bryans, Ireland (Honda) 30
3 Hans-Georg Anscheidt,
  W. Germany (Kreidler) 29

125cc
1 Luigi Taveri, Switzerland
  (Honda) 46
2 Jim Redman, Rhodesia (Honda) 36
3 Hugh Anderson, New Zealand
  (Suzuki) 34

250cc
1 Phil Read, GB (Yamaha) 46
2 Jim Redman, Rhodesia (Honda) 42
3 Alan Shepherd, GB (MZ) 23

350cc
1 Jim Redman, Rhodesia (Honda) 40
2 Bruce Beale, Rhodesia (Honda) 24
3 Mike Duff, Canada (AJS) 20

500cc
1 Mike Hailwood, GB (MV) 40
2 Jack Ahearn, Australia
  (Norton) 25
3 Phil Read, GB (Matchless) 25

Sidecar
1 Max Deubel, W. Germany
  (BMW) 28
2 Fritz Scheidegger, Switzerland
  (BMW) 26
3 Colin Seeley, GB (BMW) 17

1965

50cc
1 Ralph Bryans, Ireland (Honda) 36
2 Luigi Taveri, Switzerland
  (Honda) 32
3 Hugh Anderson, New Zealand
  (Suzuki) 32

125cc
1 Hugh Anderson, New Zealand
  (Suzuki) 56
2 Frank Perris, GB (Suzuki) 44
3 Denis Woodman, GB (MZ) 28

250cc
1 Phil Read, GB (Yamaha) 56
2 Mike Duff, Canada (Yamaha) 42
3 Jim Redman, Rhodesia (Honda) 34

350cc
1 Jim Redman, Rhodesia (Honda) 38
2 Giacomo Agostini, Italy (MV) 32
3 Mike Hailwood, GB (MV) 20

500cc
1 Mike Hailwood, GB (MV) 48
2 Giacomo Agostini, Italy (MV) 38
3 Paddy Driver, S. Africa
  (Matchless) 26

Sidecar
1 Fritz Scheidegger, Switzerland (BMW) 32
2 Max Deubel, W. Germany (BMW) 26
3 Georg Auerbacher, W. Germany (BMW) 15

1966

50cc
1 Hans-Georg Anscheidt, W. Germany (Suzuki) 28
2 Ralph Bryans, Ireland (Honda) 26
3 Luigi Taveri, Switzerland (Honda) 26

125cc
1 Luigi Taveri, Switzerland (Honda) 46
2 Bill Ivy, GB (Yamaha) 40
3 Ralph Bryans, Ireland (Honda) 32

250cc
1 Mike Hailwood, GB (Honda) 56
2 Phil Read, GB (Yamaha) 34
3 Jim Redman, Rhodesia (Honda) 20

350cc
1 Mike Hailwood, GB (Honda) 48
2 Giacomo Agostini, Italy (MV) 42
3 Renzo Pasolini, Italy (Aermacchi) 17

500cc
1 Giacomo Agostini, Italy (MV) 36
2 Mike Hailwood, GB (Honda) 30
3 Jack Findlay, Australia (Matchless) 20

Sidecar
1 Fritz Scheidegger, Switzerland (BMW) 24
2 Max Deubel, W. Germany (BMW) 20
3 Colin Seeley, GB (BMW) 13

1967

50cc
1 Hans-Georg Anscheidt, W. Germany (Suzuki) 30
2 Yoshi Katayama, Japan (Suzuki) 28
3 Stuart Graham, GB (Suzuki) 22

125cc
1 Bill Ivy, GB (Yamaha) 56
2 Phil Read, GB (Yamaha) 40
3 Stuart Graham, GB (Suzuki) 38

250cc
1 Mike Hailwood, GB (Honda) 50
2 Phil Read, GB (Yamaha) 50
3 Bill Ivy, GB (Yamaha) 40

350cc
1 Mike Hailwood, GB (Honda) 40
2 Giacomo Agostini, Italy (MV) 32
3 Ralph Bryans, Ireland (Honda) 20

500cc
1 Giacomo Agostini, Italy (MV) 46
2 Mike Hailwood, GB (Honda) 46
3 John Hartle, GB (Matchless) 22

Sidecar
1 Klaus Enders, W. Germany (BMW) 40
2 Georg Auerbacher, W. Germany (BMW) 32
3 Siegfried Schauzu, W. Germany (BMW) 28

1968

50cc
1 Hans-Georg Anscheidt, W. Germany (Suzuki) 24
2 P. Lodewijkx, Holland (Jamathi) 17
3 B. Smith, Australia (Derbi) 15

125cc
1 Phil Read, GB (Yamaha) 40
2 Bill Ivy, GB (Yamaha) 24
3 Ginger Molloy, New Zealand (Bultaco) 15

250cc
1 Phil Read, GB (Yamaha) 52
2 Bill Ivy, GB (Yamaha) 52
3 Heinz Rosner, E. Germany (MZ) 32

350cc
1 Giacomo Agostini, Italy (MV) 32
2 Renzo Pasolini, Italy (Benelli) 18
3 Kel Carruthers, Australia (Aermacchi) 17

500cc
1 Giacomo Agostini, Italy (MV) 48
2 Jack Findlay, Australia (Matchless) 44
3 Gyula Marsovszky, Switzerland (Matchless) 10

Sidecar
1 Helmut Fath, W. Germany
(URS) 27
2 Georg Auerbacher, W. Germany
(BMW) 22
3 Siegfried Schauzu, W. Germany
(BMW) 19

1969

50cc
1 Angel Nieto, Spain (Derbi) 76
2 Aalt Toersen, Holland
(Kreidler) 75
3 B. Smith, Australia (Derbi) 69

125cc
1 Dave Simmonds, GB
(Kawasaki) 90
2 Dieter Braun, W. Germany
(Suzuki) 59
3 C. van Dongen, Holland
(Suzuki) 51

250cc
1 Kel Carruthers, Australia
(Benelli) 89
2 Kent Andersson, Sweden
(Yamaha) 84
3 Santiago Herrero, Spain (Ossa) 83

350cc
1 Giacomo Agostini, Italy (MV) 90
2 Silvio Grassetti, Italy
(Yamaha/Jawa) 47
3 G. Visenzi, Italy (Yamaha) 45

500cc
1 Giacomo Agostini, Italy (MV) 105
2 Gyula Marsovszky,
Switzerland (Linto) 47
3 G. Nash, GB (Norton) 45

Sidecar
1 Klaus Enders,
W. Germany (BMW) 60
2 Helmut Fath, W. Germany
(URS) 55
3 Georg Auerbacher,
W. Germany (BMW) 40

1970

50cc
1 Angel Nieto, Spain (Derbi) 87
2 Aalt Toersen, Holland
(Jamathi) 75
3 Rudolph Kunz,
W. Germany (Kreidler) 66

125cc
1 Dieter Braun,
W. Germany (Suzuki) 84
2 Angel Nieto, Spain (Derbi) 72
3 Borje Jansson, Sweden (Maico) 62

250cc
1 Rodney Gould, GB (Yamaha) 102
2 Kel Carruthers,
Australia (Yamaha) 84
3 Kent Andersson, Sweden
(Yamaha) 67

350cc
1 Giacomo Agostini, Italy (MV) 90
2 Kel Carruthers,
Australia (Benelli/Yamaha) 58
3 Renzo Pasolini, Italy (Benelli) 46

500cc
1 Giacomo Agostini, Italy (MV) 90
2 Ginger Molloy,
New Zealand (Kawasaki) 62
3 Angelo Bergamonti, Italy
(Aermacchi/MV) 59

Sidecar
1 Klaus Enders,
W. Germany (BMW) 73
2 Georg Auerbacher,
W. Germany (BMW) 62
3 Siegfried Schauzu, W. Germany
(BMW) 56

1971

50cc
1 Jan de Vries, Holland (Kreidler) 75
2 Angel Nieto, Spain (Derbi) 69
3 J. Schurgers, Holland (Kreidler) 42

125cc
1 Angel Nieto, Spain (Derbi) 87
2 Barry Sheene, GB (Suzuki) 79
3 Borje Jansson, Sweden (Maico) 64

250cc
1 Phil Read, GB (Yamaha) 73
2 Rodney Gould, GB (Yamaha) 68
3 Jarno Saarinen, Finland
(Yamaha) 64

350cc
1 Giacomo Agostini, Italy (MV) 90
2 Jarno Saarinen, Finland
(Yamaha) 63
3 K.I. Carlsson, Sweden
(Yamaha) 39

500cc
1 Giacomo Agostini, Italy (MV) 90
2 K. Turner, New Zealand
  (Suzuki) 58
3 R. Bron, Holland (Suzuki) 57
Sidecar
1 Horst Owesle, W. Germany
  (Munch) 69
2 A. Butscher, W. Germany
  (BMW) 57
3 Siegfried Schauzu, W. Germany
  (BMW) 57

1972

50cc
1 Angel Nieto, Spain (Derbi) 69
2 Jan de Vries, Holland (Kreidler) 69
3 Theo Timmer, Holland
  (Jamathi) 50
125cc
1 Angel Nieto, Spain (Derbi) 97
2 Kent Andersson, Sweden
  (Yamaha) 87
3 Charles Mortimer, GB
  (Yamaha) 87
250cc
1 Jarno Saarinen, Finland
  (Yamaha) 94
2 Renzo Pasolini, Italy
  (Aermacchi) 93
3 Rodney Gould, GB (Yamaha) 88
350cc
1 Giacomo Agostini, Italy (MV) 102
2 Jarno Saarinen, Finland
  (Yamaha) 89
3 Renzo Pasolini, Italy
  (Aermacchi) 78
500cc
1 Giacomo Agostini, Italy (MV) 105
2 Alberto Pagani, Italy (MV) 87
3 Bruno Kneubuhler, Czechoslovakia
  (Yamaha) 57
Sidecar
1 Klaus Enders, W. Germany
  (BMW) 72
2 Heinz Luthringshauser,
  W. Germany (BMW) 63
3 Siegfried Schauzu, W. Germany
  (BMW) 62

1973

50cc
1 Jan de Vries, Holland (Van Veen
  Kreidler) 60
2 Bruno Kneubuhler, Czechoslovakia
  (Van Veen Kreidler) 51
3 Theo Timmer, Holland
  (Jamathi) 47
125cc
1 Kent Andersson, Sweden
  (Yamaha) 90
2 Charles Mortimer, GB
  (Yamaha) 75
3 J. Schurgers, Holland
  (Bridgestone) 71
250cc
1 Dieter Braun, W. Germany
  (Yamaha) 80
2 Tepi Lansivuori, Finland
  (Yamaha) 64
3 John Dodds, Australia
  (Yamaha) 58
350cc
1 Giacomo Agostini, Italy (MV) 84
2 Tepi Lansivuori, Finland
  (Yamaha) 77
3 Phil Read, GB (MV) 56
500cc
1 Phil Read, GB (MV) 84
2 K. Newcombe, New Zealand
  (Konig) 63
3 Giacomo Agostini, Italy (MV) 57
Sidecar
1 Klaus Enders, W. Germany
  (BMW) 75
2 Werner Schwarzel, W. Germany
  (Konig) 48
3 Siegfried Schauzu, W. Germany
  (BMW) 45

1974

50cc
1 Henk van Kessell, Holland
  (Van Veen Kreidler) 90
2 Herbert Rittberger, W. Germany
  (Kreidler) 68
3 Julien van Zeebroeck, Belgium
  (Kreidler) 59

125cc
1 Kent Andersson, Sweden
(Yamaha) 87
2 Bruno Kneubuhler, Switzerland
(Yamaha) 63
3 Otello Buscherini, Italy
(Malanca) 60
3 Angel Nieto, Spain (Derbi) 60

250cc
1 Walter Villa, Italy (Harley-
Davidson) 77
2 Dieter Braun, W. Germany
(Yamaha) 58
3 Patrick Pons, France (Yamaha) 50

350cc
1 Giacomo Agostini, Italy
(Yamaha) 75
2 Dieter Braun, W. Germany
(Yamaha) 62
3 Patrick Pons, France (Yamaha) 49

500cc
1 Phil Read, GB (MV) 82
2 Gianfranco Bonera, Italy (MV) 69
3 Tepi Lansivuori, Finland
(Yamaha) 67

Sidecar
1 Klaus Enders, W. Germany (Busch
BMW) 66
2 Werner Schwarzel, W. Germany
(Konig) 64
3 Siegfried Schauzu, W. Germany
(BMW) 60

1975

50cc
1 Angel Nieto, Spain (Kreidler) 75
2 Eugenio Lazzarini, Italy
(Piovaticci) 61
3 Julien van Zeebroeck, Belgium
(Kreidler) 43

125cc
1 Paolo Pileri, Italy (Morbidelli) 90
2 Pierpaolo Bianchi, Italy
(Morbidelli) 72
3 Kent Andersson, Sweden
(Yamaha) 67

250cc
1 Walter Villa, Italy (Harley-
Davidson) 85
2 Michel Rougerie, France (Harley-
Davidson) 76
3 Dieter Braun, W. Germany
(Yamaha) 56

350cc
1 Johnny Cecotto, Venezuela
(Yamaha) 78
2 Giacomo Agostini, Italy
(Yamaha) 59
3 Penti Korhonen, Finland
(Yamaha) 48

500cc
1 Giacomo Agostini, Italy
(Yamaha) 84
2 Phil Read, GB (MV) 76
3 Hideo Kanaya, Japan (Yamaha) 45

Sidecar
1 Rolf Steinhausen, W. Germany
(Konig) 67
2 Werner Schwarzel, W. Germany
(Konig) 54
3 Rolf Biland, Switzerland
(Yamaha) 30

1976

50cc
1 Angel Nieto, Spain (Bultaco) 86
2 Herbert Rittberger, W. Germany
(Kreidler) 76
3 Ulrich Graf, Switzerland
(Kreidler) 69

125cc
1 Pierpaolo Bianchi, Italy
(Morbidelli) 90
2 Angel Nieto, Spain (Bultaco) 67
3 Paolo Pileri, Italy (Morbidelli) 64

250cc
1 Walter Villa, Italy
(Harley-Davidson) 90
2 Takazumi Katayama, Japan
(Yamaha) 73
3 Gianfranco Bonera, Italy
(Harley-Davidson) 61

350cc
1 Walter Villa, Italy
(Harley-Davidson) 76
2 Johnny Cecotto, Venezuela
(Yamaha) 65
3 Charles Mortimer, GB
(Yamaha) 54

500cc
1 Barry Sheene, GB (Suzuki) 72
2 Tepi Lansivuori, Finland
(Suzuki) 48
3 Pat Hennen, USA (Suzuki) 46

Sidecar
1 Rolf Steinhausen, W. Germany
  (Busch Konig) 65
2 Werner Schwarzel, W. Germany
  (Konig) 51
3 Herman Schmid, Switzerland
  (Yamaha) 38

Formula 750
1 Victor Palomo, Spain (Yamaha) 61
2 Gary Nixon, USA (Kawasaki) 47
3 John Newbold, GB (Suzuki) 37

1977

50cc
1 Angel Nieto, Spain (Bultaco) 87
2 Eugenio Lazzarini, Italy
  (Kreidler) 72
3 Ricardo Tormo, Spain (Bultaco) 69

125cc
1 Pierpaolo Bianchi, Italy
  (Morbidelli) 131
2 Eugenio Lazzarini, Italy
  (Morbidelli) 115
3 Angel Nieto, Spain (Bultaco) 80

250cc
1 Mario Lega, Italy (Morbidelli) 85
2 Franco Uncini, Italy
  (Harley-Davidson) 72
3 Walter Villa, Italy
  (Harley-Davidson) 67

350cc
1 Takazumi Katayama, Japan
  (Yamaha) 95
2 Tom Herron, GB (Yamaha) 56
3 Jon Ekerold, South Africa
  (Yamaha) 54

500cc
1 Barry Sheene, GB (Suzuki) 107
2 Steve Baker, USA (Yamaha) 80
3 Pat Hennen, USA (Suzuki) 67

Sidecar
1 George O'Dell, GB (Seymaz-
  Yamaha & Windle-Yamaha) 64
2 Rolf Biland, Switzerland (Schmid-
  Yamaha) 56
3 Werner Schwarzel, W. Germany
  (Aro) 46

Formula 750
1 Steve Baker, USA (Yamaha) 131
2 Christian Sarron, France
  (Yamaha) 55
3 Giacomo Agostini, Italy
  (Yamaha) 45

1978

50cc
1 Ricardo Tormo, Spain (Bultaco) 99
2 Eugenio Lazzarini, Italy
  (Kreidler) 64
3 Patrick Plisson, France (ABF) 48

125cc
1 Eugenio Lazzarini, Italy
  (MBA) 114
2 Angel Nieto, Spain
  (Bultaco/Minarelli) 88
3 Pierpaolo Bianchi, Italy
  (Minarelli) 70

250cc
1 Kork Ballington, S. Africa
  (Kawasaki) 124
2 Gregg Hansford, Australia
  (Kawasaki) 118
3 Patrick Fernandez, France
  (Yamaha) 55

350cc
1 Kork Ballington, S. Africa
  (Kawasaki) 124
2 Takazumi Katayama, Japan
  (Yamaha) 77
3 Gregg Hansford, Australia
  (Kawasaki) 76

500cc
1 Kenny Roberts, USA
  (Yamaha) 110
2 Barry Sheene, GB (Suzuki) 100
3 Johnny Cecotto, Venezuela
  (Yamaha) 66

Sidecar
1 Rolf Biland, Switzerland (Beo-
  Yamaha & TTM Yamaha) 79
2 Alain Michel, France (Seymaz-
  Yamaha) 76
3 Bruno Holzer, Switzerland (LCR-
  Yamaha) 49

Formula 750
1 Johnny Cecotto, Venezuela
  (Yamaha) 97
2 Kenny Roberts, USA (Yamaha) 92
3 Christian Sarron, France
  (Yamaha) 55

1979

50cc
1 Eugenio Lazzarini, Italy
   (Kreidler) 75
2 Rolf Blatter, Switzerland
   (Kreidler) 62
3 Patrick Plisson, France (ABF) 32

125cc
1 Angel Nieto, Spain (Minarelli) 120
2 Maurizio Massimiani, Italy
   (Morbidelli) 53
3 Hans Müller, Switzerland
   (MBA) 50

250cc
1 Kork Ballington, S. Africa
   (Kawasaki) 141
2 Gregg Hansford, Australia
   (Kawasaki) 81
3 Graziano Rossi, Italy
   (Morbidelli) 67

350cc
1 Kork Ballington, S. Africa
   (Kawasaki) 99
2 Patrick Fernandez, France
   (Yamaha) 90
3 Gregg Hansford, Australia
   (Kawasaki) 77

500cc
1 Kenny Roberts, USA
   (Yamaha) 113
2 Virginio Ferrari, Italy (Suzuki) 89
3 Barry Sheene, GB (Suzuki) 87

Sidecar B2A
1 Rolf Biland, Switzerland
   (Yamaha) 67
2 Rolf Steinhausen, W. Germany
   (Yamaha) 58
3 Dick Greasley, GB (Yamaha) 58

Sidecar B2B
1 Bruno Holzer, Switzerland
   (LCR) 72
2 Rolf Biland, Switzerland (LCR) 60
3 Masato Kumano, Japan
   (Yamaha) 41

Formula 750
1 Patrick Pons, France
   (Yamaha) 154
2 Michel Frutschi, Switzerland
   (Yamaha) 132
3 Johnny Cecotto, Venezuela
   (Yamaha) 126

1980

50cc
1 Eugenio Lazzarini, Italy
   (Kreidler/Iprem) 74
2 Stefan Dörflinger, Switzerland
   (Kreidler) 72
3 Hans Hummel, Austria
   (Kreidler) 37

125cc
1 Pierpaolo Bianchi, Italy (MBA) 90
2 Guy Bertin, France
   (Motobecane) 81
3 Angel Nieto, Spain (Minarelli) 78

250cc
1 Anton Mang, W. Germany
   (Kawasaki) 128
2 Kork Ballington, S. Africa
   (Kawasaki) 59
3 Jean-François Balde, France
   (Kawasaki) 59

350cc
1 Jon Ekerold, S. Africa
   (Yamaha) 63
2 Anton Mang, W. Germany
   (Kawasaki) 60
3 Jean-François Balde, France
   (Kawasaki) 38

500cc
1 Kenny Roberts, USA (Yamaha) 87
2 Randy Mamola, USA (Suzuki) 72
3 Marco Lucchinelli, Italy
   (Suzuki) 59

Sidecar
1 Jock Taylor, GB (Yamaha) 94
2 Rolf Biland, Czechoslovakia
   (Yamaha) 63
3 Alain Michel, France (Yamaha) 63

1981

50cc
1 Ricardo Tormo, Spain (Bultaco) 90
2 Theo Timmer, Holland
   (Bultaco) 65
3 Stefan Dörflinger, Switzerland
   (Kreidler) 51

125cc
1 Angel Nieto, Spain (Minarelli) 140
2 Loris Reggiani, Italy (Minarelli) 95
3 Pierpaolo Bianchi, Italy (MBA) 84

250cc
1 Anton Mang, W. Germany
(Kawasaki) 160
2 Jean-François Balde, France
(Kawasaki) 95
3 Roland Freymond, Switzerland
(Ad Majora) 72

350cc
1 Anton Mang, W. Germany
(Kawasaki) 160
2 Jon Ekerold, S. Africa
(Yamaha) 52
3 Jean-François Balde, France
(Kawasaki) 49

500cc
1 Marco Lucchinelli, Italy
(Suzuki) 105
2 Randy Mamola, USA (Suzuki) 94
3 Kenny Roberts, USA (Yamaha) 74

Sidecar
1 Rolf Biland, Switzerland
(Yamaha) 127
2 Alain Michel, France (Yamaha) 106
3 Jock Taylor, GB (Yamaha) 87

1982

50cc
1 Stefan Dörflinger, Switzerland
(Kreidler) 81
2 Eugenio Lazzarini, Italy
(Garelli) 69
3 Claudio Lusuardi, Italy (Villa) 43

125cc
1 Angel Nieto, Spain (Garelli) 111
2 Eugenio Lazzarini, Italy
(Garelli) 95
3 Ivan Palazzese, Venezuela
(MBA) 75

250cc
1 Jean-Louis Tournadre, France
(Yamaha) 118
2 Anton Mang, W. Germany
(Kawasaki) 117
3 Roland Freymond, Switzerland
(MBA) 72

350cc
1 Anton Mang, W. Germany
(Kawasaki) 81
2 Didier de Radigues, Belgium
(Chevallier) 64
3 Jean-François Balde, France
(Kawasaki) 59

500cc
1 Franco Uncini, Italy (Suzuki) 103
2 Graeme Crosby, New Zealand
(Yamaha) 76
3 Freddie Spencer, USA (Honda) 72

Sidecar
1 Werner Schwarzel, W. Germany
(Yamaha) 86
2 Rolf Biland, Switzerland
(Yamaha) 82 ½
3 Alain Michel, France (Yamaha) 68

1983

50cc
1 Stefan Dörflinger, Switzerland
(Kreidler) 81
2 Eugenio Lazzarini, Italy
(Garelli) 69
3 Claudio Lusuardi, Italy (Villa) 38

125cc
1 Angel Nieto, Spain (Garelli) 102
2 Bruno Kneubuhler, Switzerland
(MBA) 76
3 Eugenio Lazzarini, Italy
(Garelli) 67

250cc
1 Carlos Lavado, Venezuela
(Yamaha) 100
2 Christian Sarron, France
(Yamaha) 73
3 Didier de Radigues, Belgium
(Chevallier) 68

500cc
1 Freddie Spencer, USA (Honda) 144
2 Kenny Roberts, USA (Yamaha) 142
3 Randy Mamola, USA (Suzuki) 89

Sidecar
1 Rolf Biland, Switzerland
(LCR-Yamaha) 98
2 Egbert Streuer, Holland
(LCR-Yamaha) 72
3 Werner Schwarzel, W. Germany
(Seymaz-Yamaha) 67

1984

80cc
1 Stefan Dörflinger, Switzerland
(Zundapp) 82
2 Hubert Abold, W. Germany
(Zundapp) 75
3 Pierpaolo Bianchi, Italy (Huro) 68

125cc
1 Angel Nieto, Spain (Garelli) 90
2 Eugenio Lazzarini, Italy
  (Garelli) 78
3 Fausto Gresini, Italy (Garelli) 51

250cc
1 Christian Sarron, France
  (Yamaha) 109
2 Manfred Herwen, W. Germany
  (Real) 100
3 Carlos Lavado, Venezuela
  (Yamaha) 77

500cc
1 Eddie Lawson, USA (Yamaha) 142
2 Randy Mamola, USA (Honda) 111
3 Raymond Roche, France
  (Honda) 99

Sidecar
1 Egbert Streuer, Holland
  (Yamaha) 75
2 Werner Schwarzel, W. Germany
  (Yamaha) 72
3 Alain Michel, France (Yamaha) 65

Index